Advance Prais  Out!

"We've all been there. The falls and rises of growing up, making something of ourselves, entrepreneurism, and more—it all takes a toll on even the mentally strongest. I loved meeting Janeane Bernstein and reading her book *Get the Funk Out!*. The story is refreshing and real, and encourages us to own up and reach our full potentials."—Winnie Sun, Wealth Whisperer, CNBC Financial Advisor Council, *Forbes* Contributor, Co-Founder of Sun Group Wealth Partners

....

"Finally, a common sense approach to an all too common malady. Ms. Bernstein has assembled the tools to overcome our personal demons in words that are clear and concise. When I find a good book, I usually 'can't put it down' but *Get the Funk Out!* demands time to absorb the inspirational stories and ponder the question of how faith can be so strong."—Gary Pihl, former guitarist for Sammy Hagar and current member of the band Boston

....

"I love this book! A radically transparent look that teaches us to face life's hard knocks—instead of running away—and heal from the gifts that emerge from them. This is a bedside keeper to remind you that grass grows through concrete."—Bryan E. Robinson, Ph.D., Psychotherapist and Author of *#Chill: Turn Off Your Job and Turn On Your Life*

....

"The power of self-esteem is on full display in *Get the Funk Out!*. Janeane Bernstein pulls together an unlikely cast to write a prescription for dealing with life's large and small challenges. Finding joy on the journey is possible, no matter how rocky the road."—Richard M. Cohen, *New York Times* Bestselling Author of *Blindsided* and *Strong at the Broken Places*

....

"Janeane has written a book that aims to help anyone navigating the funky pitfalls of life, illustrated with a wide assortment of anecdotes and her experience—all of it filled with humor and compassion."—Kathy Valentine, Musician, Composer, and Writer

....

"Janeane uses her own personal stories plus interviews with a variety of mental health professionals to explore life's persistent funks. Personable and engaging, she shines a light on the darkness many face in everyday life, illuminating a way out."—Vicki Peterson, founding member of The Bangles, Guitarist, Writer, and Singer

....

GET THE FUNK OUT!

%^&* HAPPENS, WHAT TO DO NEXT!

JANEANE BERNSTEIN, ED.D.

Post Hill
PRESS

A POST HILL PRESS BOOK
ISBN: 978-1-64293-069-6
ISBN (eBook): 978-1-64293-070-2

Cover Design by Tricia Principe, principedesign.com
Author Photo by Joanna DeGeneres

This book is not intended as a substitute for consultation with a licensed healthcare practitioner, such as your physician. Before you begin any healthcare program, or change your lifestyle in any way, you should consult your physician or another licensed healthcare practitioner.

Post Hill Press
New York • Nashville
posthillpress.com

Published in the United States of America

TABLE OF CONTENTS

INTRODUCTION

"Vulnerability is the birthplace of innovation, creativity and change."—Brené Brown

I am an expert on funks. Okay, so that sounds a little cocky, but after far too many funks, we all feel like pros. While I am not a medical doctor, I have my own funk-busting strategies that have worked for me and just might work for you. Keep in mind, none of my personal stories shared in this book are meant to be about "woe is me" or "Boo-hoo! My childhood sucked and I feel victimized." Well, at times it did really suck the life out of me, but I always felt things would get better. I was somehow blessed with a "stay positive and strong" mentality that has always been with me since I was a kid.

I am seriously so thankful for all the crap projected my way, all the times I had to switch into survival mode and put my big-girl pants on, and how I pushed through some of the worst experiences and fought through; it is hard to believe that my backstory is even part of my story. Too many great things have happened as a result of gobs of tears, hard work, rejection, disappointment, and the funkiness of my dysfunctional family.

At this point in my life, I consider myself bulletproof regarding any funky sh*t thrown my way. I first felt funks as a young child, as the daughter of two people who never should have married. I am honestly so thankful they separated when I was six months old,

7

because I never lived with the anger and arguing. I just heard their battles over the phone and occasionally in person, but I managed to escape the messiness of their union because I was so young. Unfortunately, the ugliness revealed itself in the tumultuous custody battles, courtroom shenanigans, and weekend visits. I never once wished my parents would reunite, because I never knew life to be any different. I probably wished they lived in other countries or planets; that would have made life a whole lot easier, because they seemed to be from totally different worlds.

There is nothing more humbling than hearing other people share their personal stories of what broke them apart and how they built themselves back up. My own life seems like a cakewalk in comparison, and I am humbled by the openness and details I have been privy to on my radio show. Having a toolkit for facing your own funks can be a great way to tackle life's rocky road, but being open to unexpected insights and advice from total strangers can be the best, most surprising gift of all.

Instead of running away from life's assaults, sometimes it is best to look at challenges as learning moments. Face them head-on. At age eight, when I decided to swing from the kitchen cabinets, like Mowgli in *The Jungle Book*, I failed big time. I know. What a surprise. Man, I wish someone had videotaped this calamity! The cabinet door abruptly twisted off its hinges. What does this have to do with anything, you ask? My mother sent me to her therapist, because she thought I had anger issues. I had no idea what a therapist was, and what this person did, but I had no say in the matter, so off I went.

I didn't think of myself as an angry kid. I was bored and wanted to make emptying the dishwasher a little adventurous and a lot more fun, of course. Who knew I couldn't swing from one kitchen cabinet to another? Mowgli does it with ease in the movie. For all of you cabinetmakers reading this, there's the future of cabinetmaking. Get your kids to empty the damn dishwasher when you install swinging doors! You know, I might even learn to love emptying the dishwasher if I could swing like Mowgli! Great idea, right? You're welcome.

Here's what happened in therapy, by the way. Not much. I sat there, sinking into the soft, brown, oversized leather chair, and carefully crafted some creative BS (baloney shnotz, as my daughter calls it) that I thought the therapist wanted to hear; this was my first and last therapy session and my intro to acting. Nailed it. I was so angry and bored sitting in that dimly lit, drab room. As revenge, I picked my nose and wiped it on his fancy brown leather chair when he left the room.

My mother shared with the therapist that I had burned her blouse while attempting to iron. For all of you parents reading this, please don't teach your nine-year-old to iron. Really. Nine is a tad too young, and I had no idea there were actual settings for different fabrics. The high setting seemed fine until I placed the iron facedown on the nylon blouse because my favorite show was on, and then I got hungry, and...forgot what I was doing. That iron was so hot, it melted that ugly blouse and left a huge sear mark on it. Between you and me, the blouse was *really* ugly. My mother should have thanked me. And as far as therapy goes, therapy at a young age meant nothing. I just imagined what I was supposed to say and spewed out improvised feelings.

My real outlet to express my feelings was inexpensive and fun—art! Specifically, finger painting and candle art, but you should probably supervise your ten-year-old if he or she wants to try the latter. I must have had a guardian angel, because the Manhattan apartment I lived in is still standing.

About a year later, I figured out that guitar playing was more cathartic than spilling my guts out to a monotone stranger. Now that I look back on my therapy experience, it was my first experience with improvisation. I started riffing about something fictional, replied with a lot of sentences beginning "yes, and…," and created stories about why I was "upset and angry over my parents' divorce." I couldn't have cared less about their divorce. I didn't know them as a married couple, and I wouldn't want these two crazy Tasmanian devil people as my married parents or really even in the same room. Phew, did I feel lucky. I think I hit the closest McDonald's after we were done.

By age thirteen, I still didn't have any anger issues. However, I caused a bigger mess than scorching an ugly nylon blouse; this was my all-time-worst doozy of a mistake. I accidentally caused an electrical fire in the Connecticut home we were renting. The incident started in my room and resulted in a massive fire that scorched the second and third floors. I found the silver lining: We were all alive and uninjured.

Two months living at Howard Johnson's wasn't all that bad. I ate club sandwiches whenever I wanted and every flavor of ice cream…at least twice a day. Cooking and dishes were never an option, so life was pretty good, except for the loss of my most prized possessions: a huge, soft Snoopy plush toy; my first guitar and handmade skateboard I made in woodworking class; and the skeleton leg bone I had found under my camp bunk. (I know. Ewwww!) I quickly learned that these were just "things" and my well-being was all that mattered. The latter would prove to be especially important when my mother would ridicule me for starting the fire in the first place; she never actually asked me how it started and just referred to me as *ferblunjit*, which means "lost and mixed-up" in Yiddish. Even though I never understood a word of Yiddish, I figured it meant "dumbass" or "moron." In my mind, I had caused a horrific accident that impacted all of our lives. I was completely to blame and needed to forgive myself; this would take a lifetime.

As an adult, I now clearly see the fire as karma. Why karma? My mother and stepfather moved down the street from my father and stepmother. When I say "down the street," I mean four flippin' houses down the street! Who does that? That's a story for another book. Let's just say the neighbors jokingly accused my dad and stepmom of starting the fire to get rid of the crazy ex-wife. My poor stepmom had decided to give away her beautiful, loving Great Dane months earlier, because they were planning on selling their home after the ex-wife moved too close for comfort. I would have wanted to leave, too.

In my mind, I knew the fire was an accident, but it was a blessing in disguise, depending on whose shoes you were standing in. Of course, I didn't own any shoes anymore after I torched the house, but deep down inside, I knew I would be okay. Dad made sure to wrap his arms around me that night and tell me he loved me. We watched the enormous monster fire ravage the old house and destroy everything in its path, but he made me feel safe and loved, as we watched the firefighters tackle the blaze and throw most of my charred belongings over a side balcony. I knew these were just "things" and all that mattered was that I was safe and loved.

Get the Funk Out! gives readers of any age life strategies and stories for avoiding and healing from almost any type of funk, and it does this in a way that these funks won't be felt the same way if they have a repeat performance. Along the way, you'll learn resilience, activities that inspire you creatively, and coping skills that we all need when faced with all kinds of loss and change.

One of my best strategies for dealing with the death of my friend since high school was not so obvious at first. I tried working out every day, crying and venting to anyone who would listen. I spent hours talking to my friend's past boyfriends, fiancés, and family members. I tried to uncover the details of my friend's death, the mental state she had been in, and any relationships that could have contributed to her depression and decision-making; it's amazing what you learn when you have conversations with a lot of close friends and family members in someone's inner circle. You listen to how they react, hear what they say and how they say it, and discover what they do not say. You also notice the people who want nothing to do with you and refuse to talk. The only truth I know now is that there are too many unknowns in this story and I will never know what happened the night she died, December 29, 2010.

My investigative mind never made the story any easier to accept, but it seemed to make me feel a little bit better. I felt like I could hear my friend speaking to me after she died, and no, I am not a lunatic. I just could not come to terms with this massive loss. I wanted answers I would never find. I wanted the truth, the facts, and some closure. "Forget it. I have to move on," I would tell myself. I would never know all of the details of what transpired the night she died, so I would do something to deal with my monumental grief. I would do something that she would think is incredibly meaningful; this would be my legacy and my tribute to her and everyone else who faces mental illness, cancer, grief, loss, toxic relationships, heartache, and any other assault life has to offer.

I am a creator; this is what I do when I am happy or sad. I made the decision to create something bigger than I was and something I never imagined; this idea would end up helping me through pain, sleepless nights, an avalanche of tears, and a huge funk, while helping others share their own stories and lessons learned. I never would have expected what I would learn about myself and from others during this journey.

Throughout this time of grief, I was considering shifting away from hosting a weekly music show I'd started in 2007 (*Momz Rock the House*) to producing a talk show. When brainstorming a new name, I came up with *Get the Funk Out!*. I could not understand how some people get so low emotionally and hit rock bottom, and they stay there for a very, very long time, alone, and never seem to figure out a way out, while others find the strength to pick themselves up and move forward.

In this book, we'll delve into the importance of mindfulness, meditation, creative pursuits, and other practices that help cultivate focus, direction, and tranquility in a not-so-calm life. By engaging in these healing practices, our minds and bodies can rejuvenate mentally and physically, leading us to better decision-making and a more fulfilled life. Funks dissolve more quickly (or at least start to) when you mix them with creative diversions, interventions, and a little fun. And to do that, you must go out of your comfort zone, be bold and brazen, and sometimes be adventurous. *Get the Funk Out!* includes stories of people overcoming their situations, making brave choices and moving in new directions; they share the lessons learned from the messiness of life.

There is no shame in failing and falling flat. At least you tried. Some of us are experts in epic failure and bombing when faced with a challenge (ahem!), but those failings can be opportunities to change and grow. We all get trampled on, but can we get back up? The moments that we find so painful and exhausting are opportunities to grow and learn. We can't avoid life's challenges. Use them to ignite your passions and goals. Run directly through the pain and out the other side like a beast! Fighting through our difficulties is how we become stronger and more insightful. We can overcome incredible, terrible odds and beat our funks to smithereens, but only if we believe we can and get started.

The creation of my radio show was my small way of helping others who faced similar situations and providing experts an arena to share advice and guidance. Eight years later, I have been able to share inspiring stories, review endless books, view films, and gain invaluable advice from health and wellness experts, filmmakers, authors, actors, comedians, writers, artists, teachers, doctors, and more. The conversations have been powerful, emotionally moving, thought-provoking, and unforgettable. I have laughed, cried, grieved, and learned along the way that it is okay to be in a funk, because life is one big, crazy ride, filled with twists and turns and ups and downs. How else can we become stronger, wiser, and more kick-ass survivors? We cannot often control what happens to us, but we do have control over how we deal with the situation. We can choose to be fighters and survivors or to cave under the weight of the situation. I believe we all have the power to fight right through the storm and into something surprisingly wonderful.

I was driven to write *Get the Funk Out!* to help others learn how to face life's challenges head-on. The book is filled with invaluable stories from guests on my show, who come from a wide variety of professional backgrounds and have a wide variety of personal struggles and expertise, offering advice to anyone at any age. After hosting and producing my radio show for over six years and facing the loss of my father to stage four colon cancer, I felt it was time to share the learning moments my guests had generously shared with me. And it was the death and grief of losing my father that brought me back to the one thing I have always loved: writing.

This book is arranged into thirteen chapters, delving into everything from the root causes of funks to how we choose to react and deal with the ups and downs of life. Personal anecdotes from a wide variety of show guests are included, as well as advice from health and wellness professionals and experts in positive psychology.

You will read stories of age-defying, fearless guests who rarely say no to a challenge or new opportunity. In fact, they've thrived by tossing away a career they spent years invested in, then jumped into something they always wanted to do. One of my eighty-five-year-old show guests runs triathlons and trains to hike Mount Kilimanjaro; she is proof it is never too late to try new things, and the only thing stopping us is…us!

No one can give you a time frame for healing or moving forward. The best you can do is take small steps and learn from your current situation. Running away from your situation and ignoring pain and personal growth don't work. From our negative experiences grow more positive changes, although at first your life might seem like a bad movie—bad thing after bad thing happening. You find out your ex is dating one of your best friends from high school, you drown your tears in Ben & Jerry's, and apparently next week your job is being eliminated. Just when you think you've turned a corner by signing up for a dance class, you fracture your ankle and miss out on that dance event you were so excited to attend with your best friend. But hold on. That ER doctor is *hot*, and things aren't looking so bad after all. There's a new position you forgot you submitted your résumé for even though you thought it was a long shot. You start next month. Cast and all. So, here's the thing. A tough period in your life can provide a new perspective. Pay attention to the details of that moment. The twists and turns of life can be scary, but our experiences shape who we are and who we can become.

This book will help you:

- Pinpoint when you belly-flop into a funk
- Determine the *what*, *why*, and *how* of your funks (what is bothering you, why, and how to stop funking around!)
- Know that being happy all the time is impossible, but pinpointing things that contribute to your happiness is key
- Make pampering yourself a priority
- Take the leap and try new things
- Express yourself when things are sh*tty
- Get out of your mindset and help others
- Nurture your relationships and kick the toxic ones to the curb
- Know the signs when tweens, teens, and in-betweens are funky and what to do and not do
- Recognize how seriously funked up midlife can be
- See how seniors put us to shame...a lot!
- Not to fear our endless array of funks, but see the awakenings they bring

CHAPTER 1

What Is a Funk? Is There a Vaccination/Magic Pill?

"My mission in life is not merely to survive, but to thrive; and to do so with some passion, some compassion, some humor, and some style."
—Maya Angelou

I have interviewed people who have lived through 9/11, who have experienced the trauma of losing a leg in childhood but now compete in yearly triathlons, and who keep me in awe of their daily routines and outlook on life. Others have dealt with the death of a loved one, while numerous guests have lost family and friends to cancer or survived cancer themselves and kicked ass. Some have faced near-death experiences or physical, mental, and emotional abuse; they have gone from being social misfits to being award-winning filmmakers. A personal crisis once led a woman to run off to become a showgirl in the Ringling Bros. circus in her youth, which led her to greater self-discovery and a music career, and many health and wellness practitioners have shared insights on how to deal with stress, practice mindfulness, meditate, and do self-care rituals in our daily lives.

Let's face it. Life would be pretty boring if we were immune to its curveballs. We experience change, trauma, loss, a reality slap—and *boom!* We are changed. At first, we are clueless as to what to do with this change, but slowly we figure it all out, or most of it, and we wing it. We carry on, become more resilient and often happier. If we are fortunate, we find greater meaning in the storm we have weathered, the pain and suffering we have endured, and the insights we have gained. We might think we look like a drenched cat in a rainstorm, but we have survived, and we are more of a warrior than we expected.

If you stop and think of how many types of funks there are, you would have an entire flowchart! Several years ago, on a very long flight from the West Coast to the East Coast, I was in the middle of my own personal funk. As I always do, I processed what I was feeling and going through by writing. I diagrammed all the types of funks I could think of, their origins, and how I could do away with them; this was before I got sucked into Netflix—which, by the way, really does help give your mind a vacation from whatever you are going through. Below is an entire smorgasbord of funks and how they make us feel (very sh*tty).

The purpose of this chapter to identify what a funk is, how you can pinpoint when you are in one, and what you can do to get out of a funk. Sorry, there are no magic vaccinations to immunize you.

Funks fall into two basic categories: personal and professional. Personal funks can be emotional, mental, and/or physical.

Personal Funks
1. Emotional funks can be triggered by:
- Depression
- Loss—the end of a relationship, due to death, a breakup, or other reasons

- Postpartum depression
- Seasonal Affective Disorder (SAD)
- Being stuck in bad/unhealthy relationships
- Stress
- Tragedy—physical and/or mental trauma to you or someone close to you
- Not taking care of yourself
- Feeling overwhelmed

When your feelings affect your life, you need to be proactive. Find strategies that help you process whatever it is you are going through. Many people find help by seeing a therapist, implementing mindfulness techniques and therapy methods that help them express what is going on inside their head. We keep our emotions wrapped up so tightly, and whatever you have going on can impact everything you do and how you feel.

2. Mental funks can be triggered by:

- Low self-esteem from childhood or another experience
- Lack of confidence due to personal baggage, loss, trauma, or other incidents
- Feeling unattractive
- A mood disorder—genetic or environmental (for example, Seasonal Affective Disorder)
- An unhealthy body image
- Anxiety
- Loneliness
- Hopelessness

- Post-traumatic stress disorder (PTSD)
- Having unhealthy thoughts that prevent you from moving in a positive direction
- Feeling inadequate, unacceptable, not good enough—comparing yourself to others and always thinking you are less than everyone else
- Unfulfilled dreams and goals
- Poor communication with family and friends
- Boredom
- Lack of a social life and work-life balance

3. Physical funks can stem from an illness, an injury, or a health/wellness issue, such as:

- Cancer
- Other illnesses/conditions
- Sleep disorders
- Eating disorders
- Depression
- An addiction to food, medication, exercise, alcohol, and so on
- Mental illnesses
- Feeling stuck in a situation that you know is not healthy
- Vitamin or mineral deficiency
- Seasonal Affective Disorder

Professional Funks

If you find yourself in a career funk, see if some of the following resonate with you:

- Career limits: glass ceiling, no opportunities for growth and change
- Poor interpersonal communication with colleagues and boss(es)
- You're socially anxious, shy, and introverted
- Career changes: fired, downsized, job change
- You're poorly compensated—leading to a financial funk
- Lack of confidence to make a career change due to low self-esteem, financial constraints, lack of opportunities
- Lack of resources
- Feeling disrespected, unappreciated, not heard, invisible, and replaceable
- Not knowing what to do next, and unhappy in current situation
- Lack of balance between professional and personal life (for example, working too much)
- Taking on more than you can handle
- Unhealthy eating routines at work (for example, over-eating, skipping meals, making poor food choices, and not exercising)

Causes

Those funks we all get into happen from circumstances both beyond our control and within our control. If you let someone control you, whether through your emotions, your behavior, or otherwise, you will see your situation differently than someone who takes control and comes up with a plan. Even if that plan fails, at least you tried. There will always be plan B, plan C, and so forth. Just know that doing nothing and wallowing in your situation will get you nowhere. Being proactive and taking steps will get you moving and on to the next new adventure. If you lose your job, your ability to bounce back will come down to how you view your situation. Wallowing in self-doubt and insecurity is understandable; thinking along these lines long-term will not help you get another job or improve your self-esteem. Take care of yourself physically, mentally, and emotionally, so you can rebound faster when sh*t happens…because it will. Believe me.

When in Doubt, Ask for Help!

There is no shame in needing help. A family member, friend, therapist, or mentor/coach can be invaluable in these situations. Some people prefer an objective person who can provide the fresh perspective and advice they need and get them back on track. Ask a colleague or friend for some one-on-one time outside of your work setting. Surrounding yourself with more creative feedback and ideas can be beneficial, as long as you don't feel overwhelmed by too many ideas and directions. Creating a plan and a time frame for your new direction also will help; then you will be held accountable for your own excuses and procrastination.

If you suffer from anxiety in social situations or public speaking anxiety, you are not alone. Some types of anxiety stem from bad experiences or can be something your mind repeatedly believes. When you overthink and anticipate an event to the point that you cancel altogether, you will never conquer this feeling. Anxiety is very common; it can be triggered at any age by trauma, discomfort, uncertainty, and more. If you are an introvert like me, you know what it is like to prefer solitude and quiet time to recharge. We get overwhelmed in social situations and having to be "on." There are specific techniques designed to reduce these issues and skilled professionals who are trained in helping people overcome their anxieties and fears. Some people have success using apps and online techniques; these strategies are certainly worth a try. However, if you feel you are not moving forward, seek the advice of a skilled, reputable professional.

We tend to worry about the past and the future, and to overlook exactly where we are in the present moment. So much thought is spent anticipating and thinking we know exactly how an event or a conversation will play out, but unless you have some special powers, let it go. Breathe, take a leap, and let all the overthinking fall to the wayside. When I discuss mindfulness, yoga, and pampering, you will understand the importance of taking care of your mental and physical health. They go hand in hand.

Staying home, declining invitation after invitation to networking and social events is another way to hit rock bottom. Reach out to your network, your family and friends, and know that as much as you might dread change, sometimes a fresh start is the best thing that could ever happen. What you thought was so devastating just might be the beginning of a new opportunity.

Usually, when we search for something tirelessly, nothing happens. When we let our anxiety go and take a more chill, Zen-like attitude, we free ourselves from stress, anger, and anxiety. We are present in the moment, and mindfulness takes over. In that relaxed state, something unexpected and wonderful can happen. The end of something that leaves you feeling down in the dumps can spin like a plot twist in a movie, leaving you facing an exciting new direction. Think of this opportunity as your chance for a fresh start that might just lead you to a happier you. Rejections in life are sometimes the best things that ever happen. Of course, we don't see this at the very moment we feel flattened and stomped on. Oftentimes, opportunities arise and something better comes your way; it just might be what you needed, not what you wanted and planned for. So, the next time you are blindsided by something sudden and a bit scary, yell, *"Plot twist!"* It just might be the next best thing you needed.

My Twentysomething Precancerous Scare (aka Holy Sh*t! I Have *What?!*)

There is goodness in this world. There is love and kindness, too. You just have to look up and pay attention; it's all around us. Recently, while traveling through an airport, I noticed a thirty-something guy traveling with anatomy flash cards. A TSA agent inquired about the small box the man placed in the security bin.

"Anatomy flash cards?" asked the TSA agent.

"Yes, those are mine," said the thirtysomething guy.

"Are you studying to become a doctor?" she asked.

"Yes, I am," he said, smiling proudly.

"What will your specialty be?" she wondered.

"Cancer," he responded.

Goosebumps. Tears filled my eyes. I had to say something. He is a gift to this world.

"That is wonderful. My dad had cancer," I chimed in.

"So do a few of my family members," he added.

The security lady said, "There is goodness in this world."

And I told him exactly what I was feeling at that moment: "You are a gift we all need. Thank you."

Cancer. I hate that word. Who doesn't? There are so many of us affected by this ravenous disease and other incurable illnesses. I lost one grandmother to bladder cancer, my father to colon cancer, my other grandmother to Alzheimer's; a cousin won her fight against breast cancer, and my stepmother did, too. A sweetheart of a man I dated in Boston died of leukemia, which started as Hodgkin's lymphoma. And most recently, we lost my wonderful and adoring father-in-law to Parkinson's.

His passing was so incredibly sad and reverberated through the hearts and minds of so many family members and friends. Losing our loved ones is one of the hardest blows of life but is an inevitable part of our existence; we experience the dichotomy of birth and life's joyous moments while wondering how we will overcome the loss of a loved one and the painful aftermath.

When you are in your twenties, you often think you are infallible. I know I did, but then my doctor told me my Pap smears were all coming back abnormal. She diagnosed me with severe cervical dysplasia and said I had a precancerous condition. I am not sure I heard anything else after she said that; it was all a blur. I learned that I had abnormal cells growing on the surface lining of my cervix, and I needed surgery. I was scheduled to have a loop electrosurgical excision procedure (LEEP). A small electrical wire loop removes abnormal cells from the cervix to remove those bad cells and prevent cervical cancer.

I had repeated abnormal Pap smears, a colposcopy, and then a biopsy; they all screamed the same conclusion: "You have bad cells! *Get rid of them!*"

My reaction? "*Eeek!* You are going to do what to my what? With what kind of procedure?!" I was terrified! The worry was consuming me and draining me emotionally.

I agreed to the procedure, and thankfully my best friend at the time insisted on coming into the doctor's office with me. She is from Australia, and we formed a wonderful bond living in the same building in Brookline, Massachusetts. I just adored her, and when she insisted on coming in for the procedure, I had a feeling she knew what was right. After all, I had no family or anyone else to look after me; she was my closest family at that moment. I had nothing to hide, and this was not the time to be shy. I felt lucky she wanted to be by my side.

My doctor was wonderful. She had me lie down on the table in the doctor's office, and off we went to remove the bad piece of my cervix. Seemed like an easy, no-brainer procedure, but the pain from the numerous shots to numb my cervix was extremely uncomfortable. My friend could see my pain, and she was great trying to distract me by sharing details of her upcoming blind date. The actual procedure had not even started yet, and I couldn't wait for this to be over. In retrospect, I really should have had this LEEP in a hospital, because what happened next was so shocking and caused post-traumatic stress for weeks.

"Do you have your period?" the doctor asked in a panic. I could see the color rush out of her face, and her concern was glaringly obvious.

"No," I said. "Why?"

My friend took one look at the blood from down under and looked faint. Now, the tables were turned, and I knew what I had to do.

"Tell me about your date tonight. Is he cute?" I asked, attempting to calm her down. I squeezed her cold, sweaty hand and I instructed her not to look at what was happening. "Just keep talking. It's going to be okay," I said. OMG. In retrospect, I think I was talking to myself. I was hoping this wasn't how my story would end.

She was speechless and frightened. We squeezed each other's hands, and mine were freezing. She stammered. I repeated that I was going to be fine, "just talk to me, please." She described the guy she was going out with, and of course, we both knew we were just trying to distract each other. I was scared for myself and more so that my friend would faint right there in that office. She probably needed to lie down next to me.

Stitches followed, after the bleeding was under control. I had to lie there for a while afterward, which was good because I had to digest and calm down from what had just happened. "Scary" is an understatement.

A few days later, I was still so traumatized, which resulted in a panic attack as soon as I entered a restaurant. My friend took one look at me and knew something was wrong. "Are you okay?" she asked. Clearly, I wasn't. I was pale and claustrophobic, the restaurant started to close in on me, and I could feel my heart pounding and sweat pouring out of me. We ran to the car and I pulled my pants down, because I thought I was bleeding profusely again, and my stitches had busted open; it was obvious I was not ready to be out in public. I hunkered down in my apartment until

I was healed emotionally and physically. Pizza and wine had never tasted so good.

When Emotional Pain Turns into Physical Pain

Emotional pain can sometimes lead to physical pain, because our insides reflect what is going on in our mind, body, and inner core. Maybe you are a person who gets stomachaches and gut issues if things are messy in your life. That's me. My entire life. Stress, anxiety, or any other emotional upset rears its ugly head in my gut, and when I am happy and content, everything is calm.

Pain can also reverberate in other parts of your body. When I heard my father's cancer diagnosis, I started experiencing a nagging pain in my left shoulder. Pretty soon my mobility was limited, and when I moved a certain way, the pain was sharp and shocking. I would lose my breath from the sudden pain and grab my arm in agony. Diagnosis: frozen shoulder. Cause: overuse and repetitive weight lifting after I lost my friend. Forecast: extremely painful with a chance of surgery.

I tend to blow off going to the doctor until something gets really bad—like, my arm feels like it is going to fall off—and my quality of life hits rock bottom. Upon the urging of my family, I finally went. The doctor said my options were physical therapy, cortisone shots, and possibly surgery if nothing else worked. I told him the last one was never going to happen. Years ago, I went through back surgery for a horribly herniated disc, but my doctor was a rock star and put my anxieties to rest. In my opinion, you should do your homework, because you have one precious body. Get as many opinions as possible. Listen to your gut and talk with people who have been through what you are going through.

Exhaust every option before surgery, but if that's your last resort, find your own rock star doctor. The bigger message here is: Take care of your body. You have only one, and if it is screaming at you in pain, pay attention. Ignoring your body can make matters worse.

Just so you know, I am a big baby and hate needles; this will never change. I once ran around the room at a doctor's office (as a child, not as a grown woman, but I have been tempted), trying to escape a huge shot. My mother sent me by myself for the physical; there's an even scarier thought. The doctor finally grabbed my arm and slammed the needle into it. The next day my arm hurt more from the punch than from the needle.

Dr. A**hole. That wasn't his actual name, but it should have been. I was so young and not sure why the office staff asked me to fill out a form that asked all kinds of questions beyond my comprehension.

Question: "Sex?"

My answer: "None."

The funny thing was, I was nine years old—clueless, and thankfully I did not know what sex was.

Back to my herniated disc (from running with sciatica—I know! So *stupid*). I declined cortisone, because I've never liked the idea of a massive needle in my back and I am a big scaredy-cat baby. Still to this day. I once changed the dates on my immunization record in high school because I didn't want shots from some really old doctor who I am pretty sure was legally blind. I guess he really was blind, because I fooled that sucker. Don't worry, this was the first and last time I ever forged any records.

I couldn't fool my shoulder doctor at all. He insisted on cortisone shots, but I was very vocal about my fear of large needles and additional pain. He insisted I needed the shots, but in hindsight,

I am not even sure they did much. He did send in a nice nurse to hold my sweaty, nervous hand.

The stupid thing was, I had brought this injury on by attending a strengthening class almost every day and doing all kinds of exercises using hand weights. I did this because my friend had just passed away and I needed a diversion from my inner pain and shock. I guess I thought I would get in better shape, too. Epic fail, because I am pretty sure I tore something in my shoulder, which then healed funny, which was not funny "ha-ha!" but more like, "Oh sh*t! That feels so not funny. What the heck did I do?" It just ruined my range of motion, and my shoulder blades moved in a lopsided way, and then there was the constant pain. Lesson learned: Don't try to diminish pain by causing more pain.

Physical therapy was great, and slowly my shoulder motion improved and the pain lessened. I did plateau to a point where the doctor said he could "break up the loss of motion in surgery, but recovery could take months, and that is where the fun begins." Not my idea of fun, so I firmly declined, because I don't have time to be out of commission (unless I am on a remote beach somewhere). I don't need my body to move perfectly in alignment. No surgery for me.

I opted for more physical therapy and something new: massage. Yes, massage had a significant impact on me emotionally and physically, especially after my dad passed away. All the stress, anxiety, and sadness while Dad was suffering, and then following his death, were stored in my body. Finally, after two years, my pain was gone. Time and self-care helped me rebuild emotionally and physically.

Facing death is up there on the list of one of the worst funks you can face. However, I had a sense of calm and relief once Dad passed. Living with the *any day now / on high alert!* signage hanging over me and racing for the phone at all hours had been weighing on my drained body; it was no secret to those who know me. I was a deep wreck in funktown.

I felt that there were two phases to my funk: before my father died and after. Before was the torturous phase, but there were also so many meaningful fleeting moments. My stepfather, whom I had not spoken with in years, called me right after my father told me he had cancer—right after I hung up the phone. I was in a state of shock and running on autopilot, so I didn't tell him the news. I learned that love can come at the most unexpected times, and at the very moment you need to know you are loved. Our renewed relationship helped me through this journey. His love healed a lot of my wounds, and on days I felt I had hit rock bottom, he listened and kept showing up with his love and compassion, phone call after phone call.

My father was a tough man, but this was one battle he wasn't going to win. When he passed on December 4, 2015, I had spoken to him four times that day. The first time, he cracked one of his usual jokes about "being on the john." "Call me back in an hour. I will probably still be here," he said. The last time we spoke, he sounded weak, but we always ended the call with "I love you. Talk to you later." He used to say there was never goodbye, just "see you later."

I was asked to write his eulogy as I flew from California to Florida. I always carry a notebook, so I wrote, cried, wrote some more, and wiped my tears off my face and the pages as the words poured out. Four pages and a lot of corrections later, I was done. The thing is, I hate public speaking and always avoid it at all costs. With barely a few hours of sleep, I walked to the podium at the funeral. A small but mighty group of close family members and friends was waiting to hear my words. And then something different happened. I looked out and I could see the heavy hearts around me, the tears, the sadness. Something occurred to me: It was an honor that I was the one speaking at my dad's funeral. I stood at that podium all alone, and it felt like a privilege.

At that very moment, I knew I needed to be heard and not crumble. I needed to share memories that others might not know about my father. As I opened my mouth and began to speak, something miraculous happened. I was the most confident and calmest person I had ever been, in any speech I had ever given. The truth was, there was nothing to fear, and I realized that my father had been coaching me for years to become more confident. He knew, more than I did, that I had the ability to do anything I set my mind to. He prepared me to work my hardest, speak my mind, and express my thoughts. My eulogy was not a serious, tearjerker speech. I reminded everyone what a goofball, workaholic, religious and sensitive big bear of a man Dad was. Between the tears, there were smiles and laughter. I wanted to capture Dad exactly the way he was, the way we all remembered. I wrote the eulogy to give us some levity on a very heavy day. Death is inevitable. Mourning is part of the process. How long the mourning takes is up to us, but at some point, we move on and treasure what we have and who we are, and what is in store.

Let's look at three guests from my show who have their own perspectives on personal and professional funks and see how they worked through them. Here are Gary Pihl of the American rock band Boston; Robin Farmanfarmaian, member of the Forbes Business Development Council, professional speaker, entrepreneur, and author; and Cindy Charlton, triple amputee, professional motivational speaker, and author. Each shares personal experiences, advice, and insightful anecdotes.

Meet Gary Pihl

"We can play funky and sing the blues, but we don't have to live it."
—*Gary Pihl, guitarist for the band Boston*

Gary has a lot of empathy for people who may be "in a funk," have "lost their mojo," or have "the blues." He knows they are not alone. Gary feels that funks have no boundaries when it comes to age, race, or social standing; a funk is an equal-opportunity malady. As a musician, Gary has seen plenty of his bandmates go through a whole range of issues, from stage fright and writer's block to social anxiety and just plain inability to get out of bed. He says, "Musicians can get away with being eccentric or weird, because people will cut us some slack, thinking, 'They're in a creative space and a bit out of touch.' We've lost some of the most influential icons of music because we didn't intervene when the signs were clearly there that this person was in trouble."

What is Gary's advice for staying out of a funk? Be active. He has been an avid runner since high school, running fifteen miles a week. He has never touched drugs or alcohol and is thankful to his parents for his Christian Scientist upbringing. He does admit to having had his first aspirin a few years ago, for a root canal! Gary urges people to help one another overcome being in a funk. And when life becomes difficult, it is best to go seek advice from a mental health professional. Sometimes people can't see their own issues in front of them, and the solutions might be diet, exercise, or something more serious. Gary doesn't want anyone to wait until a solution is too late. He encourages people to keep a watchful eye out for family and friends.

Gary advises, "When you're feeling blue, do something for somebody else! It's amazing how quickly you forget about your own troubles when someone needs your help." In addition to playing in the rock band Boston, Gary is in a charity band called December People. "During November and December, we play traditional holiday songs but in the styles of our favorite bands," he says. They do a lot of styles from A to Z. Gary says, "Think AC/DC doing 'Rudolph the Red-Nosed Reindeer,' ZZ Top doing 'Santa Claus Is Coming to Town,' Billy Idol doing 'White Christmas' like he does 'White Wedding.' You get it, right? It's family friendly, a lot of fun for the audience, and all of our shows benefit local food banks."

Find Gary and his band at *bandboston.com*

Meet Robin Farmanfarmaian

"Set goals, help a lot of people along the way, and laugh."
—*Robin Farmanfarmaian*

Robin Farmanfarmaian was continually being bullied and sabotaged at work. The torment never stopped, and the abusive behavior was never dealt with by management. She was verbally berated about her work in front of clients and told she was worthless. Robin turned her life around, because her attitude is all about resilience. No matter what happens, she knows she will survive and thrive. She always has backup plans and can find a solution quickly. She also loves to keep options open. With her wide variety of skills, there are always multiple life paths for her to choose from. Through all of life's challenges, Robin believes success is the best revenge, which makes her the overall winner already in any situation.

When asked how difficult or easy it was to pull herself out of a funk she had, Robin says it took a lot of effort. She was depressed for months, but only for part of the day. She had an exercise routine, got plenty of sleep, spent time with friends. Plus, listening to music and spending time outside in the sunlight helped her a lot. She reflected internally on what was going on externally. Goal setting is now a huge part of her daily, weekly, and yearly routine. And she gets incredible joy from helping others. Years ago, Robin had to undergo forty-three hospitalizations and six major surgeries. Her laid-back view of life has helped her believe that if it's not life threatening, then there is always a solution or a way to deal with her situation.

She is currently a patient with a severe chronic disease. Every day of her life is a struggle with pain and fear—fear of food obstructions that need surgery, fear of dehydration requiring IVs, fear of overwhelming pain, fear of catching something while immunocompromised—these are very real daily worries in her life.

Robin is a professional speaker, an entrepreneur, an author, and an angel investor. She is also a member of the Forbes Business Development Council, a vice president of Invicta Medical, a cofounder of and member of the board for the Organ Preservation Alliance, and a vice president of Actavalon.

Find Robin at *robinff.com*

Meet Cindy Charlton

"If you only look at what you've lost, you will never be able to see what you have."
—Cindy Charlton

Cindy Charlton is one of the most inspiring guests to have graced the airwaves on my show. She is a professional speaker and an author with a valuable message. Cindy has lost her husband to cancer and is living life as a triple amputee; her story of survival is nothing short of a miracle. When she speaks, she is filled with inspiration, hope, and strength. Her message: Make the most out of every moment. One of Cindy's biggest survival tools is her resiliency. She has always had the ability to bounce back no matter what the circumstances; she believes this is just part of her genetic make-up, which includes, "pure, unadulterated stubbornness. The other part comes from a much deeper place, a place of respect, specifically self-respect."

Here's the backstory of how Cindy became a triple amputee. People get overwhelmed when they hear her story, but she has a different view of herself. "I am just a person who has had adversity and has had to deal with it, not unlike most people," she says. Cindy has always been a positive person. She believes she was born with her glass half full, but she told me her mom said she was born with a glass of champagne, ready to party!

Cindy has always been very positive in her life and believes she gets her optimism from her dad; she feels very fortunate to have him as her role model. Her mom, on the other hand, would say to never hope for the very best, because when you don't get it, you won't be disappointed. Her response to that was, "Yeah, but in the time that you are hoping for the best, it's thrilling and exciting!" Cindy believes, why not live in the excitement for the moment?

When we spoke, she shared that she had recently added a new member to her family: a dog. She had been so sad, losing her tiny dog, Lilly, she'd had for twelve years. Lilly was a service dog, Cindy says. "She demanded the service, and I provided it," she jokes. "She was a gift and came to me after my husband, Michael, passed away; she was my companion." Her faithful companion would sit with Cindy in the living room, where she had been unable to sit before; she had been much too lonely after losing Michael. Cindy felt more complete with her new companion, because losing her husband was devastating to her and her boys.

For her birthday, her boys decided she and they needed a dog, and they adopted a three-year-old beagle. At first, she was not so pleased, but she quickly realized that the dog was a wonderful addition to the family. That beagle gets Cindy walking every day and helps her with her mission to get fit.

Cindy candidly shared the story of when she first realized something was wrong with her. It was February 13, 1997, at 4:55 p.m. She will remember that date until the day she dies. She says it hit her profoundly, like the Twin Towers, Columbine, and the assassination of JFK. Cindy was in her office getting ready to leave northern Denver. She was attending night school working on her paralegal degree, thinking she might want to be an attorney when she grew up. She got a piercing pain under her left arm and couldn't figure out why. During the class, she felt worse, and when she got home, she told her husband that she was not feeling well. The next morning, she was very sick to her stomach and in an incredible amount of pain. She thought she had injured her arm and thought the pain was making her sick.

They went to the ER; Michael dropped her off and took their sons, four-year-old Wes and one-year-old Colin, to daycare. The doctor sent her home with pain meds; he thought it was a virus that had settled in her arm muscle. Twelve hours later, she was back in the ER fighting for her life. Strep A—necrotizing fasciitis, also known as flesh-eating bacteria, was attacking Cindy's body.

Cindy had no idea where she had contracted this infection. She has since read a lot about this life-threatening bacteria and has even met survivors. A portal of entry into the body allows bacteria into the bloodstream, but for her there was no obvious portal of entry. The doctors were confused at first. By the time they figured it out, it was too late. The bacteria moved rapidly, and she is lucky to be alive. There were several diagnoses regarding what could be wrong, and doctors even thought it was a blood clot in her lung. That was the last thing she heard.

She was given so many infusions and painkillers that the doctors could not believe she was even conscious. Cindy shared that "the pain almost had its own identity, keeping me very focused." They gave her so much morphine that she had to be moved to the cardiac care unit. The infectious-disease doctor told her she "fell off the cliff." Her blood pressure crashed, and her heart stopped. The compassionate doctor held her hand and told her that she most likely would not make it. They took Cindy to surgery to try to combat the bacteria and remove the infected tissue.

After her first surgery, she was airlifted just a few miles away to a hospital that had hyperbaric chambers. Cindy explained that there is a theory that the intense oxygen in hyperbaric chambers helps fight the bacteria. They had to airlift her even though the other hospital was only two miles away; ground transportation did not have the equipment to sustain her life. She was airlifted, sedated from surgery, then put in a drug-induced coma for forty-five days.

She went into the hospital on February 15 in the early morning, and when she came to and figured out what was going on, it was March 31. She felt like Rip Van Winkle. When she awoke, she realized that she had no legs, had no right hand and arm, and half of her chest was gone. She could not wrap her mind around what had happened. She was extremely distraught, as you can imagine.

A doctor kept coming into the intensive care unit and calling her "Miracle Lady." The first time she heard him say those words, she looked at him strangely. Every time he saw her, he kept referring to her as the Miracle Lady. Even though she could not speak because of a tracheotomy, Cindy motioned for him to come into her room. She asked him why he was calling her Miracle Lady. He shared how he had flown in with her on the flight, and her heart had stopped twice. When they landed, the ICU team came out with a team nurse, who asked the doctor what Cindy's prognosis was, and he said to the nurse, "If she makes it through the night, it will be nothing short of miraculous." And that is why the doctor called her the Miracle Lady.

At that moment, she realized how lucky she was. She had no idea how close she had come to dying. She thought about her two young boys at home, a loving husband, a house, and two cars, and the only thing missing was her dog. She was filled with gratitude because she had survived the unimaginable. When I told her, "You are incredible!" she said she just considers herself lucky. She feels tremendous gratitude for still being here and has always felt immense gratitude for everything in her life.

Sure, she has had days of being distraught and filled with anguish, especially after losing her husband. Her boys were five and nine years of age at the time. She was newly disabled, and she was struggling to figure out how she was going to make her new life work. Cindy's and her children's grief was enormous, but Cindy shared that she has a cache of survivor tools. The first tool is gratitude. The other tool, which she recognized through her late husband's illness and what he recognized in her, is courage.

Gratitude and courage have gotten her through everything. She is courageous and does not allow fear to drive her. Her courage keeps her going.

She has tons of survivor tools, but the most used is gratitude; it's the number-one thing that keeps her focused, and the positive attitude comes through the gratitude. She has a lot to be grateful for. After losing her husband, she knew she had to be strong for her kids.

Cindy shared the story of how a close friend said it was "unbelievable what she had been though." Her friend told her that the best thing that would come out of this is that her sons would grow up to be very strong and very compassionate young men. "From your lips to God's ears," she responded. She feels so grateful because her boys are very strong and dependable, and they are all very close to one another.

When she was in the hospital, she had many people, even total strangers, sending her cards and doing things for her and her family. She told me, "I was so overwhelmed by the glory of humanity, I can't even tell you; that made me want to go out and pay it forward. And I mean spiritually, because I felt divine intervention, and I had been given a second chance at life." She said she really wanted to pay it forward, to do good things for as many people as she could.

In 1999, she met a man who was a bilateral amputee, below the knees, like Cindy. He was very knowledgeable about national legislation and was recruiting people to help work on the Prosthetic Parity bill for the state of Colorado. She volunteered to work on the committee. They wrote the bill, which would require health insurance companies to pay for prosthetic arms and legs. She testified before the Senate and the House. The bill was passed on the first attempt, and was signed into law in 2000. Since then, about thirty other states have passed the same health insurance mandate; this was a huge financial relief for so many people. As she explained to the House and Senate committees, she wears the equivalent of a brand-new SUV on her body in terms of cost! People don't realize the expense of a prosthetic limb.

Cindy has a master's degree in psychology and helped organize and facilitate an amputee support group in the Denver metro area; she is a certified peer counselor through the Amputee Coalition.

Cindy is known as the "Disability Diva," for her training programs on disability etiquette and the Americans with Disabilities Act for corporations and nonprofits. Her disability etiquette presentation, "What Do You Say to a One-Armed Lady?" has been accredited for continuing legal education (CLE). She is a contributing writer in five *Chicken Soup for the Soul* books, including *Family Caregivers, Power of Positive, Angels Among Us, From Lemons to Lemonade*, and most recently *The Miracle of Love*. Cindy writes about her life as a survivor on her blog entitled *The Survivor's Handbook*. She believes that being a mother to her two sons is her most important job and the biggest blessing in her life. Cindy is now also the program director of rehabilitation services and the stroke day program at Easterseals Colorado.

Cindy is also a columnist at *inMotion* magazine, which focuses on amputees. In 2015, her work was published in a literary journal, *Progenitor*. Her story, "My Left Breast," was nominated for a literary award called The Pushcart Prize. She hopes her writing will give people hope and inspiration. She talks about lifelines, about what or who throws you a lifeline to pull you out of the darkness and into the light. During her time in the hospital, she had so many visitors that it was overwhelming and exhausting. She was so determined to get out of that hospital after three months, followed by rehab for nine weeks. Rehab was not easy for her, especially getting up on her prosthetic legs. The physical therapy was an incredible workout but painful. Cindy had to make a decision, and hers was to move on—to go on and not get stuck in despair, pain, and darkness. She chose to step forward. She told me, "It can cost you emotionally or physically to move on, but it's worth it."

Cindy's parents stayed with her for a long time after she lost her husband to cancer. Cindy wanted to write a thank-you letter to all the people who had helped her along the way, such as by sending her cards, letters, and gifts. When she shared the letter with her mother, she noticed tears streaming from her mother's eyes. Her mother could not believe how positive she was after everything she had lost. Cindy's response: "Well, Mom, if you only look at what you lost, you'll never be able to see what you have." And she feels that if you get stuck in the dark, all you will see is darkness.

When we spoke, she was talking about her goal of training for the Paralympic Games tryouts with her cool running blades! She told me she was ready to get running to "get the funk out!" Funk? I didn't recognize any funk whatsoever. *Go Cindy!* When I asked if there was anything else she wanted to share, she concluded by saying, "Anything can happen to anyone at any time, but it's what you do with the anything that matters. If you get up every day and you find something, no matter how big or small, to be grateful for in your life, your day will be blessed."

Find Cindy at *CindyCharltonSpeaks.com* and *http://thesurvivorshandbook.blogspot.com/*

In a Nutshell

There you have it—three different perspectives from Gary, Robin, and Cindy.

Now it's your turn. What are some details of your own recent funk?

Last _____ I was _____ (profession) and everything was _____. Then _____ (person/event) happened and the sh*t hit the _____ (object). I had never felt more _____, so I decided to _____; this made me feel _____ (emotion), which was great at first and then I realized _____ is the real problem. After this reality slap, I ate a lot of _____, took a lot of _____, and watched a lot of _____ and _____, which made me feel _____, except for maybe the _____. Now I know if I ever find myself in a similar situation, _____ will help me, and also lots of _____. Plus, I do primal screaming when no one is around and yell _____ at the top of my lungs!

CHAPTER 2

Feeling Funky?
Welcome to the Club!

"Praise all scars, which, by definition, reveal that something, one thing, one thing minimum, is healed."—Thomas Lux

Let's face it: We all get in a funk sometimes. Funks spin your life out of control. One day you are fine and the next, you might find yourself diving into a doozy of a binger, a food coma, a relationship that isn't even right for you, or some other outlet that really doesn't help the situation. And guess what? No one can tell you when it's time to get out of your funk either. Funks are very personal. Some incredibly resilient people quickly pick themselves up and move on. Others lean on their friends, overeat or drink too much, call up their old loser of a boyfriend or girlfriend in a boozy stupor to yell at the top of their lungs. These things might feel cathartic at the time, but long term they don't work. The next day, you'll probably have some serious regrets. And venting on social media is another big no-no. Get a grip and don't act like a lunatic.

Then there are those who might find themselves unable to walk down either path, and instead lie down in a sea of depression filled with self-loathing, pity, sadness, drugs, and alcohol. I highly recommend therapy if you find yourself relating to this. There are numerous types of therapy, and whatever strategy works for you can be life changing. Therapy can help you sort out years of piled-up, repressed sh*t. You get a chance to discover just how complex you really are, and to work through your backstory, current story, and overthinking, stressed-out self. You'll have breakthroughs, and you'll work through habits and pent-up emotions from fear and anger to repressed emotions and memories. The right therapy will help you feel open and connected in a safe, objective environment.

No one should be in a funk forever, so find the best solution that works for you. I personally think that talking about what is troubling us is a great form of therapy. You can't find the answer to your problems in the bottom of a stiff drink or some pharmaceutical prescription. I know because I have lost several people who just could not find their way out of a spiraling funk. No matter what pill they took, no matter what anyone said, they checked out. There are so many avenues for you to explore and people who want to help you. Just take a step; it doesn't matter how big your step. Just take one step in the right direction.

I wrote this book because I'm fascinated by how some people face a crisis in their life and wake up one day with a solution that helps them move on. Unfortunately, there are others who look for answers in places they will never find answers and they experience a free fall into sadness and a life of unfulfilled aspirations. When we fall apart, it's okay. We are human. We make mistakes, and we must forgive ourselves and be our own best friend. Breaking into a gazillion little pieces emotionally gives a chance to rebuild ourselves into a better version, a version we might never have imagined. When things seem hopeless and nothing makes any sense, take a breath, because darkness can turn to light in the words of stranger, a phone call, or a sudden epiphany. Unexpected moments await all of us, and we must let go of things we cannot control. When we let life happen and take a deep breath, our world unfolds, not as we planned and expected it to.

In life, we all have choices. We can choose to get up, dust ourselves off, learn from our funks, and come out stronger and more resilient. Or there is that dark, ambiguous path to nowhere. That path keeps you down and going nowhere. You blame yourself, ignore your destructive patterns, drown in your uncertainty and self-doubt. That dark road is often necessary to find deep insight into what lies ahead, but don't feel you have to go down this challenging road alone. Depression can also be genetic, environmental, and influenced by other internal and external factors. Take a close look at how you treat your body, mind, and well-being. Seek professional help and make sure you have a supportive network of family, friends, and colleagues who want the best for you and support you. If you don't, any negativity can drag you down even further, and who needs that detrimental sh*t?! Certainly not you.

What makes me an expert on all of this? Numerous personal experiences have rocked my world repeatedly since I was a little girl, but somehow, I managed to learn from the negativity thrown my way. All the hard times made me smarter, kinder to myself, introspective, and more resilient. I have also learned the importance of taking really good care of myself, gratitude, deep reflection, and having coping mechanisms that can aid me in any situation.

Here's one of the real reasons I wrote this book. I lost one of my closest high school friends in 2010. I didn't just lose her.

She lost herself to wine, medication, insecurities, sadness, and love—or lack thereof. For as long as I knew her, she was forever chasing happiness and longing for love and to be loved. I was told she ended her life on December 29, 2010, with her mother and fiancé in the next room. There are a lot of details I will never know. The whole situation didn't sit well with me, and I wish I had more answers. Only she knows what was going through her mind that night in New Orleans, four days after Christmas. Of course, I wish I had known the depths of what was going on with her, but I learned long ago, you cannot beat yourself up with "should have, could have, would have."

My reaction when I found out? Shock. Horror. Devastation. Disbelief. And the nonstop need to cry and wish this nightmare was over. At the dinner table, I could barely speak and carry on a conversation. As a contributor to this book once said, "death is the meanest thief." I will miss her forever. She had been my best friend in high school for years, and we shared so many memories.

I knew I would have to somehow put one foot in front of the other, even though I just could not comprehend that she was gone. The truth was that deep down inside, she was always unhappy, wanting that perfect unattainable relationship. I began to see a pattern of unhappiness when she told me she was engaged for the fourth time. My gut told me to pay attention to several details: four engagements and her glowing descriptions and pictures of how great her life seemed to be—an illusion. She was thrilled to be learning to fly planes, like her late father. I could see she was living her dream, and that was fantastic. I admired her for her smarts, drive, and zest for life. Whatever she set her mind to, she went after with 100 percent of her heart. She was also part of the Free Hugs organization in Chicago, where she lived. Something in my gut told me that her wisecracking sense of humor and happy-faced pictures were a facade. I know, because friends can see through the bullsh*t.

The truth is, she had been in so many funks that they created a spiraling funnel that led to her demise. She was out of work and had lost her father to cancer in 2008, and she was crushed when he died. Even though she earned an MBA and was highly intelligent, she had no idea what she would do next. A tough job market crushes some people's self-esteem. She always dreamed of being married and in a loving relationship. Knowing that would never happen ripped my heart out.

I have come to terms with the fact that I will never get over losing her. Slowly, I have healed and moved forward, but the scar is big and deep in my soul. There are so many things I wish I could say, but don't we all feel that way when someone dies? I used to call her voicemail just to hear the sound of her voice. One day, I recorded her message, so I would have her voice with me forever. I am so glad I did.

In the aftermath of taking a year off from my radio show, I decided to switch from a music show to a talk show. I had a new direction and focus, and decided to call my show *Get the Funk Out!*. Creating this show was my way of honoring my friend and anyone else who might be suffering in darkness and despair. I dedicated my focus to her memory, not really knowing where my new show would lead. I just had this deep desire to inspire others on their own journey, especially when life gets rocky. Conversation after conversation with my show guests led me to understand that there really are inspiring ways to get out of a rough patch and move forward. But you must be willing to walk directly through that awful, crappy rough patch to see what you are made of and find yourself on the other side, where there is something better and something new. You also must come to terms with the fact that your current situation is not what you need and deserve, and that there is a happier life for you around the corner; it all depends on how bad you want to be happy and get out of your funk.

For those who have been in a deep, dark funk, you know what it is like to feel like you might never smile again, or like you might not feel joy or laugh for a very long time. Life is filled with moments that challenge us. Sometimes they are smaller challenges, which I compare to hiccups; they are annoying and unexpected. You can't control them and just want them to stop. The more you focus on stopping them, the more they persist, until you focus on something else, and then they go away. Grief is like that; it can suck the life out of you, but it is temporary if you want it to be. You must want to move forward at any speed.

Sometimes we just need to get our faces out of our phones and disconnect from our current environment. See the beauty and joy of life, be present in the moment, and feel the gratitude and love you have deep in your soul. Surround yourself with your family and posse; they know you and have your back.

There is joy in everyday moments, and especially unexpected joy. Time will help you heal to the best of your ability, as much as you will allow. Be open to the possibility of happiness around you, even in the simplest forms. Find gratitude in your life, and joy will follow. Remember to love yourself and surround yourself with people who love and respect you, because we all need a posse and a cheering section. Be kind and patient with yourself, and be open to new events and opportunities to shift and grow.

Own up to your funk. Don't hide from your feelings and issues. Admit when things are just plain sh*tty. We are not expected to walk through this life constantly happy with a permanent smile on our faces. And if you don't feel like answering the typical greeting "how are you?" with "fine," be honest. You never know who will brighten your day when you least expect it. Just don't go overboard and hurl your issues onto others! Let's say, for example, you are at your local grocery store:

Checkout person: How are you today? Find everything you wanted?

You: *No!* I did not want to find out my boyfriend [or girlfriend] *cheated on me* with *someone on Tinder!*

Checkout person: Do you need help—

You: Do I look like I need help?!

Checkout person: …to your car.

Sometimes venting to a close friend or two or even a therapist is a good start in unraveling what exactly happened and how to move forward. When dealing with a funk, understand that there are negative and positive ways to handle the situation. As you read through the following situations, make a mental note of which ones are relatable.

There are two roads people take when dealing with funks— the negative and the positive. The negative road sends you straight into "funktown"; it makes you more of a wreck and is a detriment to your recovery. The positive path, on the other hand, helps you get back on track. Negative roads are filled with negative actions and negative self-talk that are a step back in your recovery, whereas the positive road can be healing, insightful, and the path to self-love and growth.

The Negative Road

- ⟳ Overeating, not eating enough, or making poor eating choices

- ⟳ Self-medicating with drugs that can have adverse effects and cause more problems, such as antidepressants. (Did you know these may cause suicidal tendencies? Odd, but true. Listen to those ridiculously fast disclaimers.)

- ⟳ Taking medicines that enhance how you are feeling— either the wrong dose of an antidepressant or a drug that has a negative side effect. If this is you, speak with a doctor, especially someone you can open up to.

- ⟳ Drugs and alcohol (and mixing with other meds can be a recipe for disaster)

- ⟳ Shutting out loved ones—emotionally and physically

- ⟳ Dieting extremes or fad diets

- ⟳ Inflicting harm on your body

- ⟳ Not getting enough sleep or sleeping longer than usual and not being able to get out of bed

- ⟳ Compulsive purchases

- ⟳ Spending money you don't have

- ⟳ Lacking patience for others and yourself

- ⟳ Being aggressive and impulsive

- ⟳ Spending most of your time on your phone and computer and not connecting on a personal level

- ⟳ Having mood swings and anger issues that make others want to run in the other direction

- ⟳ Having poor communication skills when dealing with family and colleagues

Negative Self-Talk

- ⟁ I can't do this; I don't have what it takes.

- ⟁ I feel like an imposter.

- ⟁ I am not good enough, especially since _____ said so!

- ⟁ I just don't know where to start, and I feel overwhelmed.

- ⟁ I deserve this because I wasn't good enough for him [or her].

- ⟁ No one likes me.

- ⟁ I don't even like myself.

- ⟁ I can't, because I am too _____.

- ⟁ I am too old to do what I have always wanted to.

- ⟁ I have no skill set.

- ⟁ Everyone else is doing great things in life, and I don't know if I will ever achieve greatness.

- ⟁ Everyone else seems so happy, and I am not a happy person.

- ⟁ I am an introvert, and that can't be good.

- ⟁ I don't know what to do with my life, now that my _____ is over.

The Positive Road—aka Funkblasters!

- ⟁ Eating healthfully can change the way you feel physically and mentally. It's not a difficult concept. If you eat well, you feel better. Eat crappy? You feel like crap. Simple.

- Avoiding foods and beverages that cause negative effects (weight gain, impairment, out-of-control behavior, allergies, immune issues, and so on)

- Opening up and sharing what bothers you

- Doing things you love

- Getting off the grid and disconnecting from technology

- Trying new activities (on a bucket list or something unexpected). Why not?

- Journaling—expressing your thoughts and emotions freely

- Therapy—talk therapy, art therapy, and the like

- Socializing

- Fitness

- Religious practices

- Health and wellness activities

- Adopting or fostering a pet

- Helping others—random acts of kindness for a senior citizen, child, or total stranger

- Loving yourself—treating yourself with kindness, love, and respect. Don't depend on others to treat you the way you want and deserve if you don't put yourself first.

- Being around positive people

- Saying yes to events and doing things you otherwise might never do—don't miss an event, because you might miss out on a chance for happiness and an unexpected twist in a more positive direction

- Tossing out your clutter and donating the useless baggage in your life to a good cause
- Cleaning up your act—yourself and your home. Bathe, take care of your body, and clean your home. You don't want your dust bunnies mating. I know this from experience.
- Taking a mental vacation by attending a concert, comedy show, movie, or something similar
- Having a staycation
- Cooking
- Having a party! Consider a theme like "Suddenly Single!" or "Divorce Party!" or "I Hated My Job Anyway!"
- Pampering yourself with a massage, mani-pedi, make-over, or something similar
- Taking a walk in the beautiful outdoors or wherever you are
- Reflecting on your current situation in stillness or while walking or doing something else relaxing

Positive Self-Talk

- I can do this!
- There is nothing holding me back but me.
- The only person who can make me feel bad about myself is me.
- Yes, I screwed up, but I will get through this.
- Change is good. Change is exciting.

- ⤺ I can't wait to _____!
- ⤺ This is probably for the best, and I am excited to see what I do next.
- ⤺ Through this darkness, there will be light.
- ⤺ I am not alone. I have family and friends who love me.
- ⤺ I don't have to keep fixing myself. I am perfect the way I am.
- ⤺ I love who I am.
- ⤺ I am happy with my personal and professional life.
- ⤺ I can now focus more on me, my needs, and what I want in life.
- ⤺ I have always wanted to _____, so now is the time.
- ⤺ I am tired of doing what is expected of me and trying to please others. I need to focus on what I want, even if people don't support me. This is my life; it's up to me to live it the way I want.

This next section includes stories about how people have dealt with a funk. Some people start off in a negative mindset, because they have hit rock bottom or close to it. Others immediately think of strategies to deal with their situation in an optimistic way. These mindsets are sometimes learned in our youth. Others say that they have had a positive outlook all of their lives. Who are these people, and how did they get so lucky?

Meet Jill Santopolo

On September 11, 2001, Jill Santopolo was a student at Columbia University in New York City attending a Shakespeare lecture. From her experiences that day, she created the characters in her novel, *The Light We Lost*. The story came to life years later, as a result of a terribly emotional breakup. She told me, "It was like when your world is turned upside down and your heart is in pieces on the floor, and you are not sure what to do next." Those words are so relatable.

Jill started writing vignettes about a woman who had also gone through a breakup. In her story, her main character is not Jill and her boyfriend isn't Jill's boyfriend. However, the emotions her character is feeling are what Jill was dealing with. Jill didn't think this was going to be a novel but shared her work with a friend. "You've got the beginning of a novel!" the friend said. And Jill was off and running. When I asked her to share what she does to get out of a funk, Jill told me, "It's what a three-year-old does with an imaginary friend, just the adult version." Writing gave Jill something to concentrate on, so she was not always thinking about what was happening. She focused on the people in the other world she created. Her mom said she thinks that what Jill went through was supposed to happen, because her experience opened up an entirely new chapter in Jill's life...for the better.

Before she wrote *The Light We Lost*, Jill had been writing for a younger audience quite successfully. From 2008 to 2017, she wrote fourteen children's books. When I asked whether she was writing as much when she had been in her relationship, she said no. I told her to call and thank her ex right away! She wrote a little before the breakup and *a lot* after. Her whole world opened up because of her breakup...for the best! Life gives you gifts when you least expect them. Jill considers the departure from writing for a younger audience really enjoyable. She loves being the visiting author at schools and talking about writing, helping students find their voices and teaching writing techniques.

With *The Light We Lost*, Jill doesn't interact with young fans in schools or libraries. Instead, she connects with her adult fans on social media. The people she connects with share breakups and first loves, and how they relate to Jill's characters. What is so personal and intimate for Jill has struck a chord with other people, which is very rewarding.

The Light We Lost is the only book she has written in the first person. She wanted to capture the intimacy of having someone else hear her internal monologue. When she was in her previous relationship, she was thinking all the time about telling her boyfriend about something she had seen or experienced; he was in her head all day. She wanted to create a style that would capture that intimacy, so she uses "you" a lot in the book. The story evolved because of where she was emotionally.

When we spoke, Jill had recently been chosen to be a part of Reese Witherspoon's book club, and was mentioned by Reese on Instagram. In February 2019, Jill's next book, *More Than Words*, will be published. In addition to attending Columbia, Jill has an MFA in writing from the Vermont College of Fine Arts and is an adjunct professor at The New School. She works with the MFA students who are writing for children and young adults. She loves working with writers and helping them figure out their visions for their stories and how to shape their stories. She is also an associate publisher at a children's book imprint, Penguin Young Readers group at Penguin Random House.

When I asked if she always wanted to be a writer, she said, "Kind of. I wrote my first book at three. My mother was an elementary school teacher, and she used a laminating machine to laminate a lot of things I did when I was a child, so I still have a copy of that first book." The story is about Stacy the Cat, who is a fat cat who sat on a mat, and when you pat Stacy the Cat, you turn into a mat. Props to her mom for saving the book, because Jill always loved writing and telling stories. She wrote a lot of stories in first grade and asked her friends to illustrate her books. When visiting authors came to her school, she realized that writing was a career. Her mom's first cousin was a writer, and Jill attended book signings. The road to becoming a writer can have detours, but we always come back to what we love.

Jill shared that when she visits schools, she brainstorms a story with the kids. She provides prompts, a setting, and so on. Whatever it is, they go with it! There are no impossible stories. There is no end to our creative imaginations.

Find Jill at *www.Jillsantopolo.com,* and on Instagram *@jillsantopolo,* Twitter *@jillsantopolo,* and Facebook at *jillsantopoloauthor.*

Meet Elena Stowell

When I spoke with Elena Stowell, author, science teacher, and Brazilian jiu-jitsu practitioner, she shared the story behind her latest book, *Frango & Chicken.* She had been asked to attend an illustration workshop, and had no interested in illustrating! Her friend thought she might enjoy the class, and Elena quickly envisioned her Brazilian friend Luciano's becoming an illustration.

Having creative outlets has been a necessity for Elena. In 2007, she suddenly lost her fifteen-year-old daughter, Carly.

Her first book, *Flowing with the Go*, is a memoir she created from grief counseling. She shared her experiences with jiu-jitsu, and the writing was cathartic. Elena continued to dive into all things creative: cement steppingstones, mosaics, stenciling the walls; that is how she survived. Sometimes people hit rock bottom and can't get out. She knew it was hard, but she had to do something to face this catastrophic event.

Elena and I share the same sentiment. Once you learn life skills, your toolkit helps you face anything that comes down the road. Along the way, it's hard to put yourself out there. The support of friends helped her. "If you keep yourself open and you share, you will find so many other people who share your story and you strengthen them," she said. She could not believe she could actually help others. When they appreciated Elena, their admiration built her up. "There's a network of people who want you to carry on," she explained.

Elena found tremendous meaning in why she met her Brazilian friend Luciano. When she went to a book fair in Brazil to promote her memoir translated into Portuguese, she could not speak a word of the language; this is when she met Luciano. She was struck by Brazil and started a nonprofit called Give the Gift of the Gi; she collected jiu-jitsu uniforms. She found jiu-jitsu a year and a half after her daughter died.

She met Luciano where she went to do her jiu-jitsu training. The following year, she continued to train with Luciano and work with Brazilian children. Luciano was so inspiring to Elena! He was a double-arm amputee with a huge smile and a great attitude, and he was incredibly talented in jiu-jitsu! Less than 125 pounds of talent and power! Rooster weight is his class. His nickname is Frango, which is "chicken" in Portuguese. In *Frango & Chicken*,

Elena named the main character's sidekick Chicken. Luciano is so honored to be featured in her book—"my mom far away" he calls Elena. She sees him whenever she travels to Brazil.

Elena's books were translated into Portuguese, and she had them printed as booklets, which she distributes to kids and grown-ups in Brazil. The families she works with don't own a book or can't afford a book. She received some donations to help with the printing and brings Luciano along. He reads to the group and gives books away.

Elena has ideas for other books she would like to produce next. She's a high school teacher, but she is trying to carve out time for herself. She practices jiu-jitsu three to four days a week and teaches a women's class, and she thanks her wonderful coach for helping her get back on track. She describes her coach as an amazing individual, and the support and spirituality of the jiu-jitsu community has been incredible. She used to compete in tournaments for a while and even won a medal! The students she teaches think she is pretty cool. She would show up with bruises and injuries from competing!

When I asked what advice she would give to writers, she said her notes and doodles became her memoir. She never journaled. We all need an outlet. She learned something very important from her funks. "You have to honor your funk, and if you don't, it owns you. When you honor it, your way of honoring is that you are going to tell a story," she says. Every time she gets down and questions what she is doing, she thinks about her daughter, Carly, and feels her creative energy. "If you lean into that, you will get control back. You have to keep your mind and heart open to that," Elena said. She reached out to Luciano and focused on someone else. He was burned as an infant and lost his hands, and doesn't know life with hands. She wrote a grant proposal to the Challenged Athletes Foundation and in 2014 brought him to the U.S. to train; it was life changing for him. He did not speak English. He is amazing, and neater than most people!

Find Elena Stowell at *http://www.elenastowell.com* and at *http://carlystowellfoundation.countmein.com*

While writing this book, I was drawn to the writing of American Tibetan Buddhist nun and teacher Pema Chödrön. In her book *When Things Fall Apart: Heart Advice for Difficult Times,* she reveals her own personal crisis and reflects on the ancient teachings of Tibetan Buddhism. The following is a powerfully relevant quote from her book:

> *Things falling apart is a kind of testing and also a kind of healing.*
> *We think that the point is to pass the test or overcome the problem,*
> *but the truth is that things don't really get solved. They come together*
> *and they fall apart. Then they come together again and fall apart*
> *again. It's just like that. The healing comes from letting there be room*
> *for all of this to happen: room for grief, for relief, for misery, for joy.*

Jill and Elena both shared stories that were incredibly personal and powerful. Here's a strong takeaway. We don't have to be a victim of our situation. We can learn to spin whatever happens to us in a new direction. Just be patient with yourself and be open to what's in store for you next. Tap into what you might have done years ago for a creative outlet, especially when you were little. You never know if what you once enjoyed doing can turn into a new career path or personal journey.

Life is never smooth sailing, but when we search inside ourselves and imagine the life that awaits us, there is often the answer to what we need; it might not be what we want at first, but sometimes we discover the answers to our challenges when we least expect an answer. Imagine a solution right in front of you that you have overlooked or never considered.

We have all had painful learning experiences. Some last longer than others, but there is always a lesson in each challenging moment. The funny thing is, you are never too old to revisit your earlier funks (just don't spend a lot of time dwelling and staying in that dark place). Find the lessons you may have missed; this is one of the great things about getting older. You reflect on your journey and find meaning in the moments that tore you apart. Ask yourself, "Why did I let that person (or situation) tear me down? I am much stronger than I realized."

We can all gain wisdom from earlier road bumps in life. Some of us have physical scars, while most of us have deep emotional wounds. Either way, scars are a sign we experienced something powerful, and the perspective we gain outweighs the moment itself. Perspective and insight are invaluable and help create a better version of ourselves. Moments that seemed monumental at the time become important lessons. And here's another advantage of age: We don't see things the way we did in our twenties (thankfully!). We see how we might have overreacted because we didn't have the wisdom we have now. When we are younger, we dwell on things probably longer than we need to, and we hurt deeply. We have no idea how we will ever recover and when. The scars of life can run deep, but they make us who we are.

The best thing you can do when life gets funky is turn to your trick bag and hang on for the ride. Strap on your "I can *do* this!" attitude, put on your Ironman or Ironwoman outfit, and kick ass. Well, at first you might be a weak mess trying to figure out what just happened, but hang on for a bumpy ride, filled with twists and turns; this won't be the first time you face-plant into the muddiness of life. Let me be clear though. If you're hoping this book will include "five tips that will make your life funk-free," well, sorry, you came to the wrong book. The following chapters focus on skills that you can use at any time and in any order. Some might not be for you, while others might be just what you need or once found joy doing. You have a lot of options; it's up to you to want to move towards a happier, healthier, more fulfilled you.

The Two Roads to Funktown! Why Choosing a Positive versus a Negative Mindset Matters

A ridiculous way to express your journey
in and out of funktown!

There I was in _____, when life seemed _____. I told myself I would always _____, but _____ happened. This funk was _____, and I felt _____. Really sh*tty, actually.

I landed in this funk because I got _____. The _____ was caused by _____, and I hope they know karma is a bitch! But I am resilient, so I was able to _____ right after I _____. I now feel _____ because my funk taught me to _____, and I am _____ because of my experience, which sucked the life out of me at the time.

When I was going through this _____, I felt _____, but _____ helped me get through. If I had to relive this experience, I would tell my _____-year-old self to _____, and that would make me feel _____ instead of _____. I now know I am never too old to _____ or _____, because why not?

CHAPTER 3

The Science of Happiness

"It's a helluva start, being able to recognize what makes you happy."—*Lucille Ball*

We can't be happy all the time. That would be strange and unrealistic, like some weird *Twilight Zone* episode. We learn a lot about ourselves when we're not in a state of bliss. Reflecting on our shifting moods and mindsets allows us to analyze and make choices about the things that matter. When life is tough and you feel down, that is an opportunity for self-reflection and growth; there is a need for openness to uncertainty and newness. We would never gain wisdom and insight if it were not for failures, funks, and tumultuous times.

We open ourselves up to changes we need when we fall apart. We cannot strive to be happy all the time. Imagine a relationship that never had conflict and disagreements. Weird. Another *Twilight Zone* episode. Relationships become stronger when you work through differences and disagreements. You won't always be in a state of joy with the person you are with, but that's okay. There are ways you can grow together that don't involve being happy all the time. For example, when couples experience loss, they grow either closer or further apart. Even though it might seem impossible, some losses can bring about joy, connection, and greater happiness than before; that is the dichotomy of life. For every loss and sorrow we experience, happiness and joy are waiting around the corner.

You just need to know the right ways to achieve happiness, why it matters, and why sometimes it doesn't. Don't gauge your happiness based on your perceptions of other people's happiness. You might be seeing one version of "happy" that is far from reality. What you see could just be an illusion.

Spending your time perusing social media accounts and seeing people's glowing lives can lead to misinterpretation, and sometimes you're seeing a facade of something that's not even close to reality. Much of what we see online is a sales pitch, smoke and mirrors a lot of the time. The really happy moments are the ones not captured by a camera. You might have just rolled out of bed and you look like a wreck, but your puppy is kissing you or you are holding your newborn blissfully after only four hours of sleep, with spit-up all over you.

You see a beautiful skyline and one gorgeous monarch butterfly flies by, and the moment reminds you of someone who always loved butterflies. You get a surprise visit from someone you have not seen in the longest time, because the person just wanted you to know he or she loves you or is sorry. What matters is that you focus on what is right in front of you. You become so enraptured in the moment that you forget about sharing every detail of your life with the world. Just capture those memories in your heart and mind, because who cares what everyone on Twitter, Facebook, Instagram, or wherever else thinks? You don't need approval and accolades. Be satisfied knowing you experienced something special or even life changing that shifted your thoughts and mindset.

Experts in the area of happiness were asked the following questions:

- ⌂ Why did you decide to study happiness?

- ⌂ Were you in a personal or career funk?

- ⌂ What is happiness anyway?

- ⌂ Why does everyone want it so bad? Is it really all it's cracked up to be?

- ⌂ What is the science of happiness?

- ⌂ What is positive psychology, and how does it affect our behavior?

- ⌂ Are there skills to achieve happiness or enhanced well-being?

- ⌂ What advice would you give someone who is going through a funk right now (a personal funk and also a career funk)?

A few years ago, I heard about Adam Shell and Nicholas Kraft, who coproduced an award-winning film, *Pursuing Happiness*. These two filmmakers discovered that happiness is a feeling connected to emotions that results in many physical and spiritual reactions that make a person feel good; it is the reward we get for doing things that strengthen the connections between humans; it's like a glue that keeps us together and unites us. When we spoke on-air, Adam talked about the science of happiness, the skills it takes to achieve happiness, and how going through tough times is necessary and meaningful. If you embrace where you are and then slowly allow yourself to move out of that place into a new mindset, you build emotional strength and the ability to move through these funks with greater ease and fluidity as more of them pop up.

Happiness can be achieved in so many ways, but not all ways have long-lasting effects. Materialistic happiness is fleeting. Look at all of the people who win the lottery and are miserable. Some say it's the worst thing that ever happened to them. When happiness is achieved through hard work, dedication, and a genuine passion for what you want, the impact can be lasting. For example, kids who struggle in school and suffer from low self-esteem and anxiety but are allowed to choose learning methods that meet their needs and the teacher's educational goals have a greater chance of increasing their comprehension, self-esteem, and grade-point average. Long term, this impacts their future successes and increases their happiness quotient.

Meet Dr. Orin Davis

Orin C. Davis, PhD, is the principal investigator of the Quality of Life Laboratory and the head of behavioral science at Vervoe. He shared his research in positive psychology, including creativity, flow, and mentoring.

Dr. Davis earned his first doctorate in positive psychology and is a self-actualization engineer who enables people to do and be their best. His consulting focuses on making workplaces great places to work; his coaching centers around careers (personal branding, career trajectories, and personal and professional development); and his research is on flow and creativity. He runs the Quality of Life Laboratory and advises early-stage companies on enhancing their value propositions, pitches, culture, and human capital. Dr. Davis is also a science advisor to Happify, an adjunct professor, and a public speaker.

I asked Dr. Davis the following questions:

1. How would you describe the science of happiness?

2. What should people know about this field?

3. Why is it an important field of study? Has it been around awhile?

Here's what he had to say:

Dr. Davis:

"The science of happiness involves using rigorous behavioral research to ascertain the nature, development, and promotion of human flourishing. This field exists because knowing how to fix problems is not enough to raise the bar on the human condition, and knowing how to improve our lives and both self-actualize and self-transcend is something far beyond (and indeed separate from!) not having any complaints. The concepts of the field are ancient, going back to many of the oldest texts of the world's religions and philosophies. As a field, it was codified by Abraham Maslow and others into the canon of humanistic psychology, and in the 1990s Martin Seligman and colleagues developed an offshoot that they titled "positive psychology" (a term coined by Maslow in the 1950s). The latter places more emphasis on adhering to the precepts of experimental research methods but is philosophically a direct extension of human- istic psychology. One could almost say that positive psychology is the experimental branch of humanistic psychology."

I first heard about Dr. Davis on the Happify website, which has an app that brings positive psychology to everyone; it provides an opportunity to try out interventions that promote happiness in people's lives. He recognizes that it is challenging to go through the ups and downs of life and that we could all use some help in finding balance.

I asked him what advice he would give to people who are in a funk.

"It's not always about staying positive one hundred percent of the time," he said. It's about recognizing the negative emotions we experience and understanding their reason and their value."

He said sometimes we wake up on the wrong side of the bed. Been there! We just have to recognize we are having a tough morning and acknowledge our feelings and emotions. "On difficult days, what makes it worse is when we don't acknowledge we are having a bad day," he explained. "We are trying to push back or avoid the negative, and in doing so, this puts us in a downward spiral." Dr. Davis shared something he learned from psychology professor Todd Kashdan: "It is helpful to acknowledge what you are feeling, look at what is there and observe yourself in these moments; it makes it more manageable once you have identified what is going on."

When I asked him to explain his work as a self-actualization engineer, Dr. Davis shared that he looks into "how people can actually achieve self-actualization, get to that level of self-transcendence." He is interested in the factors that promote self-actualization and self-transcendence, how people can achieve those states; he believes this looks similar to the field of engineering. He said it's all about "understanding mechanisms, understanding which variables relate to one another, and building up a rather complex system of life and understanding how we can use the different variables, work with them to get ourselves to the fulfillment of our potential, and then create something that lasts beyond our lifetime."

Dr. Davis, as mentioned above, works at the Quality of Life Laboratory. It sounded like an intriguing place to work, so of course I wanted to know more. At the lab, he and his colleagues work on promoting mechanisms that lead to self-actualization. "My areas of focus are creativity, innovation, flow, and the different ways we can make workplaces great places to work, but also make the most of our careers, which are vehicles for self-actualization," he said. He noted that he uses the word "career" broadly and considers parenthood a career.

Dr. Davis also develops tools that promote creative ideation. He explores "how to come up with creative ideas and the mechanisms that allow us to come up with more creative ideas." When we spoke, he shared that he is researching the relationship between empathy and creativity.

I asked him to share more about his involvement with Happify, and specifically his role as a science advisor. "On Happify, we look at the interventions that promote positive well-being," he answered. "There's been a lot of talk about it, but we want to be able to do some of the gold-standard clinical trials and make sure the interventions we have at Happify are hard-core science-based. In order to do that, you need some scientists on the team."

Dr. Davis has some strategies people can use to focus on being positive. He said we first need to be honest and realistic. "From there, people have the opportunity to be more optimistic once they have a good grip on the variables, and in many cases, people associate realism with depression—and they are certainly related.

At the same time, if our optimism is entirely unbridled, and isn't bounded by what we know about, in those cases people still go off the rails." He pointed out that we must look at the things we have some influence over. We need to determine what we can do, because a lot of times, our reality "seems to look like what we can't do, what our boundaries are and what lines we can't go over, instead of looking at 'what do I have with me at this moment in my black bag of tricks that I can pull out and use here?'" He explained that most people lose focus on what is going well, and they seldom count their blessings. "They don't look at what is going right," he said. "That is often the primary first step. Be honest about what is going on but focus on what is going right."

I shared my thoughts on funks and how we all have them. I wondered what Dr. Davis does to stay out of a funk and stay positive. He shared some great insights:

> "First of all, people have funks. And so do I. The first thing is I acknowledge I am in one. Sometimes I realize I just have to ride this out—that I am having a tough time and I have to look at the emotions, see what I am feeling, why I am feeling, and once I get the whats and the whys, I begin to understand what's going on." He said usually it is "a lot easier for me to ride it out and deal with and know that there is light at the end of the tunnel."

He knows there are things he can do to move though his funk, but the number-one thing he reminds himself is, "I've done this before. I have been though a funk before." He added, "A lot of times people think that once they get in one, they can't get out. Most people have a really good track record of getting out of funks." Dr. Davis explained that that track record is something you should hang on to, because that's your "lifeline." He shared that in his deepest funks, his track record, or history, of dealing with past funks has been his lifeline. He tells himself, "I have gotten out of this before, and I will do it again!"

This is where I chimed in with agreement and said:

> "Let's face it. We're going to go through heavy-duty crap! That's part of life. And you have to figure out a set of skills to use, your toolkit to get out of that at different moments. I think it's okay to wallow. Sometimes we gain insight and we learn, but after all, you have to start moving and change your perspective and start working on it."

Dr. Davis said that he sees people repeatedly ignore their track record. He works with college students, teaches business school students, and coaches professionals, and he finds that people over and over again do not pay attention to their past funks and how they recovered. "You have a track record of success," he noted. "You have a track record of getting out of funks. You have a track record of doing what you need to do at the times you need to do it, and you need to hang on to that."

Right. Because the older you get, the harder the funks get. Let's face it: There are different career funks and personal funks when you are in your twenties and someone breaks up with you than when you're older.

"Yes, people of all ages have to deal with different situations; it's mostly about what you are facing relative to what you are able to handle," Dr. Davis said. "But you have a track record of taking on increasingly hard challenges, and if you look back over your life, almost everyone does." He finds it ironic that people ignore that track record. "I am not saying that that is going to make it easier, and I don't want to suggest for a minute that that makes things look positive or easier. All I am saying is, you've got that lifeline."

Next, I asked Dr. Davis to talk about the organization Happy Brain Science.

He shared that Scott Crabtree is the founder. Scott focuses on bringing the neuroscience of happiness to the workplace. Dr. Davis considers him to be a great guy who does incredibly brilliant work. "It's an honor working with Scott," he said. "He brings great experience to what he does. He mixes the science of positive psychology with years of experience in the workplace to make workplaces better."

When I asked Dr. Davis how he decided to pursue a doctorate in positive psychology, his response was thought-provoking.

He was always interested in the fulfillment of human potential. He would wonder how far we can go and what we are capable of doing. Some of that came from his impressive experiences with hypnosis in his childhood. "I got into it at six years old and kept at it and actually published a few papers on it," he said. He continues to publish papers on the topic. He has been focused on this area almost his entire life. "I am Jewish and coming from a Jewish background where a lot of the Jewish wisdom is about fulfilling your potential, and how people can do that." He said we were created to live our lives to their fullest; this viewpoint was very inspiring for Dr. Davis and drew him to the field of self-actualization. He is very interested in discovering what works for people, how they can thrive and use whatever tools they have to make an impact in their lifetime.

Dr. Davis originally thought he would be a premedical chemistry major at Brandeis University. He loves chemistry to this day, and this field inspired both of his TED Talks and many lines of his research. His interest in behavioral medicine and lifestyle medicine had not caught on yet back then, and he was a lot more interested in research than medicine. One of his mentors convinced him to go for a PhD, and it was a perfect fit!

Dr. Davis has a lot of experience working in the areas of human capital, creativity, and innovation. I was curious to see if he thinks it's hard for people to find time for creativity as they get older and get caught up in their busy lives.

"I don't know if it is as much about age as it is about getting so swamped in all the details," he said. "And there is always so much to do, and in many cases we don't map out the time and we think we have to fulfill obligations." He said we are so focused on "the short term, not the long term, and creativity is very much about the long-term view." He shared that most companies don't provide employees with opportunities to be creative, but this really works against them. He added, "This is at the expense of the company's growth, but still we don't make time for it because we don't see it as a priority, mostly because the value is not seen in the short term."

Here's my take on that. If you have a creative pursuit and you take time to do it, whether it's guitar, cooking, sculpture, or something else, you are going to be a happier person and you are going to be more productive in what you do on a daily basis.

He agreed and added, "Absolutely, because you are being more yourself. There is a connection Maslow made a long time ago; there is a relationship between being creative and being self-actualized."

Of course, I was curious whether he had creative outlets. Here's what he shared:

"I love writing. I love music, and I am a ballroom dancer. I love doing ballroom dance." He dances a couple of nights a week.

"For me, that's both my gym and my mental health. Even though I was slaving away in grad school, there was my dancing night every week, and no one touched my Thursday nights!"

Without creative outlets, it is difficult to regain and maintain happiness. Having some kind of outlet brings about feelings of satisfaction and overall well-being.

Dr. Davis says that outlets are an important part of his life. He explains, "If I am not writing and I am not dancing, definitely something feels kind of tight inside. I really need to get out and do that."

I agreed and responded, "You turn kvetchy! (*laughter*) I know I do!"

"Pretty much!" he said relating to my sentiment.

Here's where you can find out more about Dr. Orin Davis—his TED Talks, research, consulting work, his thoughts on breaking glass ceilings, and more: *www.qllab.org*.

Meet Adam Shell

Adam Shell is an award-winning documentary film director and the creator of *Pursuing Happiness*. His work has been featured on *This American Life* with Ira Glass and honored with over two dozen awards across multiple categories around the globe including best documentary, best director, and best editor; his personal favorite is a Creative Spirit Award. Starring in *Pursuing Happiness*, which is the story of his journey across the United States, Adam interviewed over four hundred of the happiest people in the country and has become a well-educated and enthusiastic purveyor of happiness. Adam says that one of his favorite things to do is share what he has learned with everyone who wants to know how they too can become one of the happiest people in America.

Adam continues to share his passion for happiness and to spread what he believes to be one of the most important messages by presenting his findings to audiences around the world. He was honored to be a chosen speaker at the United Nations in celebration of the International Day of Happiness, where he gave a presentation to the General Assembly chronicling his journey and sharing selected clips from the film.

Adam has also appeared on countless TV shows, podcasts and radio shows, including *The Today Show* with Maria Shriver, *Good Morning Arizona*, *Good Day* in Dallas, and has been featured in *Live Happy* magazine.

Adam's goal is to help create positive change on a one-on-one level by engaging with people and sharing the many, many life lessons he was so fortunate to learn. By being a positive force—sharing this wealth of knowledge, spreading these ideas, and helping to create programs to strengthen our communities—Adam strives to help make the world a happier place, one person at a time.

In their film, Adam and Nicholas sought answers to the following:

- ⟲ What is happiness in the first place?
- ⟲ How exactly do we achieve it? And when we do, how do we hold on to it?
- ⟲ Despite being a country that grants its citizens the right to pursue happiness, America surprisingly is not among the happiest countries in the world. Why not?
- ⟲ Why is happiness so elusive? What are we doing wrong?

They discovered some answers while traveling across the country searching for the happiest people in America. Their film is filled with funny moments and tearjerker memories. Those profiled include a young woman battling stage four colon cancer, a single dad who lost both of his arms, an impoverished painter single-handedly revitalizing his condemned neighborhood, and two vigilante artists fighting to save their bankrupt city. These are among the happiest people in America.

I thought Adam would be perfect for this chapter, and he was a fascinating guest on my show. Here's our Q&A.

Janeane: What made you decide to study happiness?

Adam: I wanted to make a film that would be able to help people find their joy. I also wanted to make a film that resonated with me. By my nature I am a happy person, and I like to spread that happiness wherever I go. I figured if I was going to spend several years of my life making a film, I wanted it to make me happy. And what better subject than happiness itself to do the job? The fact is, there is more information about the subject of happiness than ever before in history, and I thought it could not only be highly educational and helpful for a lot of people, it would also be a fun and exciting project to work on.

JB: Were you in a personal or career funk?

AS: I don't think I was in a funk, though my wife does tell me that after working on this project, I did become a happier person. Truth be told, I was in a career transition, and that definitely can cause anxiety, which I guess could be perceived as a funk. Though I did make films prior to this one, they were always side projects to my full-time job. This was the first time in my life when film-making was my full-time job.

JB: What is happiness anyway?

AS: Oh man, I get asked this question a lot. The answer is one that took me several years to fully grasp and an eighty-minute film to fully explain. That said, I can share this with you. Happiness is a feeling; it is an emotional feeling that causes many physical and spiritual reactions making a person feel good. In its primary function it is basically a reward for doing things that further the human race. Just like fear can lead to fight or flight, which can help preserve you when being chased by a lion, happiness is the reward we get for doing things that strengthen the bond between humans; it is the glue that keeps us together. For being together, acting together, and living together is our greatest strength. Happiness brings us together.

JB: What is the science of happiness?

AS: The science of happiness quite simply is the study of happiness—the physiological, psychological, chemical, spiritual, and emotional study of how happiness affects us and relates to us as human beings. As I said in the film, as of 2016 there were eighty-eight thousand books on Amazon with just the word "happiness" in the title. Now, those aren't all scientific, but it sure is a lot of information that we have amassed.

JB: Are there skills to achieve it?

AS: There are indeed. I think one of the most exciting things about studying this subject was learning the answer to this question. Simultaneously, it was the biggest letdown. I only say it was a letdown because what I discovered was not some big secret that has been evading us for millions of years. It was information I already had and skills I had already learned but mostly just hadn't practiced enough. It was nice to have a bunch of different voices putting images to these concepts and being able to watch them play out in living color.

One of my favorite moments was when I was talking with life coach and author Gary van Warmerdam, who said, "What you put into the world is your experience." Most of us are familiar with the ideas of karma—what you give is what you get. With karma, the belief is that the energy you put into the world will one day find its way back to you. I absolutely love this concept and believe in it fully, but the idea Gary was presenting was a much more immediate and somewhat more attainable concept. He said that "as you express yourself, you are feeling the emotions of those expressions at that very moment. So if you express hate, you feel hate; if you express love, you feel love." So thereby, if you simply change your expression in any given moment, you can change the way you feel. He did admit that it was not always as simple as he made it sound, but it is a skill that can be learned and practiced.

JB: What advice would you give to someone who is going through a funk right now (a personal funk and also a career funk)?

AS: I would say this: Funks are part of life. We have a very vast emotional spectrum, and a part of living life, love it or hate it, is experiencing the range of those emotions. Sometimes trips to darker places last longer than we would like, but I think it is extremely important to accept where you are and realize that things won't always be like this. Feeling those emotions allows us to move through them. When we resist and we feel sorry for ourselves or get saddened by the sadness, it compounds and creates an inability to move through it. The only way out is through, so embrace where you are and then slowly allow yourself to move out of it into a new place. This builds our emotional strength and enables us to move through these funks with greater ease and fluidity as more of them pop up in our lives. I am boiling this down to make it sound really simple, and I know sometimes it is not as easy as it sounds in a sound bite. Most times, understanding a concept is easier than putting it into practice, but it is the first step.

Find Adam Shell at *www.pursuinghappiness.com,* and on Facebook at *https://www.facebook.com/PursuingHappinessMovie* or Twitter *@PHdocumentary*

Meet Scott Crabtree

Scott is the founder and chief happiness officer at Happy Brain Science. We spoke on my show and the conversation continued off-air.

Janeane: Tell me how you became a happiness officer at Happy Brain Science.

Scott: Well, really through luck, Janeane. My wife brought me to Powell's bookstore a year ago in Portland, Oregon, and I saw a book turned sideways called *The How of Happiness* by Sonja Lyubomirsky. I bought it and read it, and it was my introduction to the fact that there was a solid peer-reviewed science of happiness, that real scientists were doing real research with random assignments, placebo control, and all that makes good science good science. That science found choices we can make to bring us more happiness. And if we make those choices, our brains fundamentally work better in most situations.

I felt like I had discovered the most amazing thing ever and really wanted to learn it. I finished the book and thought, "I want to know this science; I want to live this science. I want to be happier and enjoy all the benefits that come with it." About five seconds later, I thought, "You're not going to do that, Scott! You're going to forget ninety-five percent of it in six months, the way we forget ninety-five percent of most things in six months. So how can you not forget this?" I happen to be the kid of two teachers, so I thought, "If you really want to learn something, you should teach it."

I started pitching software development conferences and video game development conferences, because I was in software development and specifically the video game development world. I started pitching them with talks like "The Science of Happiness in Software Development." Conferences kept saying yes, so I kept learning more and more, and the experience essentially went viral.

JB: I love the name Happy Brain Science.

SC: Thank you. I was working at Intel when I discovered all of this, and Intel is a wonderful company; it is also a very engineering-driven, data-driven, skeptical kind of place where it's like, "Yeah, prove it to me."

JB: Sure.

SC: So, I could not go out there with a presentation like "Just Be Happy! Yeah! And We'll All Put on Clown Noses!" (*laughter*)

I needed to prove this to my Intel colleagues who I wanted to make happier. The former CEO of Intel, Andy Grove, had a quote that we often repeated at Intel, which is, "Everyone has an opinion. Some people have data." So, I developed a very data-based approach to all of this, where I try to give as little of my opinion as possible and guide people to as much solid peer-reviewed science as possible.

JB: I love how this carries into corporate, where you are bringing this into different environments, workshops, and things like that. Can you talk about that?

SC: Absolutely. We spend most of our hours at work. If someone [reading] this is working full time, like it or not they probably spend more time at work than doing anything else in their life possibly outside of sleeping, but most of us work more than we sleep. And certainly for the time that we are conscious, we are spending more of our time at work than anywhere else. We are spending more time with our colleagues than anyone in our lives, and in my experience too often that is an unhappy work experience.

People suffer from nine to five, or whatever their working hours are, and they are telling themselves, "I am doing all of this so I can make money, so I can be happy on the weekend or the evenings or on vacation." Well, I think life is too short to be suffering through the thing we do the most in life. I am not here to criticize Intel, but I was not terribly happy at Intel. It was not my corporate environment, so to speak, and I saw a lot of people who were really unhappy there and other places. To be completely candid with you, I have had family members of mine, and myself at times, be quite unhappy in life and we suffer. We don't do work well when we are suffering, but solid science suggests when we're unhappy, our brains figuratively shrink, and the parts of our brain that look more like your average mammal, the limbic system and the brain stem, come to the front burner; this happens when we're stressed or sad.

And our uniquely wonderfully, human creative layers of logic and more in the neocortex just under our scalp largely go to the back burner when we're unhappy. When we are unhappy, we are at work thinking more like your average house cat than your average human. I wanted to help people be happier because life is too short to suffer at what we do most. I think that all of us deserve to be happy at work. But also, we do much better work when we're happier—not in one hundred percent of the circumstances, but [in] the vast majority we do better work with a happier brain.

JB: What I hear you saying is that you had a little bit of a funk at Intel?

SC: Yes.

JB: Okay. So, what advice would you give people that are in a funk—personal funk, professional funk—because I believe there is a toolkit that people can have to help them find their way out. I am not saying that they have to have this permanent smile and be blissful, because that is unrealistic.

SC: Exactly.

JB: But just to know there are certain things they can do. What would you suggest?

SC: Absolutely. Great question. First of all, I have eight or so different workshops. I go to corporations and conferences delivering them, and only one is called "The Science of Being Happy and Productive at Work." That one typically takes a half a day, so this is obviously an abbreviated answer. For people who want to learn more, I have a recommended reading list of science-based books on happiness that is free on my site HappyBrainScience. com. That is where you will get a longer answer.

I organized the science of happiness workshop into four themes. The first one is to reduce stress, second is practice positivity, three is flow to goals, which requires a little bit of explanation, and four is probably most important, prioritize people. They are all important. Reduce stress means that when you are stressed out, your brain is figuratively shrinking and some of your not-so-valuable real estate is leading the way. I try to help people stop stressing about stress. Moderate stress can actually be helpful to us.

JB: Yes.

SC: And then cope effectively, because science says a big difference between high-stress, low-happiness people and low-stress, high-happiness people is how we cope with life's inevitable stresses and hardships. And you said it well. The goal of all this is not constant bliss.

JB: No.

SC: It's unrealistic, unhealthy, and not helpful. We can choose to be happier. A big way to do that is to cope with the funk that life gives us, right?

JB: Right.

SC: Bad things happen to us and people we care about. The question is, how do you cope? How do you bounce back? Science says cope effectively. If you are drinking, eating, smoking, gambling heavily, there are better ways to deal with life's hardships. Those include exercise, talking with friends, mindfulness, and humor—whatever works for you and is a healthy coping strategy. Cope effectively with stress and hardship.

JB: I would like to interject something. Everybody has their own personal time frame for how and when they are going to get out of that funk. The important thing is not to dwell in that vortex for too long.

SC: Exactly. When we can't tolerate any funk at all, we tend to make ourselves even less happy. "I am unhappy! This is horrible!" But hey, this happens to all of us.

JB: Yes.

SC: This is not about eliminating misery. As you wisely put it, Janeane, it's about not getting stuck in your funk.

JB: Yes.

SC: The three other sections are practice positivity; this is basically a bunch of corny-sounding stuff about positive attitude. So, why would I include a bunch of stuff about positive attitude when people have heard clichés about positive attitudes before?

Because if you watch television for an afternoon, you can hear that happiness comes from sports cars and prescription drugs and perfumes. What science can sort out is what really brings us happiness. Science says that all that corny stuff about looking on the bright side, being optimistic, seeing the best in each other, focusing on the positive—all of that really works. So bring the positive attitude.

JB: I always say we tend to say no to a lot of things when we are in a funk. Try to just say yes! I know I am guilty of that too, where we are very comfortable staying home in our routine, and we don't want to drive. We are overthinking and analyzing how the evening is going to play out, and we are not mind readers.

SC: Yes.

JB: But we think we know. And I find that when I do push myself and I do go, I have a really good time. Being with people is one of the best ways to get out of a funk.

SC: Absolutely. In the fourth section of my happiness workshops, that's when I tell people, "Here comes the cliché line when the guy says, 'If you only remember one thing I say today, remember this: Warm relationships fuel happiness.'" According to Harvard professor Daniel Gilbert, if you had to boil the science of happiness down to one word (we can't, and it's not that simple), but if we did the word might be "social." We are social creatures. When we are in a funk, as you pointed out, we often do not want to reach out to people, and in fact that is often when we need to the most. Social support is huge. Happiness and unhappiness are contagious, and there are great ways to invest in happiness at the same time, including kindness, forgiveness, celebration, savoring, and lots more.

JB: I want to add that sometimes with certain professions… for example, I am a writer. I can become very antisocial. I tend to be an introvert, and when you get into that zone, that cave of writing, and you are not socializing, it is not good for you. Even though you might think you are fine, you forget how to interact. I recently went to a film festival, and I had the best time meeting people from all over the world. I had these intriguing conversations, and it brought me a little brightness in my life.

SC: Yes, it's amazing the power of it. I was fortunate enough to have dinner last summer with Sonja Lyubomirsky, the woman who wrote *The How of Happiness* and who is a happiness researcher. It was me and a few other people, including a fellow researcher who asked Dr. Lyubomirsky, "What unpublished research are you excited about?" Keep in mind that this is unpublished research; it has not been through the peer-review process, so you can take this with a big fat grain of salt. Dr. Lyubomirsky said that she and some of her grad students have been running an experiment that found the biggest boost to any well-being on any happiness intervention they had tried so far. And the instructions, loosely speaking, were: Act like an extrovert.

JB: Oh!

SC: Introverts like you are thinking, "But it's exhausting. It's hard for me."

JB: Yes.

SC: I know. I get it. I totally get that we have different styles, but what she has found is that both introverts and extroverts get a massive boost in well-being, and introverts do not get as exhausted as they predicted they would. My own experience is similar. I am a bit of an extrovert and a bit of an introvert, depending on the time of day or whatever is going on. I heard some scientists say that if you have to boil down the science of happiness to one thing, treat every elevator ride like a great social experience.

JB: Oh, yeah!

SC: Which is unnatural for us, right? We get into an elevator and it is like, "I'm on my phone and I don't want to talk to you. What if you are crazy or mean?"

JB: Sure!

(*laughter*)

SC: I feel hesitant to talk to people, but because I know the science, I push myself. Not always. Sometimes I am not in the mood and I get it, but I will often push myself and start a conversation with someone in the elevator. I'll say, "How's it going?" or anything like that, and ninety-nine percent of the time I get out of the elevator in a better mood than when I got in.

JB: Sure.

SC: We don't feel like being social, especially when we are in a funk, and yet it's one of the best ways to get out of a funk.

JB: It is. I think you just imagine there is a person behind you going nudge, nudge, or kick or shove!

SC: At the times you really do not want to be social, that brings us to the fourth thing I have not explained yet. "Flow to goals" is about the very productive zone that psychologists call flow, where you are deeply immersed in work that is challenging but possible for you. You are making progress towards a clear and important goal, and you are doing as little multitasking as possible. Science says multitasking makes us stupid and miserable. If you just do not feel like being with people, the question to ask yourself is: can I get really into something that challenges me? Usually, when we get immersed in a challenge, what we find is a delightfully productive experience.

JB: I can give you an example of that. I was working on a screenplay for many years and I thought, "Is this really worth doing? Is this going to come to fruition?" I was determined to tell this story. I would be so happy when I submersed myself in my writing.

SC: Yes, exactly. For those who cannot or don't want to choose human contact, choose immersing yourself in work. Part of why I get so excited about the science of happiness is that we sometimes make choices that are not good for our happiness. For example, most people given an opportunity for a new thing will choose relaxation over something challenging. We will choose to watch TV, for example, or spend a lot of time on social media. The evidence is, neither one of those tends to make us less happy, and something hard—playing chess, making a piece of software, writing a screenplay, a book or an article...they are harder, so we have less appetite for them when we want to kick back and relax. Challenge is invigorating for us and gives us that experience that results in being happier, because we chose to work hard.

JB: If you choose a passive experience, like sitting back and watching Netflix, it is not as fulfilling, is what I hear you saying; it's not like you start creating something such as working on a nonfiction story.

SC: Yes, often true. Look, I watch TV too, but I try to do it with other people, not all the time. Watch something interesting and not just mind numbing.

JB: Things that are going to engage your brain.

JB: Exactly. We think we are going to be happy when we just kick back—"Please just let me just lie on a beach and drink mai tais for a month"—but....

(*laughter*)

SC: I know a lot of people listening are like, "Try me!" But what science says is: When we get total relaxation, we end up kind of bored, kind of sad. We end up feeling happier and more alive when, as you put it, we are engaged, we are challenged, and we are connected.

JB: I want to add to that as well. I always feel like with social media, people might compare themselves, their level of happiness, to the people on Facebook.

SC: Yes.

JB: There is an illusion. I call it smoke and mirrors. There is an illusion of "happy": "Look at me! I am here! I am there! I've got this! I've done that!" You know, at the end of the day, these people have their own unhappiness as well, and you cannot compare to that.

SC: Yes, exactly. I try not to talk about the things that make us unhappy too much. I prefer to focus on the things that lead to happiness. But you are right on. The science says that comparing yourself to others is a great way to be miserable. I am not anti-social media. I am on Facebook, Twitter, and LinkedIn, but if you spend too much time there, especially on Facebook, you are comparing your real life to other people's highlight reel—"This friend is on vacation in Italy. This friend is in Hawaii. And this friend's kid just won an award. *My life sucks!*" (*laughter*)

I am anti-social comparison, because the data suggests it's a great way to be miserable. Anytime you catch yourself thinking, "Why can't I have a life more like this person?" or, "Why can't I be like this person?" it's a mistake. And if anyone is a leader at work, please do not tell a colleague, "Why can't you be more like Jennifer?"

JB: Oh, yuck!

SC: That is a great way to make people miserable.

JB: Absolutely!

SC: And therefore cut their productivity about twenty-five percent, by the way.

JB: I cannot believe that! It is almost like we are children again when someone says, "Why can't you be more like Suzie?"

SC: Exactly.

JB: What advice would you give people who want to work on maintaining their level of happiness at work?

SC: Number one, connect with other human beings. When I worked at Intel and other large organizations, a lot of people would call into meetings, even ones one hundred yards down the hall. Go in person. Make some eye contact. We thrive on human connection, and too often we deprive ourselves of it by thinking, "I don't want to walk" or, "I can get some other work done while I am at this meeting if I stay here at my desk." We just choose the misery of multitasking and lack of human connection when we could be choosing happiness, and studies suggest a boost in productivity. This is not choosing happiness just to be happy, which is good enough of a reason, but you will be more productive, more creative, and a better work citizen. You will be more resilient. All of these benefits come from happiness. Choose human connection. Manage stress. Do not multitask. Immerse [yourself] completely into challenging, meaningful work and bring the positive attitude, whatever that looks like for you.

The other thing I say, as I am dishing out all of this science-based advice, is I try to guide people through the science so they can thrive at work, but everyone's path is different. I cannot tell them what to do. Science cannot tell them what to do. Science can tell us what works for most people, most of the time, but every brain in the world is different. Every person in the world is different, and people need to figure out what works for them.

JB: Absolutely.

Find Scott Crabtree at *www.happybrainscience.com* and on Twitter *@scottcrab*

In a Nutshell

- ⟳ Have you ever managed to stay positive in a situation that would have derailed you in the past? What did you do?

- ⟳ Are you living an illusion of happiness and not very happy on a day-to-day basis?

- ⟳ What techniques do you use to maintain and/or increase your happiness?

We are not expected to be happy all the time. Being unhappy or neutral is okay, because working out your underlying problems increases your chance of greater happiness or at least decreases your misery! Some of our best adventures happen because we were unhappy. As difficult as it can be, try to embrace your challenging times and seek ways to cheer yourself up or at least divert your attention—temporarily and long term.

How do you measure happiness? Having good values and a moral compass will lead to greater happiness and resilience when life throws you curveballs. Happiness should not be fleeting; it should be something we know how to maintain and strive to achieve while juggling all the moments that rock our worlds. Your happiness meter can vary from over-the-top joy to having a pleasant, calm, happy demeanor, because things seem to be going well. Knowing how to take care of yourself and strive for a level of happiness that meets your needs and expectations is key in life. One person's level of happiness is not someone else's. What makes one person happy can make another person miserable.

Sometimes it takes a lot to make a person happy, and the simple everyday moments seem to go unnoticed. Everyday experiences that might be so mundane to one person might bring bliss to another. Ever take a walk in a beautiful area on a gorgeous day, but you're in such a bad mood that all you stare at is the ground or your phone? You are missing an opportunity for some amazing mood-changing, mindful moments! Focus on being present on everything around you, from the sights, sounds and smells of nature to the gift of clean air and your ability to be able to take that walk. The simplest things can bring you joy if you open yourself up to receiving joy. Be present and take it all in.

The Road to Happiness

The following is a list of activities that can spark some happiness in your own life:

- Volunteering—at a food bank, homeless shelter, or pet shelter, delivering meals to seniors, and the like
- Meeting new people
- Attending a party
- Going to a film festival
- Seeing a movie or theatrical performance
- Attending a health and wellness event

- ⌂ Keeping a gratitude journal to remind yourself of all the goodness in your life
- ⌂ Trying something new
- ⌂ Laughing (attending a comedy show or laughing with a friend or two)
- ⌂ Creating a list of long-term and short-term goals
- ⌂ Going to a workshop that will teach you a new skill or encourage a new way of thinking
- ⌂ Starting a conversation with a total stranger
- ⌂ Practicing mindfulness, meditation, yoga, and Pilates
- ⌂ Saying yes more! Turning down invitation after invitation leads you down an unhappy road all by your lonesome
- ⌂ Creating a vision board
- ⌂ Staying away from toxic people and negativity
- ⌂ Taking walks in nature
- ⌂ Spending time outside
- ⌂ Taking a bath and trying aromatherapy
- ⌂ Doing activities in nature—gardening, hiking, swimming, sailing, rowing, and the like
- ⌂ Exercising
- ⌂ Starting a new hobby
- ⌂ Trying new fitness classes
- ⌂ Dancing
- ⌂ Striving to create mental, emotional, and physical well-being

- Seeking advice from a professional—a life coach, mentor, or psychiatrist

- Attending support groups

- Participating in therapy—a group or individually

- Eating a healthy, well-balanced diet that makes you feel good and perform your best. Getting rid of foods that are not good for you. What you eat affects your mood, health, sleep, and overall well-being

- Sleeping! Lack of sleep can bring out the worst in us. Aim for seven to eight hours a night.

- Playing with a pet

- Connecting with people of your own faith or another religious affiliation and attending services or get-togethers during holidays and throughout the year

The Happiness Pledge

1. I will start each day by taking a deep breath and focusing on my gratitude.

2. I will work on myself every day by taking care of my mental, physical, and emotional well-being.

3. I will strive to instill happiness in my life, because happiness makes me a better person in my relationships.

4. I will strive to achieve realistic goals and fulfill my ambitions, but not feel derailed if they do not come to fruition.

5. I will trust my gut and stay tuned to when things do not feel right.

6. I will not change myself to please others.

7. I will live my life according to my own internal compass.

8. I will tell myself I am worthy of love, happiness, and joy, and I will love myself.

9. I will surround myself with people that make me happy (my tribe, my posse, my people).

10. I will try things that are new and different, because the unexpected can bring joy.

Looking for Happiness in All the Right Places

Insert the preferred pronoun below.

There once was a _____ named _____. _____ (pronoun) was so happy until _____ (pronoun) lost his/her _____. _____ (pronoun) tried to get another _____, but _____ just couldn't. _____ (pronoun) started staying home and not making time for _____ and _____. _____ (pronoun) grew unhappier, until a friend suggested _____. _____ (pronoun) declined at first, saying he/she was too _____, but a friend said, _____! So, _____ decided to give _____ a try.

After a few _____, _____ felt _____ and met a lot of new

_____. _____ became more
_____ and signed up for _____
Every day _____ would _____
after work or in the evenings. _____
(pronoun) said yes to more social events and became a lot more
_____ in the end. Now, _____
is an expert _____ and has scheduled events
each _____ at _____
(pronoun) house. Creating a vision board and journaling helped
_____ visualize the life _____
(pronoun) _____, which included:
_____, _____, and
_____. One day _____ real-
ized that _____ (pronoun) had turned a corner
and his/her life was _____!

CHAPTER 4

Why Pampering Yourself Matters

"Art enables us to find ourselves and lose ourselves at the same time."—*Thomas Merton,* No Man Is an Island

We are happier in our personal and professional lives when we take care of ourselves physically, mentally, and emotionally. Even if you have limited time, carving out a little bit of space for yourself every day and having "me time" is crucial for your well-being and your relationships. If you are a creative person, you already know how important it is to nurture your creativity. For those of you who are athletic, working out changes your outlook for the entire day and how you handle whatever is thrown your way. This chapter provides strategies for shifting your mind away from whatever it is you are struggling with and taking care of yourself inside and out. Along the way, I share some of my own stories and expert advice from others who have found their own ways to shift gears when life gets bumpy.

You will find it difficult to stay in a bad mood forever when you shift your focus elsewhere. I learned this from an early age.

After my short, sporadic visits with my father, Sundays were always depressing. We would end the weekend with a beautiful dinner at my grandmother's house or at the local Howard Johnson's; we'd have an early dinner of fried clams, ice cream, and a bunch of goodies on the way out—a cute doll, M&Ms, and Juicy Fruit gum. Those M&Ms and doll were my saving grace when we said our goodbyes. Who can be miserable chewing a sugary wad of colorful gum and laughing while trying to blow bubbles with sweet rubbery gooeyness, and giggling as the gum hits the windshield? I figured out that even the simplest things could help me with those Sunday moody blues. And those little tricks would carry me through life, even if I did develop a bad gum, candy, and fast-food addiction.

During a bad breakup when I was in my twenties, I was a wreck even though it would be one of my best decisions to end that stale, unfulfilling relationship. My father always said, "Don't confuse love for weakness." I was initially too weak to end a relationship I knew was wrong, and when I finally did, it took me years to realize that being brave hurts. We hang on to old relationships like worn-out baby blankets or a ragged old teddy bear; they served their purpose once, but it's time to move on and grow the funk up.

I quickly realized I had to celebrate my newly single, footloose and fancy-free self; it was time to put myself first and focus on the road to happiness. I was not out to find another relationship, but instead I wanted to focus on myself—with some pampering, self-care, and time off from dating.

The next day, I joined an all-women's gym and went almost every day. I enjoyed the sisterhood of the bulging pants camaraderie. Everyone was warm, chatty, and sometimes moodier than I would have preferred. Getting myself in a daily routine of exercise was an important first step to pampering myself and taking charge of my expanding waistline and sad moods. I was long overdue to break up with Ben & Jerry, because I was turning into a chunky monkey.

The plus side was that I got in shape and formed great friendships with a few members and instructors, which led to lots of laughs and great adventures. I was no longer doing everything solo and had created a network of new friendships and alliances. I knew that if I was ever going to venture out into the dating world again, I needed to work on my excess emotional and physical baggage.

Based on my own experience trying to de-funk myself, I ventured into all sorts of activities, some of which were hobbies I had long forgotten and wanted to get back into. I explored playing electric guitar, joining group pottery classes (throwing clay is incredibly cathartic) and dance classes, hiking, biking, camping (as long as there was a shower nearby), and even joining an all-girls band.

Pampering yourself physically, emotionally, and spiritually can be gratifying and a major stress relief. We are composed of so many layers of emotions and experiences. Self-care should be a necessity, because it allows us to unwind, decompress, and process things we struggle with, and take a good, hard look at the influences that drain us. Taking care of ourselves helps diminish our anger, sadness, grief, and disappointment and get to our center core. You might not like who you find when you get there. You might be denying the person you are at your core, but moving forward requires you to go there—to the place that is uncomfortable or suppressed. From the honest admissions of who you are, you'll be ready to work on rebuilding yourself from the inside out; it takes guts and determination. You got this. Now *stop funkin' around!*

Here are some strategies to pamper your mind, body, and soul that will make you feel a little less sh*tty while you're funkin' around:

Do Yoga

You do not have to be in incredibly great shape or know anything about yoga to take the leap into this wonderful spiritual and physical journey. I was extremely uncoordinated during my very first class (anything new makes me feel like a dork). I thought I stood out like a sore thumb. As a newbie to yoga, just start off slowly and see where your abilities take you. Yoga is a great stress reliever and a fantastic way to get in shape; it helps improve your posture, decreases your chances of heart issues, increases bone strength, wards off osteoporosis, increases mental focus by teaching you to be present and less distracted—especially for those whose minds tend to be all over the place (ahem!)—and improves sleep. Plus, you might meet some new friends while you are learning how to do Downward- and Upward-Facing Dog and Tree Pose. *Namaste.*

Practice Mindfulness and Meditation

We live in a fast-paced world in which we're constantly connected to our phones, computers, and other gadgets. We're incessantly texting our every move, posting on social media, liking and commenting on posts, and so on; this is all the more reason to disconnect for a while. Take some time daily to sit quietly and get in touch with your breath. And no, I am not talking about your halitosis. I am referring to your breathing and how you feel in your body during different moments throughout the day.

Find a quiet area that can become your consistent space each day; try meditating with music or without, by yourself or with a friend. Look into taking a class (online or in person) and trying out an app on your phone; this practice helps you find clarity and calm first thing in the morning and starts your day off on a positive note. For most newbies, the challenge is to focus on the breath and quiet a busy or distracted mind. When you catch your mind wandering off, redirect your thoughts to your breath. "By repeatedly bringing your attention back to the breath each time it wanders off, concentration builds and deepens, much as muscles develop by repetitively lifting weights," writes Jon Kabat-Zinn in *Full Catastrophe Living*.

Get Good Sleep

We all need sleep, but do we get enough? Probably not. The quality of our sleep is just as important as the quantity, if not more so. Without seven to eight hours of sleep, I am a dragon witch. Okay, maybe just a wobbly, cranky weirdo with no mojo or get-up-and-go, and I am certainly not my sharpest, happiest, most pleasant self. Coffee please? Some people are fine with six hours, but I feel off-kilter and not my best self. Sleep is healing, mentally and physically. Trying to combat emotional exhaustion with caffeine and sugar will just end up making matters worse.

When you are feeling down or stressed, sleep can rejuvenate you and enable you to feel refreshed and inspired. The power of sleep, especially REM sleep, affects every part of you. However, if you can't get the proper amount of sleep you need at night, consider a nap. I know some of you might be saying, "I feel lousy when I sleep during the day." I hear you. I do too, but if you are so fatigued you cannot function, your body is trying to tell you something. Close your eyes and shut down.

Some of the benefits of napping are: stress reduction, improved mood, better focus and alertness, and better memory and recall. Adults sometimes say they don't like to nap because they wake up "out of it" and groggy. Even just a short nap (ten to twenty minutes) can lift your mood and improve the quality of your day. Ignoring your exhaustion and downing more caffeine will not help you in the long run.

Not having enough sleep is a recipe for disaster. When I have a lot on my mind, I usually do not sleep soundly. In fact, I sleep-walk...and sleep swear. Yup. At first, I was embarrassed because that crazy woman yelling (I don't know her) wakes me up and everyone in my house is startled. Of course, I have no idea what I am doing and who is yelling like that! Thankfully, my kids are teenagers and they think I am half funny and half a lunatic. I just tell them it's my wicked twin sister with the potty mouth again. Couldn't be me. "Go to sleep, kids. Mom's fine," I muttered when I heard them ask me if I was okay. (A sleep analyst is having a party right now.) The worst time was when I yelled, "&*^%! ^&%$#! A snake!" Sound asleep. Freaked the kids out, because they actually thought there was a snake. There was no snake. Just me, the sleeping lunatic.

You are not alone if you are like me (I just hope you don't sleep swear). Getting a good night's sleep can be very difficult for a lot of us. You toss, you turn, you spend too much time on your phone or watching TV. We all need a routine and downtime.

Nighttime should be all about rituals for relaxation to wind down and prepare for sleep. Quality sleep recharges us (keeps us from yelling "&*^%" at top volume) and relaxes the mind and body. Setting up a sleep schedule is key, but more important, you need to stick to your strategies. You might try soothing music, a bath or shower before bed, some light reading, journaling, or playing a musical instrument. But ditch the phone for the night.

Get Moving

No, I am not talking about packing up and selling your house (unless that would make you feel better). Call a friend for a walk, run, or hike, or go solo while listening to an inspiring audiobook or uplifting music. Working out is one of the best antidepressants. Boosting your serotonin is a start to improving mood and decreasing depression and anxiety. Choose activities you love or would like to try. And you don't have to work out alone. Joining an exercise class or finding a reliable friend is a great mood booster.

Low serotonin at any age can lead to anxiety, hopelessness, and depression. Find something you like doing and get going. Don't have a lot of time and money to join a gym? Get a bike, walk, take a self-defense class, exercise out in nature. Do you have a yard and plenty of space? Using a small trampoline is a great way to get moving and feeling like a kid again. Jumping has cardiovascular and lymphatic benefits and helps build bone mass. You just might lose a few pounds in the process. Of course, if you have knee or back issues, better check with your doctor first.

Listen to Music

Find new music or music you love. My teenage daughter says that music is art and poetry. Absolutely. I believe that listening to music is the greatest vacation for the mind. After just a few notes, you can be in a more relaxed and soothing state or transported to a wild, rockin' universe.

Music is an absolute healer for the soul. Find different musical styles that grab you at certain times of the day. Need something meditative while writing or walking? Indie rock or alternative to bring on the weekend? Stream music at any time from any location. Plus, check your local radio stations and see if they are giving out free tickets to some of the bands or musicians on your playlist. You never know. You just might score a pair of tickets to a favorite new band.

Get a Massage

Another technique that's effective in reducing stress and anxiety is massage. Here are some types to consider. Do your homework and see which ones work best for you.

- Deep tissue
- Swedish
- Aromatherapy
- Sport massage
- Hot stone massage
- Prenatal
- Reflexology

- Shiatsu
- Thai
- Trigger-point massage
- Chair
- Couples

Massages help to decrease stress, tension, anxiety, and pain; promote relaxation; and improve overall mood. Depending on which type you choose, you might also experience better flexibility and sleep. Do your homework when looking for a massage therapist. Ask family and friends for recommendations and look at reviews online. You want a reputable professional who knows what he or she is doing.

The right massage therapist will figure out what is best for you and where your weak areas are. You need to be vocal about what you like and do not like, how hard or soft you want the massage, and your own comfort level. If you have shoulder, neck, or back issues (and your doctor says it's okay), getting a massage is a great way to ease tension and pain dramatically. Pain and stress can go hand in hand. Pay attention to when you are most uncomfortable and what your trigger points are.

Get a Makeover

Maybe you have been wanting for a while to switch up the way you look. There is no better time than now. Consider a new cut, color, or style for your hair. Look through some magazines or online for a change that might suit you. Then consult an experienced, reasonably priced stylist. On a budget? Some salons have students who need experience as part of their training, and the prices are fairly reasonable, but again, do your homework first.

Treat yourself to a manicure-pedicure. Can't afford it? Check out Groupon and ask your friends and family whom they would recommend. A little pampering can go a long way. Overhaul your wardrobe and try out some new styles. Maybe have a clothing swap party with friends. Share with your close circle what you want to do and start a new tradition by swapping clothes and enjoying the chance to socialize.

Read

Select some books from a bestsellers list. See what is popular online in some genres you enjoy. Look for new authors on book tours. Ask friends and family what they are reading. Visit your local library and see what's new in print and in audio format. I have spent hours at my local library, reading, writing, and discovering many great authors. Look online and see what new authors are hot right now. There is a world of diverse authors and topics to choose from. Reading is transformative and inspiring. The wonderful thing about reading is, you often end up wanting to write and explore new ideas and outlets you never imagined.

Write

Writing in a notebook, expressing your thoughts and feelings, is very cathartic. Journaling is a great way to process your internal dialogues and work through issues; it boosts creativity, self-esteem, mindfulness, and writing skills. According to Hayley Phelan of the New York Times,

Once the domain of teenage girls and the literati, journaling has become a hallmark of the so-called self-care movement, right up there with meditation. And for good reason: Scientific studies have shown it to be essentially a panacea for modern life. There are the obvious benefits, like a boost in mindfulness, memory and communication skills. But studies have also found that writing in a journal can lead to better sleep, a stronger immune system, more self-confidence and a higher I.Q.

Some people have started incredibly fulfilling careers by writing fiction and nonfiction during a funky time. Don't ignore what is going on in your inner life. Being in a funk can be tumultuous, and self-awareness through writing can bring about incredible insights (for example, personal flaws, weaknesses, and suppressed ambitions); it is never too late to switch gears in your life and do something you always wanted to do. Pay attention to what you are feeling by having a daily writing ritual; this routine will help you move forward in a positive way.

Take Classes

Learn how to draw, paint, sculpt, sing, dance, cook, and the like. Don't dismiss something new because it looks hard. You never know what you can achieve until you try. You are never too old to learn something new or revisit an earlier passion. Taking classes is also a great way to make new friends and create a weekly routine you can look forward to.

Cry!

Yes, I meant what I said. We all need a good cry sometimes; it's cathartic, so let all those emotions out. Holding your emotions in is awful and stressful. Having a good cry can be a release and emotionally necessary. You might even need a nap afterward, but crying is very cathartic, and those tears and sobs are your body's way of closing a painful chapter in your life and moving on.

Do a Primal Scream

Seriously. Try a primal scream sometime. Just not so someone feels the need to call 911 or near your kids or pets. I had my first primal scream experience in college with one of my closest friends. She took me to the edge of a beautiful hill and said, "Okay, let it rip! Let's primal-scream at the top of our lungs!" Best. Experience. Ever. If anything, you will laugh really hard afterward and feel very exhilarated. Shut your windows first though if you do this indoors, and warn your family. Better yet, try it alone when no one is around for the full effect. Put your dog outside first though. You don't want to scare the crap out of your pets.

Hit the Road, Jack/Jackie

Whether you have the time and budget for only a brief road trip or can swing a big trip out of state, any kind of mental break will be beneficial. When you step out of your surroundings, magical things can happen if you let them. Go with a small group or a close friend or even go solo. Some of the best travel experiences I have had were solo. You never know who you will meet on your adventure, and the change of scenery is healing and rejuvenating.

Eat Well

Nothing says "mood lift" like a complete diet makeover. Cleaning up your bad eating habits is an excellent way to improve your energy and overall well-being. Make sure most of your diet consists of plenty of real, clean foods, such as veggies, whole grains, and fruits. There are all kinds of diet trends, from keto and paleo to Mediterranean and vegan diets. Be smart and do your homework before jumping into a new routine. You want the best diet for you and your long-term goals.

Start by taking a close look at what is in your fridge and in your pantry. Read labels, and if you can't pronounce something or don't know what it is, dump it. It probably doesn't belong in your body. Processed foods—and anything else genetically modified or artificial—can take a swan dive right into your trash. Everything you eat impacts your health and well-being, and the same goes for your family. Be smart and make good choices. Don't be fooled by marketing and the slick ads on TV. Convenience foods don't make sense in the long run, because your health will be impacted by your shortcuts and choices for convenience.

If you are considering starting on a new diet to lose weight, check with your doctor first; it is important to keep tabs on your bloodwork and make sure your body is functioning normally and all your blood levels are healthy. Your doctor can run a panel of tests that check things like:

- Cholesterol—HDL (high-density lipoprotein) and LDL (low-density lipoprotein)

- Triglycerides and your cholesterol ratio (total cholesterol number divided by HDL cholesterol number)

- Kidney and liver function

- Anemia
- Vitamin D
- Thyroid function

If you are experiencing any sensitivities to foods or want to see if you have food allergies (for example, to gluten, dairy, peanuts, or something else), contact your doctor and request some allergy tests. Be sure to mention any genetic conditions that are prevalent in your family, such as cardiovascular disease, hypertension, auto-immune diseases (such as lupus and rheumatoid arthritis), cancer, and diabetes.

Remember, what you eat affects how you feel, how you sleep, and how you perform mentally and physically. If your diet meets your dietary needs, chances are you will feel a lot better, too.

Get Plenty of Vitamin D

Lack of sunlight can cause depression and mood changes. If you live in an area where there is less sunlight in the winter months, you could experience Seasonal Affective Disorder (SAD). Pay close attention to how much sunlight you get and keep tabs on your mood changes. There are simple ways to treat SAD. Consider getting your blood checked to see if your doctor thinks your vitamin D level is low. The solution is easy.

Adopt or Foster a Pet, Or Get a Low-Maintenance Pet (Such as a Goldfish)

A pet is a great companion and shifts your focus to nurturing and caring for something that needs you (all right, maybe not so much if it's a goldfish). A cat or dog can be a great source of love and companionship. Life is a little less lonely and even humorous when you dive into pet ownership. Just make sure you have the time, energy, and resources to care for your pet. Whether it's a rabbit, dog, or guinea pig, it's not fair to be unrealistic about whether you can give your new pet the time and attention it needs. Be clear on what is required with pet ownership, so your new roommate doesn't feel neglected.

Get Musical

Pick up that instrument you used to play! It's never too late to rock out, study the blues, pick up your guitar again, or whale on the drums. Used gear is relatively inexpensive, too. Want lessons but can't afford them? There are plenty of free lessons on YouTube and other sites such as Songsterr and TrueFire. There have been many nights that learning a Beatles song or an Aerosmith riff brought a smile and a boost to my mood, and helped me get a better night's sleep.

The idea is to shift your thoughts elsewhere. As we get older, we lose our sense of childlike wonder, creativity, and playfulness. I am here to tell you that you are never too old to play like a child again. Sports, arts and crafts, coloring, and revisiting a skill you used to love can boost your mood. Taking a pottery class and pounding the %^&* out of clay is a great stress reliever. You never know who you will meet while learning a new skill and having a great time. Sometimes while you are wallowing in your funk, there is something or someone new right around the corner.

It is very easy to neglect yourself, your loved ones, and your responsibilities when you are in a funk. Let's face it, your world has been rocked. Depending on how hard you have been emotionally body-slammed, sometimes it is hard enough to get out of bed and take a shower. Just remember, there are some basic things you need to do to keep yourself on the conveyer belt of life.

Shower or Bathe

You will feel only as good as you smell and look. Really. Not washing your hair and not taking care of your personal hygiene screams "*I have fallen apart and can't find all of my pieces!*" Do something nice for yourself. Treating yourself to something special can be a quick pick-me-up and just what you need. If shopping in a store is not your thing, go online. Just don't spend beyond your means. The last thing you need is a financial funk.

Shop online if you don't want to leave the house, and send yourself a care package. Remember the days when you were younger and received a care package? You don't? How sad! Send yourself one *now!* And make it a great one! Pamper yourself with some affordable self-care products or that new item you've had your eye on. Even little purchases can brighten your mood and give you a little lift. Just shop wisely, and you can even act surprised when your packages arrive.

Clean

Don't clean just yourself. Keep your abode clean, too. A messy home can reflect what you are feeling. A clean home can make you feel energized and productive. I went weeks without cleaning my room when my father passed away. I didn't care, and my feelings showed. I had so many dust bunnies, they were probably mating and having a party under my bed with their relatives. Windows were filthy, and I wore a lot of the same clothes over and over. "Who the hell cares?" I thought. "I am going to recycle my wardrobe as long as I want, because I feel sh*tty. Oh, so sh*tty." I was upset and there were a lot of things on my low-to-no-priority list. Laundry? I did loads of laundry but never made the time to fold any. Mounds of clothes were strewn across my bed, and I would sleep next to the piles like they were roommates. By the time I got around to folding my kids' clothes, they had forgotten they even owned their missing shirts and pants. It was like a nice surprise when I finally handed them clothes that had been missing for a few months. I guess I went missing, too.

Now, back to the cleaning suggestion I made earlier. The sight and smells of a clean house make you feel better. Open your windows, air out your house, let some fresh air in and let the stuffy negativity out. Some people believe in the power of lighting sage to clear the bad vibes in a house, and it's a form of aromatherapy. Someone gave me a large sage stick, and I learned that Native American tribes use sage for healing and smudging, which is a spiritual house cleansing. If this isn't your thing, try baking. Seriously. Nothing beats the smell of brownies.

Cleaning can also mean decluttering. I know I have much too much clutter in my life. You should see our garage. Better yet, forget it. You would go in there and I would never find you. Nothing feels better to me than getting rid of old things I never wear and use. The clutter makes me feel claustrophobic, like it's closing in on me.

I added to my emotional-clutter pile when I decided I could not part with my dad's old clothes, fraternity hats, and basketball uniforms. What was I going to do with his old stuff from the

1950s? No idea. I finally decided to gather up a lot of his belongings, give them one last hug and smell them, and donate them to Goodwill. I was initially not able to let go because these were the last bits of Dad I had, but they were only things. I had him in me, and that's all that mattered.

As I bagged up his belongings, I felt that maybe the spirit of my dad would enrich someone else's life. I imagined someone else getting great use out of my dad's old athletic jacket and fraternity gear. His oversized sweaters and jackets were too painful to wear. I decided to let someone else benefit from them; they were doing nothing sitting in my closet. I hope his adventurous, hardworking spirit will be instilled in the person who adopts my dad's things— that his intensity, love of life, and drive will be felt by the person wearing his beautiful brown suede jacket. It sounds woo-woo and silly, but why not let someone else benefit from his things I really won't use? They are just painful reminders that he is gone. One person's sorrow can be another person's joy.

Plants, Pets, and Epiphanies

During a very lonely time in my life, I was living in Boston and was recently unemployed and suddenly single. Actually, my relationship was so old, it was stale. You know it's time to break up with someone when you are lonely, bored, taken for granted, and neglected…repeatedly. My dad always said, "Don't confuse love for weakness. And don't think you love someone when you are really just used to them." Of course, at the time his wisdom went in one ear and out the other. Years after our parents give us advice, we all realize that they were our age once. Your parents know a thing or two about whether someone is good enough for you, and you think that person is the best you deserve. We never want to admit our parents are right, but sometimes they just are. Own it.

To body-slam my unemployed, single, and sad self, I did several things. I found freelance work through a network of people I knew. I started working out at least four to five days a week. I signed up for guitar lessons. I ate more healthfully. I tried to brighten my surroundings by buying planter boxes and hanging them outside my windows, but that didn't last long—great idea though. I went to Home Depot and bought small planter boxes about two and a half feet long and tied them to the ledge outside my windows. When I looked out my living room and bedroom windows, I could see multicolored flowers that put me in a much brighter mood. The usual view was a busy Brookline street filled with cars, concrete, and not much else. I colored my world with beautiful flowers that began to change my landscape—at least until the management told me planter boxes were not allowed. Bah humbug. Other residents told me how pretty they looked, but the management wanted them removed immediately. Total buzz-kill. Last, I found a kitten. I guess you could say he found me. We rescued each other. If you are an animal owner, you get me. The kitten was lost, emaciated, and screaming for help. I helped nurse him back to health, and he showered me with love and affection. Best roommate I ever had.

A Sloppy Mess—Yoga after Loss

When I first started taking yoga in my forties, there was a time in the class when I would lie in complete stillness…and then the tears would come. Memories of my late mother or something more painful would flood my thoughts. I felt like a child, hurt and needing comfort (a battle scar of my childhood, I admit). I was embarrassed that I was a tearful mess and tried hiding my meltdown; it was obvious I needed some healing from the inside out. Over time, more yoga classes brought renewed strength and a feeling of greater self-awareness and improved self-esteem. In stillness, I no longer felt a flood of emotion and a tidal wave of tears, but instead a feeling of calm, focus, and serenity. Plus, my butt was looking better in those yoga pants while I was doing Downward Dog.

The next two guests from my show both had a lot to share about their experiences with yoga and the transformative powers of this practice, no matter what level someone is at.

Meet Lauren Lipton

Lauren Lipton is an award-winning journalist who covers style, trends, and travel. Her work has appeared in *The New York Times*, *The Wall Street Journal*, *Allure, Town & Country*, *Condé Nast Traveler*, and numerous other publications. Her book *Yoga Bodies: Real People, Real Stories, & the Power of Transformation*, a collection of interviews with yogis of all shapes and skill levels, with photographs by Jaimie Baird, was published by Chronicle Books in March 2017. She is the author of two novels, *Mating Rituals of the North American WASP* and *It's About Your Husband*. She holds a bachelor's degree in English and anthropology from Occidental College and a master's degree in print journalism from the University of Southern California.

I asked Lauren to share the backstory of how she decided to write *Yoga Bodies: Real People, Real Stories, & the Power of Transformation*.

"I have been practicing yoga for about six years," Lauren told me. "A lot of times when people practice yoga and get into it, they want to spread the gospel to the whole world. That's the point where they quit their job and become yoga teachers. I thought I could use my skills as a journalist and bring the gospel to the world that way."

She has diverse subjects in the book, and I was curious about how she selected them. *Yoga Bodies* includes portraits of and interviews with roughly eighty people who practice yoga; there is a wide variety of body shapes, sizes, and yoga abilities. "Anyone can practice yoga. You don't have to look like the girls on Instagram. You don't even have to be flexible," Lauren said. What a relief! I am not very flexible at times—I'll be perfect.

As we age, we might think it's too late and too difficult to do yoga, but there are all different levels of yoga, and as Lauren points out in her book, everyone has a different story of who they are and what led them to yoga. One woman in *Yoga Bodies*, Michelle, stuck out to me; she mentioned that she'd lost her aunt and gained a lot of weight.

Michelle shared with Lauren that her aunt had been like a mother to her. The loss was devastating. In the aftermath, Michelle gained a lot of weight and was very open with Lauren about her feelings and, specifically, her depression. She was interested in yoga, but her weight hindered her physically. Within nine months of starting yoga, she began to see a difference. Lauren has a beautiful picture of Michelle in a complicated yoga pose; she is standing on one leg, holding the other leg high in the air. There is a huge smile on her face!

I am not even close to being that flexible, and I know I wouldn't be smiling. Lauren and I agreed that Michelle had incredible yoga skills and a wonderful, positive attitude.

Lauren pointed out something interesting about Michelle's story. "She started doing yoga to lose weight, and I never asked if she had lost any weight or not." Lauren thought Michelle would have said, "I realize I am worthy of love no matter what my weight is." Who doesn't love that?

I mentioned to Lauren that I took time off from doing yoga before my dad passed away, and then I finally went back. I felt I needed to soothe myself and take care of my physical and mental well-being, but I found myself crying a little during class. I felt like a mess, but I moved through the emotions, and yoga helped me in so many ways.

A lot of people opened up to Lauren about death. "A woman lost her dad and used her yoga as he was dying—which I can't even talk about without choking up," Lauren said. "She used her breathing and sat in bed with him as he was crossing the threshold. Another woman who lost her mother used her time to commune with her spirit. I think it is the contemplative aspect of yoga that really helps."

I have heard people say you need to calm your mind and tune in to your breath. Makes total sense. Some people might not understand the practice of yoga—the benefits and how healing it can be. I asked Lauren to discuss her experience and insights.

"It's hard to define what yoga is, but I have boiled it down to this: It is the practice of paying attention to what you are doing right now without moving ahead in your mind or to some other time zone or whatever." Yoga can be challenging because you need to quiet your mind and focus your attention on your breath and your body. Our minds are busy and overstressed and overstimulated. Lauren says you can practice the notion of staying focused and present when you do any activity, such as walking or gardening. "The poses in yoga play into that meditation, because during a complicated yoga pose, I cannot think about anything else," she said. "I am standing on one leg, trying to balance and not fall over, and that really keeps my mind focused. It's a mini vacation, in a way. After you have done yoga for an hour, your head is clear." Lauren says over time, that feeling flows into your everyday life. You learn to find serenity in the chaos of life.

I have found that yoga definitely has a calming effect on me. If someone upsets me or confronts me, I am a lot more chill. When Lauren mentioned that it helped her with road rage, we both had a good laugh. So true. "Now, if someone flips me off, I can be like, 'Whatever! It doesn't matter,'" she said. Agreed.

I asked Lauren to tell me about another special person in her book, a man who was seated in a wheelchair doing a variation of Locust Pose. "That's Rudra," she says.

Lauren is a journalist, and some people in her book are fellow students or teachers of hers. She knew there were people in wheelchairs who practiced yoga, and she wanted to meet some of these special people. One of the things that makes Lauren's book so special is her attention to diversity. "The book includes diverse ages and ranges. One of the yogis, Bunny, is ninety-one! My son thought she was fifty. Bunny is politically active, brilliant, and does yoga every day. She is really good! She can't do everything, but the head-to-knee pose she is doing in the book is a pretty difficult pose for anybody." Apparently, not for Bunny!

I asked Lauren to tell me more about a father-and-son picture in her book: Sean and Tommy. "They were doing Wheel Pose, a very difficult backbend," she said. They are both smiling at each other as they focus on their pose.

Lauren's parents introduced her to yoga when she was a teenager in the 1980s; she enjoyed the experience but wasn't quite ready for it. "It was too quiet for me," she said. "I wanted excitement. I could do all of the poses, but I didn't want to clear my mind. I wanted to ruminate on everything. Years later, I tried yoga again and it stuck."

I was curious as to whether yoga has helped Lauren remain calm in the craziness of life?

She mentioned that she suffers from serious anxiety. "A lot of people take medication—I do, and it helps. But the combination of medication and yoga has really been a life-changer for me. I am less anxious. I can talk myself out of anxiety that I know does not need to exist. I am much nicer to people. Yoga is a great thing, and I would absolutely recommend that anyone who hasn't tried it give it a try and see if it works." She believes yoga helps with everything, even in a small way.

I told Lauren that I am amazed at the power of stretching in yoga. There is a feeling of relaxation when I stretch, but also a releasing of stress and tension in my body. Whatever emotions and pain I am holding on to are gone by the end of the class. She agreed and said that she is even more flexible and stronger than before, and added: "You can actually be too flexible for yoga and cheat your way through poses for which you really need to develop strength."

Lauren believes that "the world would be a better place if everybody did yoga. We would all be slightly calmer or more accepting." I believe that, too.

She added, "What makes me happy is when someone says, 'I saw your book and I showed it to my mom; she says if those people can do yoga, so can she!' If I have helped even one person believe that, the book is a success."

I asked Lauren to share advice for people who are a little intimidated and don't know where to start. She suggested they start with classes at their local YMCA, because that is where she began. "Keep trying until you find a yoga class that you like. There are a million different kinds of yoga and teachers. Just keep trying until you find the one that works for you," she said.

Find Lauren Lipton at *www.laurenlipton.com*.

Meet Jake Ferree

Jake Ferree is a yoga master and personal transformation expert. He is a highly sought-after yoga instructor, personal trainer, and healer who discovered yoga after going through a challenging personal experience. The practice of yoga has been a life-changer for him, inside and out. I asked Jake to share his journey that got him to where he is now and whether he was influenced by something he was going through.

"Any of my moments of being down led me to fitness and eventually to mindfulness and yoga," he said. "The big thing for me was, I had to leave college." Around the age of nineteen, he discovered the power of exercise and mindset. He started lifting weights and used fitness to shift his mood and outlook when he felt down. He was going through a personal funk, and he found that going to the gym helped him significantly. He just had no idea what he would do next. He knew working out gave him a feeling of assurance that everything would be all right. Exercise shifted his mindset, and he became more focused on whatever he was doing. He shifted from, in his words, "feeling like a loser and inadequate" to finding a new, more fulfilling career path.

Fitness gave Jake a greater awareness of the power of focus and the importance of mindfulness. Whether he was doing yoga and focusing on his breath, meditating, or just connecting to the moment, he learned to be present in everyday fitness activities. He explained to me that being present is everything.

"My mind was usually somewhere else, and I kept telling myself, '*Focus!*'" Focusing on the breath was challenging for Jake and didn't make sense right away. Even though a yoga instructor would tell him to breathe, he wasn't able to grasp the importance of the breath until about five years into the practice. Once he did, Jake created what he calls "a sort of dance between the breath and the movement to connect the body." He explained how the practice of yoga becomes a seamless dance where the breath and body work together in unison. "Once you are able to move your body with the breath, it becomes a seamless flow, and it feels more like you are dancing than holding poses or moving through poses," he said. "The transitions become seamless, and it brings you fully present, because when you are present and connect to the breath, you are fully conscious of what is happening while you are breathing." He shared that getting the body and breath to work together allows someone to become fully present. "It is a magical thing once you are able to connect those two," he said.

I shared with Jake that my experience with yoga felt like being in "the zone." My breath and body were connected, and I felt more open to the benefits and joys of the practice. Yoga and being mindful are things I continue to practice, but there are moments when I am not focused on the poses and not connecting mindfully.

Jake explained that we tend to "hold stuff in," which makes our breath shallow, and we feel as if we don't have enough air. His solution is insightful: "When you get to a place where you bring awareness to your breath and turn into the breath to create calm-ness and relax the breath, you make the inhale and exhale longer. You can't help but mirror what is happening with the breath. If you take the time to calm the breath, the body and the mind will start to calm down as well."

On more than one occasion while taking a yoga class, I started getting very emotional and thinking about my childhood. I felt like I was having a pity party for one. I asked Jake if that happens to a lot of people, and he said, "It does! Yoga makes you that way." When he started doing yoga, he was "not looking for any spiritual awareness or any awareness in general," he said. He was just inter-ested in stretching his tight muscles, but what he didn't know was that yoga has a way of getting right into your mind and body. He calls this "sneaking in." Jake said that some poses open up parts of the body. He explained, "We hold emotions in certain places, and yoga has a way of opening up the body, and that makes the emotions arise and come to the surface."

When Jake shared this insight, I had an "aha!" moment. I wasn't the only person who fell apart (emotionally and physically) during Tree Pose or Downward Dog. "Sometimes you might be in a pose and start to cry and have a memory," Jake said. "In those times, there is beauty. If we can allow ourselves into that place and trust the process, the emotions are ready to be released. We can allow ourselves to heal a lot of things." Jake shared that when he started yoga, he was scared. He didn't want to feel—because, he said, "I was taught not to feel anything. I always wanted to hold things in, because I was taught that guys don't express their feel-ings." When he first became emotional during yoga, he was "a little freaked out but...also curious." Jake shared a valuable lesson from his experience about "stirring the pot." As he practiced yoga, "it started to stir the pot and get off some of the scum of the pot. My emotions started to come up, and I had to deal with a lot of stuff I wasn't aware of at the time." He found this process to be very cleansing. And now, as he practices yoga, he doesn't have a lot of "stuff" to deal with anymore, because it has all come to the surface and he has dealt with it. After you deal with what comes to the surface, your practice becomes more of a meditation and there is a calmness. "At first, if you are holding on to stuff, it will pop up and you can't hide your stuff. Your emotions will pop up with your mindset," he said. You might be crying, he said, or even laughing. Yoga stirs up a lot of different emotions; it's important to be aware of what triggers these feelings, pay attention to what surfaces, and then sit with it. "Don't judge it," he said. "Just listen to it." Jake said that when we allow ourselves "to be open to the process, we are able to learn. Through that learning, we can own up to it and empower ourselves to move through it."

I told Jake that when things come up emotionally, I feel that's a spot inside myself that I need to focus on and work on. He said it is important to listen to what is happening inside. When he teaches yoga, he looks around the room and sees how his students are reacting. "You don't learn the most from all the yoga poses you can do right and perfect," he said. "You learn from the ones we mess up in and fall out of. How do you react to falling? Do you give up? Get upset [or] frustrated and fall again?" He sees this as a continual pattern. Jake is fascinated by how people work though the practice of yoga, "because it's a good indication of how you work through challenges in your life. If we fall down, can we learn from it and get back up again? How we respond to it is the biggest thing." Jake explained that yoga teaches us how to change our responses by becoming aware of them: "We become aware of what happens when we fall out of something, and how we react to it. If you don't like the way you react, then we now have a place where we can change it, but it all starts with awareness first."

I shared that I often lose my balance while attempting a one-legged stance. I silently berate myself, usually by saying, "Duh! Stop thinking about something or someone else and focus!" Jake said that if I am not "in the moment," I will fall. When we are not paying attention to what is going on or we don't have awareness, it is easy to fall. He said, "They tell us when we are working on our balance in the yoga practice to find a spot that you can look at, called your *drishti*. You find a spot that you can put your attention and focus on. When you allow yourself to become more focused on something, you become more precise and more in the moment and become more balanced in that moment." I told Jake that I feel finding a *drishti* applies to life itself. He agreed and explained that things that happen in yoga relate to what happens in life. "How you react in yoga correlates to how you react in everyday life, or our perception of what failure is."

Jake is a very strong guy, and I was curious if he has always been this fit or if yoga has enhanced his fitness level. His answer was enlightening.

> *"In the past, my strength was an armor. I thought I had to put it on to look stronger and more masculine—to honor myself as a protection. As I have been practicing yoga, my strength is coming from the inside. Although my body may still be strong and defined, it's softer and more movable, and a more functional body. I do my best to be aware of my feelings. My body reacts to my feelings, and I can move a lot easier."*

When he used to compete in bodybuilding competitions, he just wanted to look his best, lift the most weight, and get as big as possible. There was never any stretching, only lifting. In retrospect, he sees that he wasn't in the best shape after all. "When I first started yoga, I couldn't reach my arms over my head," he told me. "I couldn't bend down and touch my toes. I couldn't intertwine my hands and clasp them behind my back. I might have looked good, but functionally I had not much movement." Over time, his body softened, allowing him to move more and create a softness within. He stopped being so hard on himself and on others. He became more forgiving and compassionate.

People judge others by how they look, but they are unaware of how someone might be crumbling inside. We have the persona that people see, and then we have who we really are. I can understand how yoga has brought Jake an inner and outer strength. Jake said yoga has taught him to look inside himself. When he is immersed in his yoga poses, he can't help but see what is happening within. There is a transparency of emotions and feelings.

With so many different types and levels of yoga, I asked Jake how people can get started.

He suggested trying various types of classes and teachers to find one that works. "Some people might want a slower class or a restorative class. You might get in a pose and lay there in a very relaxing way. Other people might want a flowing class where you connect movement with breath, or a power class where you bring in a strength component." He suggested that beginners start with a basic class, even if it's online. He said starting something new can be hard, so be patient.

His first yoga class was enlightening. He thought that because he was physically fit and used to working out routinely, yoga wouldn't be so hard. "I just thought there would be a lot of stretching. I chose a level-two class, three being the top one." The result? His whole body was shaking, and he couldn't keep up; this was a humbling experience. "I was next to an older woman, and she was gracefully moving through everything and holding poses with ease," he said. "I just kept shaking, looking at her, and hating her. That was my anger that needed to get out!" Jake encourages people to just do the best they can, because over time, the body learns the poses and things become easier. Just find an instructor that works for you.

In Jake's practice, he also focuses on healing and massage. He traveled to Thailand three years ago and completed a Thai massage course. He fell in love with the practice, and returns to Thailand each year to continue his training. He explained that Thai massage is "a beautiful combo of yoga and massage, also called 'yoga for lazy people.' You let someone else move your body and play with the trigger points. Thai massage finds trigger points throughout the body." In the practice, you stretch and find areas that need more movement. Jake incorporates Thai massage into his yoga practice, and clients see the benefits. He sees the healing power of massage and the power of touch. Having your hands on someone's body helps that person connect to the breath, heal, and bring more energy to areas that hold tension. His clients can then focus their attention on the areas that need to move more and release stiffness; this practice brings awareness to the body. Jakes feels that with awareness, we can empower ourselves to make necessary changes. He said, "Your body is amazing, and so is your mind. When you connect the two, you can create miracles."

I shared with Jake that yoga makes me feel thankful and helps me put things in perspective. I get this message that things will be okay. He said that some poses are created to do that. An instructor might put us in an uncomfortable pose, and we need to sit in that pose. We breathe through our discomfort, and as soon as we release ourselves from the pose, we learn how we react to things that are uncomfortable and stressful. Sitting and breathing through something uncomfortable, and staying calm and relaxed, correlate to how we deal with things in life. Jake said, "Freaking out in life does nothing to help your balance and the situation."

I share this sentiment exactly. Yoga makes me more centered and calm so that I don't flip out over the little things. Well, most of the time. I am a work in progress.

Jake discussed his daily morning rituals that make mine look ridiculous. I was so interested in how he starts each day calm, with focus, and with a positive mindset. He said, "It takes work to stay positive and keep yourself in a place of staying authentic and setting yourself up for happiness and success."

The first thing he does when his alarm goes off: "I meditate for twenty minutes. I connect to my breath and my body. I go right into my meditation state, then I reflect on how I am feeling and if I can direct my mind and body to a place of positivity." Sometimes he makes a list of things he is grateful for, such as his breath, his dog, his body, or friends and family. Then he writes something about his present moment—what he is feeling, what he wants to focus on during the day. He also finds time to read an insightful book he has shared with and gifted to numerous friends, called *The Book of Awakening: Having the Life You Want by Being Present to the Life You Have* by Mark Nepo.

I was curious as to whether people listen to music while meditating. He shared that he has been doing the Oprah and Deepak 21-Day Meditation Experience. I'm putting that on my list! He said they do a free series that is a guided meditation. "They give you a mantra, and there's a silent part where you are basically sitting with it. There are other times I just sit and listen to my breath and see where my mind goes. I have been meditating for at least eight years and every single day for three to four years," he said. He added that he still has moments when he catches his mind somewhere else, but he can reel himself back in to focus. Jake feels that meditation "teaches us how to redirect things and how to notice things. We go through life and we make mistakes and don't realize."

When people say they don't have time to mediate, Jake tells them, "It's just ten to twenty minutes a day. We all have that, and I feel meditation helps create more time. We become more efficient. My mind doesn't get pulled way. I am more efficient, present, and more productive." Things that normally would take more time take less. He has become more efficient and productive with his time. He believes that meditation has a way of paying you back. Whatever time you have to put in, you create more time in your life and more focus and positivity.

I was curious if it's possible to meditate while walking or doing other activities. He said it just depends whom you ask. He believes that just being present in the moment is a meditation. Walking, yoga, gardening, or lifting weights can be meditative, as long as you are present.

I wanted to know more about his practice of Reiki and reconnective healing. Jake told me he was certified and went through attunement. "You become aware through a sense of touch and feeling energy and redirecting energy throughout the body," he said. "You figure out where people are holding more energy, and send light into that area so it can be released. Reiki and reconnective healing and breathwork training can be very powerful and meaningful. I take the parts that make sense to me, and I try to share."

Jake added, "Everything comes down to awareness—taking the time to sit with yourself and notice what is going on. We have plenty of tools to do that, whether it is through movement or connecting your body to the breath. These are all ways to be more aware of ourselves."

Jake was inspired to start a blog because he wanted to create something meaningful. He first started writing on Instagram but wanted to write longer posts with personal insights. As a child, he loved to write beautiful books and had a wonderful imagination, but then his writing took a back seat to other things in life. Jake is loving his return to writing, saying, "It's a great way to collect the thoughts and to redirect things and reflect."

Jake teaches online, in person in yoga studios throughout Los Angeles, and in the summer...on a West Hollywood rooftop! With the accompaniment of an incredibly talented violinist, he takes yoga to a whole other level. Students focus on the sound of Jake's voice and the lovely music from his violinist while viewing a beautiful Southern California sunset. I look forward to meeting up with Jake in person at one of his many transformative yoga classes.

Find Jake Ferree at *www.JakeFerree.com*.

As a side note, I finally went back to yoga days after I spoke with Jake. I needed time to deal with a lot in my life, but I realized I was neglecting my own mental and physical well-being. I always loved the way I felt after taking yoga classes. After a long hiatus due to waiting for my shoulder to heal, losing my dad, and helping my younger daughter through a rough patch, I fully embraced every pose and breath. During my first class back, all I could think of were Jake's words describing the power of breath and the connection with the body. My conversation with Jake was a gift and a story I really needed to hear. Plus, every time I found myself a little wobbly in a pose, I kept saying to myself, "Find your *drishti!*" And it worked.

Answer the Following:

- ☁ What strategies do you already use when you need to de-funk yourself?
- ☁ What would you like to try for the first time? Or what is something you would like to do again?
- ☁ If you could do something out of your comfort zone, what would it be?
- ☁ What scares you? Why?
- ☁ What holds you back from being brave?
- ☁ What baggage do you have that limits you from getting rid of your funk permanently?
- ☁ What is the best thing you ever did to get rid of a funk? Why did it work so well?
- ☁ How do you deal with ambiguity and uncertainty?
- ☁ How do you deal with mistakes, disappointment, and rejection?
- ☁ Are you able to own up to your weaknesses and mistakes, instead of beating yourself up?

We learn to not repeat the same mistakes and to become stronger, wiser, and more resilient, unless we like the idea of poorly thought-out, repetitive choices that leave us feeling like we're on a hamster wheel going nowhere.

Pampering Yourself Is as Important as a Great Night's Sleep and a Health-and-Wellness Routine.

Make yourself a priority and do things that make you feel great! Here are some ideas to get you going:

- Try a yoga class or meditation workshop
- Write in a journal—note what you are thinking and feeling—and make a list of what things make you happy
- Exercise—walk, run, hike, bike, swim, surf, and so on. Get moving!
- Put your phone down and take a break from social media
- Play with your pet
- Take a relaxing bath
- Try a spa-type facial mask—the sillier you look, the better!
- Get a massage
- Get a haircut or makeover
- Get a manicure-pedicure
- Take a bubble bath
- Sit in a Jacuzzi
- Throw a party for no reason (or celebrate the end of something, such as a job or relationship, and the excitement of a new beginning!)

- Try something new—an activity or a place you've always wanted to visit
- Take a solo trip or travel with a friend
- Have a staycation
- Take a mental health day

CHAPTER 5

It's Never Too Late to
Try Something New

"A bend in the road is not the end of the road...unless you fail to make the turn."—Helen Keller

Remember what it was like to learn something new as a kid? You learned to ride a bike, speak a new language, or play an instrument. The truth is, it is never too late to learn a new skill and bring back that childlike love of learning. Think about taking a refresher in a language you learned years ago or enroll in that self-defense class you heard about. Start a hobby that you always wanted to pursue. Maybe you've dreamed of rocking out on an electric guitar. You're never too old to learn. Stop dreaming about wanting to do something, and start *doing*. Inaction leads to nothing, so what are you waiting for?

Get comfortable being uncomfortable. Stand on the edge of your fears, hesitations, and insecurities, and take that damn leap to stretch yourself. Pay attention to your dreams, because your subconscious just might steer you to the answers you are looking for. Look at this moment in your life as a chance to reinvent yourself and be bold! Revisit what you used to like to do and start doing it again. You might even discover that something you resisted doing all these years (such as owning a dog) will bring you incredible joy (with the endless affection, and adorable antics). The only person that can hold you back is you, and you are in the driver's seat. You don't have to become an expert, so start off slowly and see where this new adventure takes you. And if you decide you don't like something you started, pick something else. No biggie.

This chapter will feature an eighty-five-year-old French woman who is not slowing down anytime soon. Three to four days a week, Jackie Krisher is busy doing CrossFit training. I feel like a lazy slob when I hear about her bold adventures! She has competed in triathlons, and she didn't start swimming until recently. Her goal is to be able to go to Africa to hike Mount Kilimanjaro to raise funds for an organization that fights leukemia. Jackie believes anything is possible, and her life proves it! We should all take on Jackie's view of life.

Meet Jackie Krisher

Jackie Krisher was born in France. She has lived in the United States since 1965. She is about five feet tall, is a triathlete, and participates in CrossFit. She is eighty-five years young.

A few years back, I had a chance to speak with her when she was starring in Claire Imler's *Jackie Krisher: No Limits* film, which won numerous awards. I wanted to catch up with Jackie again because she is always doing amazing and challenging things that I could never imagine. Here's our Q&A.

Janeane: When I first met you, you were starring in Claire Imler's film *Jackie Krisher: No Limits*, which was so exciting, and

I know the film received some incredible awards. What was that like, being the star of that film?

Jackie: It was unbelievable, because that was my first time and I didn't know what to expect. We were nominated, and I didn't know we would win. I can't express how I feel. There were about two hundred people, and you go on the stage and (*heavy sigh*) your legs are kind of like falling under you.

(*laughter*)

JB: Wait a minute! You can withstand all of this running and everything you do, and you get onstage and your legs are noodles?

JK: Yes! Exactly (laughter)—because that was my first time going on the stage, and it was a beautiful one, too. After that, I went to a film festival in Los Angeles. Again, we were nominated— Claire was nominated. She was the one doing all the work.

JB: She's amazing!

JK: She's amazing!

JB: At what age did you start doing all these athletic endeavors? Running, swimming....

JK: In my eighties. I tried to swim so many times, and I paid for lessons with a coach. I love the water and I love the pool, but I never go where it is deep because I cannot swim. The reason I could not swim is because I could not put my head under the water.

JB: Why?

JK: I try to do that many, many times. I taught my grand-daughter to jump in the pool when I was there and taught her how to swim, but Grandma did not know how to swim. She was in the water anyway, as long as my feet were on the bottom. I tried so many times. The last time it was after we finished the half mara-thon in Puerto Rico. Monica, the coach, came in and said, "Jackie, we are doing swimming lessons. Would you be interested?" And I said, "Is it free?" (*laughter*) "Yes," she said, and I said, "You bet!"

I didn't know what I was doing. So, I did, but I still did not know how to swim very well. I had to put my head under the water, and I said, "Oh My God! That is terrible!" A month or two months later, I was told, "Jackie, you have to sign up." "Sign up for what?" I said. "For the triathlon!" I said, "*What?*"

JB: The triathlon?

JK: I said, "I didn't know that!" And they said, "That's why you don't know how to swim." I said, "Oh my God! I had to do the swimming, the bicycling, and the running, and that was no problem. My first triathlon, the only one I did, was in Newport Beach on the Back Bay. It was cold and raining. I was freezing, and I was thinking, "How could I do that?" Two weeks earlier I was going to quit.

JB: Really?

JK: One of the girls said, "Jackie, what is wrong with you?" (*laughter*) [I thought], "I can't make it! I am never going to do this!"

JB: What year was this?

JK: In 2015, when I was eighty-two. That was three years ago. Every year I do something. This year I did the race in Oregon. Last year I did the hiking in Yosemite. The year before, I did the bicycling. You see, that was four summers ago.

JB: Let me clarify—when you say, "I just did a *little* biking"... in 2016, you did a fifty-mile bike race for the Leukemia & Lymphoma Society.

JK: Yes.

JB: In 2017, you did the hiking in Yosemite, and this year you did a half-marathon in Sunriver in Central Oregon; it's a forty-two-hundred-foot altitude. And you're planning on Mount

Kilimanjaro, over nineteen thousand feet, if your health will allow you. In 2020, you are going to be eighty-seven.

JK: I will turn eighty-seven in August, and that is the best time, because it is not as cold. So, that is why I want to do it.

JB: And you'll be the oldest woman to do it, along with raising funds for the Leukemia & Lymphoma Society. Now, were you always a little bit athletic when you were younger, or did something happen in your life and you decided to do this?

JK: Yes, when I was younger, I was in school and we had the gym. When I was seventeen or eighteen, I was part of the Catholic youth and we would be in the gym. We did all kinds of things, and it was a big thing in France. I was crying because I could not jump the pole. I did jump that pole many times, but that day we lost because of me. I did jump the pole, but the pole went down with me.

JB: Oh....

JK: You are supposed to be jumping over the pole. I was not that much taller than I am now. I was crying because we didn't win because of me. From that, I stayed away from lots of things. Later, I met my husband, got married, and raised the kids. I didn't do anything whatsoever. I did some bicycling when I was in my twenties, but not that much. Very little. And then, all those things I started when I was seventy-nine years old.

In 2000, I was in my first marathon at age sixty-seven; this was in Maui for the Leukemia Society. In 2013, I competed in a half-marathon in Los Angeles for the New Year. It was the Saturday before New Year's Eve at Dodger Stadium. It started at nine o'clock at night.

JB: (*gasps*) What? At night?

JK: We did not start until 9:30 p.m., and we finished at 1:22 a.m., which was eight minutes before the cutoff. I was sick the whole night; it was supposed to be beautiful in the dark. They took us into Dodger Stadium, and we stayed for hours running and walking. I couldn't even run, because my tummy was hurting so bad. The three of us—Jennifer Shramo, Dani Daniels, and myself—crossed the finish line together at 1:22 a.m.

JB: Awful.

JK: It started downtown and then into Dodger Stadium. It was not the most beautiful place.

JB: I have never heard of a race starting at 9:30 p.m. and ending at 1:30 a.m.

JK: It was the first inaugural Dodger Stadium half-marathon New Year's Eve race. That is what got me going, and from there I have not stopped.

JB: You were in your seventies when you did that?

JK: I was seventy-nine. That was 2013. In 1999, I got a flyer in the mail inviting me to go and join a group of runners in the Leukemia Society and raise funds. I said to myself, "I am going to do it. I need to lose weight."

JB: Okay....

JK: I never lost a pound. (*laughter*) I told my daughter what I was going to do. She said I should hold off on this because she thought Jacob, a family relative, might have cancer. Jacob is my son-in-law's nephew.

JB: Oh, no!

JK: He was about ten months old or something like that. I told them I would do the marathon for Jacob. When I did the first marathon in Maui, I was by myself. Too slow to go with the group, too fast for the other ones. So, I was by myself. And then I was tempted to run, and every time I was thinking, "Jacob. Jacob.

Jacob." I said, "I am not going to run." I signed up for walking, not running. I got second place.

JB: Second?!

JK: Yes, second [in] the age bracket from sixty-five to sixty-nine.

JB: Amazing! Oh my gosh, Jackie!

JK: The athlete who won first place was a runner, not a walker, and she was only nineteen minutes ahead of me. When I was coming in, I was far away, and I hear on the loudspeaker, "From El Toro, California, Jackie Krisher!" (*laughter*) How the hell does he know I am from El Toro, California, and it's me?

We will return to Jackie's story in Chapter 11, when we focus on senior citizens doing extraordinary things.

Every evening after work, this next guest would arrive home from work and spend his evenings not curled up in front of the TV or perusing Facebook. Instead, he would try something new every day. A new film. A new musical project. Working on something new gave him creative freedom and expression and proved to be a great way to decompress from work.

Meet Charlie Visnic

Charlie is an editor and a creative tinkerer. He found himself in a bit of a creative rut and shared how he turned his life around.

Janeane: Describe the funk you were in. What happened? What caused it?

Charlie: I think when I decided to start my blog, I felt like I was just getting a bit old and I wasn't in the place that I'd imagined myself to be when I was younger. I felt a bit like I was in a rut and creatively stagnant. I wanted more focus, plus I wanted to quit smoking, which I had been doing for the past twelve or so years. So, I decided to put myself on the spot and put the pressure on to get something done—to make something happen for myself. And that's how the idea for the blog came about.

JB: How did you turn your life around?

CV: I don't think my life was necessarily turned around by the blog. I definitely learned some great lessons about myself and how to work creatively, but I think quitting smoking was probably the most "life changing for the better" for me.

JB: How difficult or easy was it to pull yourself out of your funk?

CV: It wasn't as hard as one might think to do the task of one creative thing a day. For me, I set myself a date for when to start, my birthday, so when it was finally time to begin, I was excited to get going. It was harder in the middle of the year when time was not on my side, and I still had to figure out something to do and document it as well.

JB: What did you learn from this experience? What did you learn about yourself, if anything?

CV: I learned a fair amount about myself and the types of things I find interesting. I learned a lot about other things, whether it was art techniques or mechanical things. I also gained a love for trying things for no reason whatsoever. For example, attempting to carve a face into the lead on the tip of a pencil. It seems extremely tough to do, and my results were certainly less than mediocre, but I did carve a tiny face into that lead, and I really enjoyed the challenge. Doing something without expectation can be surprisingly rewarding. So, I guess I gained an affinity for experimentation and doing things "just because" and not because I expect anything from it.

JB: Do you have a mantra or quote you live by?

CV: I don't have a mantra or quote that I try to live by. I guess the Eagles song "Take It Easy" comes to mind, because I do try to always take it easy.

JB: How do you keep calm when life gets rocky?

CV: I am lucky. I have good parents that have given me a wonderful life. Whenever I get worried that I might lose my job, that money might run out, that we could lose everything, I remember that I am lucky. I have a place that I can land and start over if the worst were ever to happen. I try to remember how lucky I am whenever life gets rocky. I also don't need much. I live to provide for my wife and kids, and we all try to work together if the going gets tough.

JB: Advice for others?

CV: Whenever I think of imparting advice, I imagine it's always aimed at some young kid who's just getting his or her start, but really I think the advice I have is better imparted to someone older like me. And that advice is: Don't lose your ambition. When you're young and driven, you are full of ambition, but as you get older and life happens around you, it's easy to settle into your bubble—to just want to come home, watch a little TV, and hit the sack. And that's fine to some degree, but as you fall asleep, remind yourself of the plans you want to make. And then after that, take things bit by bit. Some ideas feel impossible because they seem so big, but the only way to do it is bit by bit or piece by piece. Like that Shel Silverstein poem about Melinda Mae, the little girl who ate a whale. She finally finished at eighty-nine, and she did it by taking small bites and chewing slowly. Ha!

Meet Peter Zheutlin

Peter Zheutlin is a freelance journalist and author whose work has appeared regularly in the *Boston Globe* and the *Christian Science Monitor*. He is the author of several books, including *Rescue Road: One Man, Thirty Thousand Dogs and a Million Miles on the Last Hope Highway*. We spoke about his latest book, *Rescued: What Second-Chance Dogs Teach Us About Living With Purpose, Loving With Abandon, and Finding Joy in the Little Things*. Here's our Q&A.

Janeane: I got a puppy five or six months ago, and I had sworn I would never get a dog because it is a lot of work, but she's helping my daughter with anxiety and she is wonderful. What made you decide to write the book *Rescued*?

Peter: I finally got on board with something we had never done as a family, which was to adopt a dog. For the first twenty-five years of my marriage, I was adamantly opposed to getting a dog; it was a real leap for me to agree in the first place. By the time I wrote *Rescued*, we had three rescue dogs, and they were all wonderful additions to my life.

JB: Why were you adamantly opposed? I bet I am in the same boat.

PZ: Because I thought it was going to be too much work. We had young kids. I do a lot of the housework in our house, and I just thought this was going to be another thing to take care of.

JB: Right!

PZ: I knew I would be the one to get up early to walk the dog, do the cleanup. Everything. I just felt like it would be too much. Six years ago, once my kids were grown up and the younger one was about to be a senior in high school, the switch flipped. We were about to become empty nesters, so I agreed to get a dog. I had no idea how to go about it. We ended up going the rescue route. I knew nothing about rescue dogs. I had no idea what we were even talking about. Once we adopted Albie, who was our first of three, I just couldn't believe how connected and in love with him I was. I was also curious why we had adopted a dog from Louisiana. I didn't really know anything about the problems down there or why these dogs are coming all the way to Massachusetts from down South. That is what made me curious, and that is what led me to write two books about it, *Rescued* and *Rescue Road*. They are an attempt to answer my own questions about the whole process—how it happens, why it happens, and how these second-chance dogs contribute to and improve our lives.

JB: Sure. So, it is so interesting because you were not always a dog person. How have you changed after becoming a dog owner?

PZ: Oh my gosh! I am so devoted to these dogs. They are a big part of our life, especially with three of them now, all rescues and all from Louisiana. It is deeply satisfying to me because I know that if we had not stepped up for them, and nobody else had, they would be gone. It's a very tender relationship. I think having a dog you know might have been headed to a bad end, as opposed to getting a dog through a breeder or other means, makes the experience even more poignant. Just to know what might have been for these creatures you love so much adds a lot more to the experience.

JB: Do you feel there are emotional benefits of owning a dog for teenagers that are going through issues with anxiety and depression?

PZ: I only know that anecdotally. I talk to so many people, from teenagers to older, who talk about their dogs' being therapeutic. We talk about therapy dogs, who are trained to come into difficult situations. After talking to a lot of people, I came to the conclusion that every dog is a therapy dog in one way or another. Our third dog was originally adopted for our son, who is now a young adult, who was having some issues with anxiety. As it turned out, she came to live with us because he realized it wasn't fair to the dog living in an apartment in Boston and working most of the day. He has since moved back to Louisiana, where he went to college, but I don't think there is any doubt that there can be huge benefits. For people in difficult circumstances, a dog is a nonjudgmental companion; they are never judging you. I can't say it works for every kid who has issues, but there are certainly endless stories about dogs that have been a therapeutic benefit to the people they live with.

JB: They give you so much love, and it's not like they give you grief. They just want to smother you with kisses.

PZ: It's not only the love, but I talked to a number of people for *Rescued* and they say when you have a dog, and there are days when you don't feel like getting out of bed or it's hard to get motivated, the dog still needs to be cared for. The dog still needs to go out for its walk, so just the fact that it needs to be tended to gets you up and out. Everyone knows that people with depression or who are going through grief, when you get up and get out for a walk, that itself can be therapeutic. The dog requires that you get up and do those things.

JB: Yes.

PZ: It's not just the companionship aspect but the motivation to do things that is beneficial.

JB: Right, because you wouldn't normally get up and do it for yourself if you were alone and in this depression. Knowing that you have this responsibility of a dog makes you do it, and then it becomes a benefit to you.

PZ: Right. Exactly.

JB: Is there anything people should know about adopting a shelter dog?

PZ: The notion is common, and I had it myself, that shelter dogs are somehow damaged goods or second-class citizens, that you are destined for years of struggle with the dog's anxiety or their behaviors. It's just not the case. I often tell people, dogs are like kids. You get no guarantees. There are no absolute guarantees with any dog, wherever it comes from. But ninety-nine percent of the time, these adoptions work out beautifully. With any dog, you must understand the dog is an individual. Some have anxieties, just as people have anxieties. Some of them are not explained by past experience. One of our rescues, for example, was adopted as a young puppy, and she is scared of little kids, but she has never had a negative experience with a little kid. She is just scared of little kids. It requires great patience. You wouldn't give up on your kid when they are struggling, and don't be quick to give up on a dog either. When you do adopt a dog through the shelter system or one that has had a difficult past, you have to understand that it might take that dog a period of time to feel acclimated and trusting, and at home. Some will adjust almost immediately, and some won't. But when you go into it, you don't go into it with the idea that "you know, I will try it out for a week," like you're buying a TV and if "it doesn't work the way I like, I will return it."

JB: Right.

PZ: It's just not fair to the dog. Look, there may be times when, despite all your best efforts, it doesn't work out. But just don't give up easily is the main point.

JB: Exactly, it's not like you can return a dog so easily; it's kind of selfish to take on that responsibility and then throw in the towel.

PZ: Look, there can be legitimate reasons. I never want to say "never." People get very excited when they are about to get a dog, and they have these visions in their head of what it is going to be like, and those are often "perfect." You know, like Hallmark visions of life with a dog. Life with a dog can kind of be like life with kids. They may get in trouble. They may chew your favorite pair of shoes (*laughter*); they might soil your favorite carpets. It's not a bad dog. A dog is not a human being. It doesn't speak English. The bottom line is yes, a dog needs to learn to live in a household, but more importantly, you need to learn how to live with a dog.

JB: Oh *yes!*

PZ: It's a two-way street. You can't just expect the dog to completely adapt to your lifestyle; you have to adapt to living with a dog. So that would be my main advice. Go into it with reasonable expectations; it's not always a perfectly groomed golden retriever puppy running through the fields of wheat.

JB: (*laughs*) With hair flowing!

PZ: Yeah, one of our dogs suffered a severe laceration a month ago, and it's still not healing properly.

JB: (*gasps*) Oh!

PZ: Bandages are being changed every day, and she's not happy, but that comes with the territory. You have to accept that just as you would an injured child.

JB: Exactly. Just like a child.

Find Peter Zheutlin at *www.peterzheutlin.com.*

Creativity and new experiences feed our souls and invigorate us so that we think about something other than our daily grind. If you allow yourself the freedom to not judge yourself and accept that whatever you do is right, you will feel a sense of levity and joy in whatever you do. Now that I am a dog owner, I see that I really don't care what I look like at six in the morning, which is similar to how I felt when I first had kids and my breast milk was leaking profusely onto my mismatched clothes and I was an exhausted mess. Now, my mornings are filled with fur balls, scratch marks, and muddy paw prints; my dog couldn't care less what I look like in the early morning hours, just as long as she gets some love and her breakfast. I have never experienced an animal so happy to smother me with kisses, and my entire life has changed. She loves me more than I probably love myself at that hour. I just love my coffee.

While you delve into trying new activities in your life, from exercise to creative endeavors, consider revamping your food choices. Expanding your palate with new foods is a great way to change things up a bit and incorporate mood-boosting and beneficial nutrients into your everyday meals. However, be attentive to what foods rub you the wrong way. Too much caffeine can be a culprit of bad moods, anxiety, irritability, and poor sleep. If you can't give up coffee completely (that would be me), know your limit and never have your favorite cup of buzz in the afternoon, because you just might find yourself tossing and turning at night.

Sometimes the body tells us what it needs and doesn't like. For example, you might have irritable bowel syndrome (IBS) and not even know it. If you constantly feel like what you are eating is not making you feel well, then it's a wake-up call to change your ways. Throwing down a couple of antacids just to tolerate that spaghetti sauce is not the answer. Be a detective and adjust your food choices. You might even have a food allergy you never knew existed. Just because you love eating double-chocolate cake doesn't mean it's the best choice if you find yourself with stomach issues. The same goes for any food you love, because the aftermath isn't worth it. See your doctor or be a detective with what's up with your most prized possession—your body.

What Are You Waiting For?!

I have always wanted to _____, because it looks so _____. I used to love to _____, but I stopped because _____ (excuse). The biggest thing holding me back in trying _____ is _____. If I weren't so _____, I would do it!

The three things that I dream of doing are _____, _____, and _____. No one would believe me if I told them I wanted to _____, especially _____. But _____ looks like it would be something that would be really _____ and make me _____, so I am going to go for it even though I break out in _____, _____, and tend to _____ when I get nervous trying new things. I also always wanted to own a _____, but it's a lot of work and I am filled with excuses. Au revoir/adiós to my _____ funk!

CHAPTER 6

Express Yourself

"The best way to cheer yourself up is to try to cheer somebody else up."—Mark Twain

When you're faced with one of life's many funks, it is often best to talk to someone you know and trust, such as a therapist, friend, or confidant. You do not have to deal with trauma and life's assaults on your own. Sometimes things are just too tough to process solo. That's okay. Closing off and shutting down are just not healthy or productive in your healing process. When someone asks the standard "How are you?" we all tend to answer, "Fine." But are we really fine? What if we responded with how we really felt? Of course, not with a snarky insulting answer or in freak-out mode, but something brief and more indicative of what was truthful. Of course, sometimes people don't want to hear the real answer. They are dismissive or not listening at all. "Fine, thanks" is an automatic, empty response; it reveals nothing.

Express what is going on in your life, because you never know who has advice you never considered. Just don't get overwhelmed with too much advice all at once. You don't have to jump at any suggestions thrown your way. Sometimes we need to sit and digest what we are going through and move at our own pace. People might want to fix you and throw all kinds of solutions your way, but you might want to vent and share your thoughts and feelings. Keep a journal and write down what you are experiencing. Consider expressing yourself in a creative way. Sometimes people draw or paint as a form of art therapy to convey what is going on inside their funky minds or as an outlet to take a break. There are no right or wrong ways to express yourself creatively, just as long as the way helps you move forward.

Leading up to my father-in-law's passing, our entire household was emotionally distraught and saddened by what we felt was coming. I decided to try to shift our daughters' mindsets one weekend and asked them to join me in the backyard. They knew I was up to something. I think they expected me to make them rake leaves, but I had another plan, and they were onto me when they saw the colorful paints I had bought.

Pointing to our six large clay pots, a big wooden toy box, and an old wooden ladder, I instructed them to paint anything with any color. We put some music on and spent the next few hours outside, brightening our outdoor world and switching our mindsets. Our indoor world was cloudy and dreary, so this was the next best thing to a change of scenery, and a much-needed emotional vacation.

A big sense of calm came over us, and we talked about how pretty everything looked, what a great change of pace this was, and what else we could paint next. Our old, worn-out wooden ladder had a face-lift with a coat of popping green paint, and the pots were now gorgeous pink, orange, and blue shades. We used the ladder as a place to hold the newly painted clay pots and other items. For just a few hours, we were able to take ourselves away from our sad state of mind and constant thoughts of losing their adoring, wonderful grandfather. Coloring our world for just a bit got us outside together and gave us a break. My kids are no fools. They had known what I was up to all along.

Lost your job or want a new one? Ambiguity and being in limbo are part of life, but your negative self-talk that leaves you insecure and doubtful, and your critical view of yourself, will not be helpful long term. Look at your struggle as a requirement, a moment in time to get you where you need to be. Everything that happens is necessary, even if that rejection in a relationship or that job dismissal has rocked your world. You might feel as if changes are socking you in the stomach, but they are there to elevate you to where you need to be. In our failures or challenging times, we elevate ourselves to something new, something scary, and something wonderful. You just need to be open to the possibilities and keep moving forward. A rejection or negative experience in one aspect of life can open doors the next day.

Find a networking group and connect with new faces in new industries. You might find a new path you never expected. Connecting with a group of people who can be your "think tank" of mentors is also very helpful. Set up a weekly or monthly schedule to get together and share your goals and aspirations. People who love and support you are the best network of people to have in your life. Toxic and critical people are useless and should be kicked to the curb quickly. No one needs those people, especially when you are sorting through a rough patch. Be selfish with whom you choose to spend your time. You certainly do not need additional duress and drama to add to your already stressful situation.

Post your affirmations. I had a roommate in college who loved those Hallmark posters with kittens, horses running wild, and rainbows. They had these annoyingly cute, inspirational sayings like, "A smile can make your day and someone else's too!" Honestly, I wanted to throw up when I saw these posters plastered over every wall. I felt like I was trapped in a greeting-card-factory nightmare. Don't be that person. Consider creating your own poster board with your favorite quotes or musical verses; words can connect with where you are in life and where you would like to be. Put up images and words that move you and find a mantra you like or create your own. Switch things up a little. Change is good.

Last, please don't keep everything pent up inside of you until you feel as if you will implode. You must vent. Venting is good. Venting is healthy. Venting lets you express, share, hurl, and laugh at all your suppressed or unexpressed emotions and feelings. Sometimes when I vent to my stepmother, for example, I laugh at how chaotic and comical my life is. My material sounds like an award-winning sitcom with a whole bunch of characters, including a nine-week-old puppy who barks way too much at three thirty in the morning; ants that seem to invade every crevice of my house as I am looking extremely sleep-deprived; and my husband, who steps in dog doo at five in the morning and walks through the house unknowingly, and I almost throw up trying to figure out the source of the horrendous smell that has invaded our home. Unbeknownst to him, his shoe is clearly covered in dog evidence, but we make the discovery a little too late. Barf.

The wonderful thing about venting is that my life makes my stepmom laugh harder than she has in a long time and gives her a chance to thank her lucky stars she does not have my life! "You're welcome," I say, and we both laugh. She is thankful and filled with appreciation for her beautiful, quiet, uneventful life. I tell her it is all about perspective.

Meet Jay Silverman

"It is the act of making art that heals the broken creative heart."—
Julia Cameron

Some people turn to creative expression when faced with an emotionally challenging situation. Jay Silverman, a successful Los Angeles director, producer, and filmmaker, took an all-encompassing crime and turned it into a gift. About five years ago, he was struggling to cope with the horrific date rape of one of his daughters.

As a filmmaker, Jay is obsessed with telling stories. At the encouragement of a friend, he was asked to write about himself, and the result was a candid story about how he and his daughters were dealing with post-traumatic stress. Jay knew that PTSD is so prevalent and that his story might help others going through similar circumstances.

Believing that movies have a huge impact, Jay began the process of jotting down each step of his family's journey, honestly and cathartically. Expressing about a real, personal event and transforming that expression into a meaningful movie was Jay's parallel goal, while helping his daughter recover. He didn't realize it at the time, but he was healing by making his film *Girl on the Edge*. As a result, his daughter began to open up more and reveal her journey. The two have also traveled to Washington, D.C. and spoken to members of Congress about the importance of residential boarding schools in the recovery of young people from PTSD, date rape, bullying, and the like. *Girl on the Edge* has had a powerful impact on audiences; it is currently available on Showtime, Amazon, and iTunes. Find more info at *www.girlontheedgethemovie.com*.

Meet Jenna Torres

"Find out who you are and do it on purpose."
—Dolly Parton

The words of Dolly Parton inspire musician and singer-songwriter Jenna Torres, giving her strength and the courage of her convictions. Jenna was in a painful and difficult marriage. She longed for personal freedom and needed to find the courage to move on. She was at her rock bottom, but even that was not enough to catalyze the change that she would have to go through to get to the other side. She was the mother of a young child and could not imagine how she was going to take care of herself and her child.

On the morning of September 11, 2001, the sky was clear and the air crisp on a beautiful fall Manhattan day. Jenna and her husband dropped off their child at school, less than two miles away from the World Trade Center. Moments later, Jenna stared up at the sky as the first airplane hit the tower. She and other frantic parents rushed to find their children. As they ran back home, their neighborhood was no longer a haven but a war zone. She knew beyond a shadow of a doubt that if life could be taken in an instant, then it was her responsibility to be brave and take every chance there was to take. She needed to stop playing it safe. In the midst of sheer terror, Jenna found peace and clarity. She knew what she had to do, and she was ready to do it.

Within a few months, Jenna separated from her husband and started a new job in real estate. Her first gig was to fill up a building that teetered on the edge of the gaping hole that had once been the World Trade Center. The building had been abandoned by 97 percent of the occupants. Each day, she would sit in silence, alone with just the souls of the departed, waiting for a tiny trickle of the brave and the curious to pass through, wondering what it would be like to stand so close to an open wound.

These apartments were not for everybody; they were for hardly anybody. Jenna knew it takes a special soul to want to be part of the healing of a neighborhood and our world; this meant she had hours of time to spare, so she brought her guitar to work without anybody's ever noticing. During that period, Jenna wrote the songs that ended up landing her a contract with Warner Music.

Jenna believes that if you keep looking for ways to be who you are called to be, life turns around for you and with you. Pretty soon, you are in lockstep with the life you are meant to have. Jenna learned that life is lived one day at a time, one step at a time, one scary challenge at a time, one kiss and one breath at a time. Satisfaction comes from walking straight in the direction of your fears.

Find Jenna Torres at *https://www.jennatorres.com*.

Meet Adrien Finkel

Adrien Finkel is a photographer, writer, and comedic television producer. When not producing television shows, she devotes her time to a project called My Naked Truth, a visual catalog of quotes, personal confessions, and advice shared with her by friends and strangers.

Adrien Finkel has always loved conveying her thoughts and feelings through words, poems, and lyrics. The *My Naked Truth* project is a photo journal similar to Humans of New York. Adrien started the project in 2010, and her work has evolved into a recently published book, My Naked Truth. She started the project because when she was younger, her love of words and sayings became how she expressed herself. How she felt was reflected in personally meaningful words, poems, and lyrics, and this is how she spoke to people.

In college, Adrien attended a challenging acting conservatory. Her focus was theater, and she was planning to become an actor when she moved to LA. However, after she booked a show and was on TV, Adrien realized she didn't want an acting career after all. She didn't know how to express her feelings and tell everyone, because she had told them she wanted the acting career in the first place. Two years later, she switched gears and enrolled in cooking school and got a cooking job. But after a year of working in a cooking position, she still felt she had not found her calling. Still unhappy, she found that all of the words she had collected over the years didn't seem to make sense. Wanting advice, Adrien turned to Facebook and posted that she was looking for words, phrases, and poetry that gave people hope when life seemed meaningless; this is how her My Naked Truth project began.

"You think you want one thing, and then you get there, having achieved it, and you still are not happy, but you don't want to tell anyone! They might think you've lost it! You move on to something else and see where things go," she explained.

"When someone is going through a challenging time, they don't always share what is going on, and it feels like their world is crumbling," Adrien said, "When you speak to other people who feel lost, you find out that we are all technically lost and searching. That's the point of being here. We are searching for more meaning, depth—and whether you have a job or not, we are human beings having a human experience, and we are all pretty much the same no matter what." Adrien's remarks hit home for me, because there have been times in my life when I was so excited to achieve a specific career milestone, but once I got there, I felt…empty. Then I thought perhaps people were judging me because I had not achieved a certain level of success. The truth is, we are all looking for happiness and achievement and are often worried about what others think of our decisions. Adrien's My Naked Truth project is incredibly beautiful, poignant, and grounding. Adrien said, "The only thing that matters is what makes you happy. You shouldn't do what people expect you to do."

When Adrien invited people to share their words with her, she recognized that some of her subjects had very successful careers. She was embarrassed to tell them how lost she felt. Surprisingly, she discovered that many were not as happy and satisfied as she imagined. "Even if you make a lot of money, life is never what you expect, and we are all searching for more. We all have our strengths and weaknesses," Adrien concluded.

Once she connected with people on Facebook, they met with her and allowed Adrien to write personal quotes on their bodies. She came up with this idea because she used to write words and quotes on herself as a kid. "I thought it would be funny and exciting, and put them outside of their comfort zone; this evolved over time, and everyone who was involved helped me create the project. The project started from conversations, and one thing led to another." Some people shared very personal thoughts. "They wanted to mark this moment with these words, and this promise by writing on themselves," she told me. From that moment on, Adrien realized the project was bigger than she had first thought. "The words and pictures became time stamps for people," she said. Adrien recognizes that we are all going through something and that having a "safe space" where we can open up our hearts is so important. This was an opportunity that most people never get a chance to have. "How are you doing?" "How are you feeling about your life?" Adrien pointed out that these questions are not typically asked: "It's hard to ask those questions and really listen." As a result of asking these questions and listening to people share their feelings and emotions, Adrien experienced personal growth.

She noted that her subjects were partially or completely naked on the outside, but also naked emotionally. She was never really comfortable with the idea of having people naked, and some chose to not be fully unclothed; this was a personal choice. Some people were more than happy to take their clothes off and be free of clothing. Adrien shared, "We are just bodies." When she photographed some subjects in New York, people would stand on the rooftop and take everything off, and she would take their pictures. She said, "They don't really know how powerful and special it is. We hide behind our clothes, hiding who we really are."

When I saw an image of a very buff, handsome man with the words "I still seek the approval of others" written across his chest, I was surprised. Really?! Adrien shared with me that people need to know that other people have insecurities and personal pain. My Naked Truth is so brave, especially in a culture in which everything is about image. Adrien continued by noting, "This is a brave, personal moment that cuts through the noise of social media, which is just fluff."

My Naked Truth has been a life-changing project for Adrien. She feels that each one of her subjects is so beautiful. She was on a quest "to meet anybody who would love a lovely picture of themselves. Some people don't want to be a part of the project because they don't feel good about themselves right now, but I am a photographer and I can light you properly and you will get a photo of yourself that you like, I promise," she said. The project is not about beauty; it has always been about sharing our humanity.

Adrien knows we are all so critical of ourselves. She imagined all her photos as beautiful headshots. Before even taking her subjects' pictures, she spent the first half hour talking to each person. Then she had a better understanding of who they were, and they felt more relaxed and open. After seeing the pictures she took, people usually told Adrien, "These pictures are more me than the pictures I have of myself." She explained that they got to a place where they were more relaxed and honest and real—just themselves—and it shows in the photos. They were more comfortable.

My Naked Truth has allowed Adrien to learn about the things she truly cares about. She has spoken to people who have been oppressed, as well as victims of racism and rape and others going through personal pain, such as divorce. Her connections with these people have made her rethink things like marriage and other life experiences. Adrien shared that when her therapist was trying to help her figure out what she should do with her life, the therapist would ask, "What are you good at?" Her response: "Nothing, but I like talking to people. It's just not a thing." But was she wrong! Adrien realized that not everyone is good at asking questions and listening, and she certainly is. She has the ability to listen and provide a safe space where people can open up and reveal who they really are. Adrien is compassionate, empathetic, and a great listener who helps people share their naked truth.

Find Adrien Finkel at *www.mynakedtruthproject.com.*

Meet Melanie Brooks

When Melanie Brooks, a writer, teacher, and mother, was in her MFA program in 2013, she decided to write her difficult family story. In 1985, when she was thirteen, her father—an accomplished surgeon—had a heart attack at age forty-two. They were living in Canada at the time; this was three months before Canada started screening blood for infectious diseases. Her father underwent a quadruple bypass surgery and contracted HIV and then AIDS.

The climate in 1985 surrounding HIV and AIDS was a very different climate than today. There were a lot of stigma and fear fueling a very intolerant society. Her father feared for himself, what people would think of him and his family, so he decided he would keep his illness a secret. He expected he would die within months, because people were dying of AIDS very quickly. Her dad thought he would be dead within a year. He lived for another ten years. The family lived with the secret for almost all of that time until Melanie's parents wrote a book and their story became public only a few months before her father's death.

I had Melanie on my show when I read about her in *Poets & Writers Magazine*. She wrote the book *Writing Hard Stories: Celebrated MemoiristsWho Shaped Art from Trauma*. She interviewed many different writers and learned what they went through, and for the first time, shared her own very personal and painful story. Here's our Q&A.

Janeane: What inspired you to write this book?

Melanie: It started as a very selfish quest during the third semester of my MFA program. I was having a really tough time with the writing. It felt too painful, too frightening to really look at. I wanted to see for myself that these writers, whose stories

I'd been reading and found to be so resonant with the embedded pain in my own, were still breathing even after having looked at their own painful experiences directly, written about them, and put them out into the world for others to read. I didn't begin with the purpose of writing a book at all. These conversations were originally just for me. But what happened was in talking to these writers—I ended up talking to eighteen memoirists—the wisdom and the encouragement that they gave to me became something that I recognized I could not keep to myself. And I realized that if someone had given me a book like *Writing Hard Stories* at the beginning of my MFA program, when I set out to write this story, I would not have felt nearly as alone as I did. I would not have felt like there was something wrong with me in the way I was responding to the writing I was doing. That was really my purpose in deciding to turn this into a book. I felt like it was something other writers needed. A companion for them through this difficult process of telling hard truths.

JB: It must have been a remarkable feeling of enlightenment and healing to listen to the stories of other people who had gone through so many other painful experiences. What did that feel like, interviewing all these different people?

MB: Well, I think what I have discovered in the year since the book was published and going out and talking to other people is that we are all kind of thirsting for stories we can relate to. I think that is why the memoir is so popular. I think any of us who are experiencing something difficult want to know that we are not by ourselves in that process. I think that is what talking to these writers did for me; it was a sense of companionship, and they were all kind of able to say, "I have been where you are, and I understand what you are going through. And you will get through this." That was exactly what I needed to hear.

JB: Was your mom always a writer? Was your dad always a writer?

MB: No.

JB: Really?

MB: My dad had great literary skills, and my mom as well, but neither of them were writers. They sat down and tried to put a narrative to their journey. Their book that they published was sharing "Here's what happened to us." They published it at the time with the same purpose of why I think many of us write— maybe people going through this experience will benefit from it. I think at the time the stories that were being published were different than the story my parents were living. The literature that was coming out about HIV/AIDS was coming primarily from the LGBTQ community. So, my parents had a different angle to this story that I think was important to put out there, to say that we don't need to put the same face for everyone who is suffering from this disease. That was important to them, and I think it was important for readers.

JB: I find it remarkable, as I am sure you did, that your dad survived ten years after he was diagnosed.

MB: Right. For me, this is at the heart of the book I am writing; nobody knew he was going to live that long, and so we were all just kind of waiting. At that time, HIV/AIDS was a death sentence. There was no hope that he was going to survive. We all knew his death was pending, but we didn't know how he was going to die. We didn't know when he was going to die. We didn't know what that was going to look like and when that was going to come, so for ten years we lived with this anticipatory grief of what was coming.

JB: Horrible.

MB: Yes, it was horrible.

JB: I say that because my dad had cancer, and I remember feeling that every day, any moment is an "any day now," and you are just holding your breath. And it's a terrible way to live.

It sounds like writing has always been cathartic—your way of dealing with life, processing, and finding meaning.

MB: It has been, and it began with reading. I was a voracious reader when I was a child. I found my escape through books, and I kind of latched on to these characters I loved. I really found companionship in the characters I loved in the books that I was reading. I think that built a foundation for me to eventually become a writer, because I recognized what words could do in terms of comfort and expression and being able to kind of give understanding to experiences.

JB: I always share with people, especially when I have writers on my show, that all you have to do is travel with a notebook, a little small one in your bag or you are on a plane and jot down things that move you. Anything.

MB: I think a lot of writers have a great memory, and I have a particularly good memory. I have a tendency to store things as images in my mind, and I think that what happens to me is I have this storage bin in my head of these images that I know at some point are going to find a place in my writing. That is kind of what happens. Things come up. I wrote a piece last week in connection to the anniversary of the Haiti earthquake that I had kind of carried for eight years; it's the story of a student of mine who lost his sister in the earthquake, and our interaction during that time. You know, it took eight years to find a place to write that, but it's been sitting in my head waiting for that to happen. What I discovered when I began writing my own memoir was the storage bin of memories over a ten-year period and then subsequently the almost twenty years after my dad died before I started writing about it was dramatically big!

(*laughter*)

JB: Huge!

MB: And to kind of dig into that storage bin was very overwhelming; it's like if someone made you sort through someone's house that you really didn't know what you were looking for, but you had to sort through everything, and that's kind of what happened to me in the process of beginning to write this memoir.

JB: That is so intriguing.

MB: The process of writing this made me feel horrible. I was thinking, "What am I doing? Why am I doing this?" That is part of the reason why I thought of these writers. They kind of helped me dissect that.

JB: I think there is always a reason for everything. And I think obviously you were meant to do this; it was meant to be your project for so many reasons.

MB: I think I always knew I would write about it, but when my parents wrote their book, all of us in the family considered that the official story. So, I don't think I really recognized that I was going to be writing a different kind of story about this and that my story was not the same as the "official" story. Looking at it through my lenses, it is a different kind of story than what my parents lived or my three brothers have lived. Coming to that recognition can be exuberant but also terrifying, because for the longest time—I think this is the nature of secret keeping—you don't realize you have a voice in a circumstance. You don't realize that there is something for you to say about it, because you have been kept from saying anything about it. I think for me, trying to uncover the voice that I have in this story has been more traumatizing than anything else, I think, because it is trying to find a sense of confidence in what you have to say when your whole nature is, you're not supposed to say anything.

JB: To have to live for ten years knowing something that you can't tell anybody and holding your breath for ten years is...I can't even imagine. The strength you must have had at that age.

MB: Thank you. You know, I think one of the things I try to make clear is, when you are living that experience, when you're just living it and it's what you are going through, it wasn't like for ten years every day was trauma. My parents worked very hard to create a sense of normalcy for us, and they tried to make our lives as rich and full as they could in the midst of this. When there is always that underlying thing, it makes it hard to completely embrace the life you are living when you know that there is this other thing lurking around the corner. I think that is what I have been exploring, not this horribly terrible childhood, because it wasn't, but this experience of kind of shutting down this piece of myself that was expecting, anticipating, waiting, fearing, and so confused and uncertain.

JB: If you could look back at your thirteen-year-old self, what do you think it was that kept you positive? Perhaps I am sure you were not always positive, but what were the things that kept you sane and happy at times?

MB: First of all, one of the roles I played in my family and have played in my family is to be the bearer of joy. My middle name is Joy, and my dad's nickname for me was "Melanie Joy Bells."

JB: Awww.

MB: I kind of moved into that role very easily. My personality put me in that place, but I think I very much defined myself by that and worked very hard to play that role in my family. For me, at times, that became suffocating, but it enabled me to kind of figure out a way to experience the things that I was experiencing and really see the positives in them—see those experiences for what they were.

My parents and my brothers, we were a close family—a close-knit family—and we did a lot of things together. There was not a lot of sitting around looking at each other wondering, "What is going on?" We were very busy. We were living a very full life in the midst of this, so I think that was helpful.

JB: That's good. What advice would you give people who are aspiring writers?

MB: One of things I would say, especially if they are writers of memoir and memoirs of difficult topics: Be prepared. Be prepared that it is not going to be such an easy process. Recognize that you don't have to cope with all of the residual feelings and repercussions of what comes up in the writing process by yourself. I am a huge proponent of finding a writing community, finding people who understand what it is you are doing, so they can be a support to you.

Find other ways to deal with whatever the emotions are that are going to come up, but also this is what I kept hearing from the writers that I was talking to, and it happened for me. There will come a place in the process where you have recognized that you have gotten over the hump of the trauma, not that it is gone or you've purged it from yourself. But you have gotten to a place where you see the direction you are headed and you recognize what it is that you are trying to do for readers.

Taking the story out of yourself and putting it on the page in a way that you have taken control of it, that enables you to then bring it back into yourself and know how to tell that story differently. I think that is where you are headed as the writer. That is what you are hoping to do. You are hoping to open up space for readers to enter into your story, to lean closer, to pay attention so that they can share something of themselves through that too.

JB: You know, that is a really important statement, and it makes me think of when you write and the first thirty pages are garbage, and then you get to the meat of it and you go, "Oh, yeah! This is where the story should start!"

MB: Right.

JB: A lot of times we write, and we figure things out about ourselves and the story and where we are going, and then you have that "aha!" moment and you have a new direction.

MB: Right, and for me, I kept hearing from these writers that you are going to feel differently than you do right now.

JB: Yes.

MB: That is what they kept saying to me. Initially, my response was, "I hope you are right. I really hope you are right." Part of me didn't believe them, but I did get to that place. Now I can say that to other writers, too. I have had the opportunity to talk to a lot of emerging memoir writers and to be able to say that to them and actually mean it, and understand that that is true is a gift for me.

JB: Let's talk about your backstory. You are a teacher.

MB: Yes.

JB: So, tell us a little about what you do.

MB: I have been teaching college part time for the last fifteen years. My daughter is turning fifteen tomorrow. I was pregnant with her when I began teaching college. I was a public school teacher before that. I began teaching college and teaching college writing. I teach at three different schools. I teach at the community college here in Nashua [New Hampshire], and I also teach at Northeastern University in Boston and at Merrimack College in North Andover [Massachusetts].

Since the book has been published, it's kind of afforded me the opportunity to go and do a lot more workshops and conferences and book talks.

JB: I read about you in *Poets &Writers*.

MB: Just this week, it was very exciting, because Random House Penguin has a blog called Signature Reads, and on Thursday they posted a blog [post] called "The 16 Best Books for Memoir Writers," and they included my book with some unbelievably stellar writers who are all kind of my writing heroes, so I was deeply humbled and honored to have been included in that list.

JB: Congratulations! That is fantastic.

MB: Thank you!

JB: Where can people find out more about you?

MB: At *www.melaniebrooks.com* and on Twitter *@melaniejmbrooks*.

JB: Any last bit of advice?

MB: You can do it!

(*laughter*)

JB: All right!

MB: When it feels as hard as it does, you can do it. I say this not just to writers, but I say that to people who are going through tough experiences, because not everybody is going to write about them, but they still want to know from other people who have gotten through those things whether they are going to survive that, and you will survive that.

JB: Yes!

In a Nutshell

We all have personal ways of expressing ourselves when faced with challenging times. What do you do? Are you artistic? Adventurous? A creative filmmaker, writer, chef, or musician? There is nothing better than expressing your feelings through art and creative pursuits. Talking to your friends, family, and a trusted therapist are also great ways to process whatever life throws your way. You need to have an outlet for expressing your feelings and emotions. Mine is writing and playing electric guitar with different effect pedals. What is your go-to strategy? Sometimes music can give you a mental vacation, and another time you might throw yourself into a ceramic masterpiece (or an epic fail on a pottery wheel!). Find the strategies you can turn to whenever you need to bust out of your funk!

There are so many ways to express yourself creatively, and other ways that are not so creative but cathartic. I once took all my old letters from a boyfriend and threw them onto a lit hibachi grill. I have never laughed so hard and felt so free. When my roommate came home and asked what I was cooking, I laughed and told her, "Love letters! Want to add any of your own? I feel so much better!" The symbolism of that event was just what my soul needed, and I was ready to move on.

Here are some other ideas to think about that don't involve hibachis:

- Take a class once a week in the evening at your local college or university.

- Pursue a degree you've always wanted or recently been thinking about.

- Be a detective and see what events are happening in your area. Ask friends and colleagues if they know of any great classes. Try not to choose online classes, because that does nothing for you socially with zero interaction.

- Get out and meet other incredibly uncomfortable and awkward strangers like yourself. Step out of your comfort zone (even if you are kicking and screaming inside!) and in front of new faces. Battle through your introverted routine and venture out there.

- If creative endeavors are your thing, do not limit yourself by your critical thoughts regarding your age and skill set. You are never too old to try something new or pick up something you used to love doing.

- Take music lessons—music is a great healer. Try ukulele, guitar, drums, piano, violin, songwriting, or voice— group or individualized instruction. Look on YouTube for a gazillion free lessons.

- Write a song (it doesn't have to be an award winner— just so cathartic!).

- Write a play, screenplay, or pilot (or take a class on how to do it).

- Produce a short film, feature, webisode, or pilot.

- Create a vision board.

- Enroll in an art class—ceramics, drawing, glass blowing, jewelry making, or the like.

- Take a photography class—learn new techniques in digital photography, from proper shooting and lighting to digital effects and editing.

- Learn to write—for example, screenwriting, creative writing, nonfiction, fiction, memoir, sketch, or TV show.

- Take acting classes—such as improvisation, commercial acting, voice acting for commercials and animation, or theater.

- Consider certification programs—business, health care, technology, or art and design.

- Attend a TED Talk, lecture, or inspiration workshop.

- Try a yoga, Zumba, Pilates, tai chi, jiu-jitsu, or other class.

- Learn creative and healthy cooking techniques.

- Feel empowered with a self-defense class—nothing says confidence like kicking the sh*t out of your funks.

- Learn a new language—for work or for fun. Learning a new language is a confidence booster and an excuse to try it out in new settings, locally and internationally.

- Become computer savvy and learn about social media, app design, and more.

- Try a basic computer class.

- Take a business class to learn how to start a new business, and delve into marketing and branding.

- Enroll in public speaking classes.

- Join a club (such as biking or hiking).

What you can achieve is limited only by your imagination. The bottom line is, whatever your interests are, pursue them. Have a life outside of work, and find something that brings added joy to your hamster-wheel life and boosts your creative imagination. Consider any activity that feeds your mind, body, and soul. Just take that first step, mix it with lots of motivation, and watch that life-changing momentum take over.

CHAPTER 7

Get Out of Your Mindset and Go Do Some Good

"Hope is not about proving anything. It's about choosing to believe this one thing that love is bigger than any grim, bleak sh*t anyone can throw at us."—Anne Lamott, Plan B: Further Thoughts on Faith

If you are fortunate enough to have a meaningful career, and your life is all about helping others and giving back, you have figured out a career designed with compassion and empathy. Sometimes people go through a personal trauma that affects their emotional and physical well-being; this experience impacts them personally and professionally, and they change in ways they never imagined. They experience a shift in their lives that allows them to be a part of something meaningful and fulfilling, and to create a life mission focusing less on themselves and more on what they can do for others. They might even set out to redesign their life to include numerous acts of kindness and generosity of time and spirit.

A great way to take a break from whatever it is you are dealing with is to step away from your situation and help others, because bringing joy and happiness to someone else's life makes your life a little brighter. Volunteering, giving your time to charities and organizations that need you and your talents, is a selfless act of kindness.

When life shakes us up, oftentimes we are brave enough to start new adventures. Deep down inside we might be unfulfilled, and this is the time to start anew.

We can feel like a part of us is fading away and there is a void in our meaningful endeavors and professional life. The beautiful thing is that these shifts in perspective come about unexpectedly. Even though we tirelessly search for meaning and happiness, they are not so easily found. When we redesign our lives to think less about ourselves and more about others, and what we can contribute and help with, there is a positive change; the focus shifts away from ourselves and our current situations, and we adopt more of a selfless attitude.

Giving back to others is a tremendous way to step outside of your own life and bring joy and happiness to others; it gets you out of your own cluttered, messy headspace. Instead of worrying about your own stuff, give your time and energy to others in need. It is a great way to redirect your energy; it might even give you some direction in life. Getting involved with organizations and people aligned with your values and interests is a great way to shift your mindset. You will end up meeting new people, feeling good about yourself, and having a sense of purpose.

There is a lot to offer at any age. Just when you think your situation cannot get any worse, if you take a break to do something for someone else or a group of people, you just might figure out how to make sense of your own life. Answers to our trickiest, most complex issues can come to us when we least expect them to.

Meet Kalifornia Karl

Karl Detken, also known as Kalifornia Karl, has worn a lot of career hats. He is a *Star Search* winner, is featured in a movie called *Duets* playing a singer with Gwyneth Paltrow, and was a highly successful marketing executive at Pioneer Electronics, where his DJ division earned half a billion dollars a year. However, his best and most rewarding gig isn't filled with glitz, glam, and mega-bucks; it's filled with love and the power of music. Karl's Joyful Noise Music program brings joy to retirees. Best. Decision. Ever. Karl switched gears and now sings to the elderly for a fraction of what corporate executive life used to pay, but his happiness level is off the charts. He is 1,000 percent more fulfilled professionally and personally from the joy his latest gig brings to the people who need it most.

Karl says it's no secret that music can help seniors and hospital patients feel better. His set list includes songs from every decade and style—from Bing Crosby to Bruno Mars. His show is a lively performance filled with opportunities for interactivity, move-ment, sing-alongs, laughter, and more. Karl describes his gig as "engaging and entertaining activities, which I call 'engagetain-ment.'" Since 1975 he has performed over 11,400 shows and is now one of the most sought-after music providers in America for health-care facilities.

Here's Karl's backstory:

Karl discovered the power of music in fifth grade when during recess his classmate was playing guitar surrounded by adoring cute girls. He started playing guitar, then played in garage bands, then got professional gigs. Poison, Night Ranger, and Metallica are some the bands he opened for. In the '80s, Metallica opened for his band. He went on to win *Star Search* and fifteen minutes of fame in the movie *Duets* with Gwyneth Paltrow.

He worked for Pioneer Electronics in the DJ division to lead the company in marketing and product development. But how did he land his latest gig singing for seniors in nursing homes? His mother had fallen and broken her hip, and he had gone into a nursing home to visit her; this was the first time he had been in one. He saw a woman playing guitar and singing to the residents. His dad was there with him and started bragging about his *Star Search* son. The woman tried to coax Karl to come up and sing a song. He declined, but when she said, "Do it for your mom," he could not refuse.

He got up and didn't know what he would play but decided on a 1950s song called "La Bamba" by Ritchie Valens. He jokingly encouraged the residents to get up and dance. They had walkers, canes, and wheelchairs, and he didn't think they would, but they did. When he finished, everyone was clapping and the room was filled with joy. One of the ladies, named Ramona, threw her hands up in the air and shouted, "I'm gonna live forever!" Karl described this moment as "a gift." At that moment, he realized how amazing his experience was. He had spent years playing in front of so many people in huge venues. His biggest audience was fifty thousand people at Stagecoach. He had never felt more warmth than at that moment. He realized just how powerful music can be at any age; this led Karl to realize there is a science behind music and what it does for people. "Music literally changes your brain chemistry," Karl told me. "Our brains respond to music, and we are wired that way, which means, for example, listening to pleasant music boosts your serotonin levels, the brain chemical responsible for good feelings. Processing music involves both hemispheres of the brain.

Listening to music engages the part of your brain that handles long-term memory storage, which is why when you listen to old songs, you get a flood of memories and emotions that you might have forgotten." He explained that even people with Alzheimer's or dementia can recover memory from listening to music. Karl mentioned the science and research behind what he does and what his audience experiences. "Music can help with addiction, pain management, dramatic brain injury, Alzheimer's, dementia, autism, and learning disabilities," he noted.

When I asked him if he had a career funk along the way and whether it had helped him, here's what he had to say:

"Yes, and after having so many 'successes' as measured by societal standards. Success was measured by the number of CDs sold, applause, awards, requests made, standing ovations, but none of these equaled to what happened that day in the nursing home." He was in a personal funk until he discovered his impact on the seniors. "I love introducing and reintroducing the music from the past, because it brightens their day," he said. "Every performance is unique and magical." His routine includes sing-along lyrics on a big flat-screen TV, maracas, tambourines, echo microphones passed around the audience, wigs, and funny props—all designed to engage people. He also incorporates trivia and shows old-time popular people, entertainment, and landmarks, weaving in his comedic sense to make his audience laugh.

During one performance, playing for patients with dementia and Alzheimer's, many of them were slumped over in wheelchairs and some were in stretchers. He played and there was no participation, no applause, no smiles, or anything to show they were connecting with the music. He felt disappointed he had not brought some joy and gotten engagement. As he packed up his stuff and made his way towards the exit, a care worker approached him and thanked him, because she noticed that a man had started singing when he played "Delilah." Karl did not realize this had happened. She told Karl, "What you don't know: He hasn't spoken in a year!" The song had triggered something in the man that made him sing.

Karl has had his career highs in the corporate world and as a professional musician, but the greatest achievement was on that day making a connection with a resident. "I live for that," he said. "It's a labor of love." There are no big budgets in nursing homes, but he doesn't dwell on this. Karl feels blessed, because his new gig gets him out of his own funk; it doesn't matter what he has had in the past, because now he experiences a tremendous path of healing and insight into how music can do so much more than he ever imagined. He smiled and said, "I am having the time of my life, Janeane!"

Karl now knows he wants to be "effective in retriggering their minds," he said. In this new role jump-starting the elderly mind, he is the silliest and most creative he has ever been. He admitted he would never act the way he does in front of his peers! He gets so much joy and positive energy from doing what he does with the elderly. "Bringing memories back to people is a powerful gift," he said.

His daughter, Cambria, who is also an accomplished singer, songwriter, and musician, sang along with Karl the very first time, when the resident Ramona yelled out, "I am going to live forever!" This father-daughter experience is now embedded in their hearts and minds.

Karl never could have imagined that this is where he would be now. Joyful Noise has pulled him out of his funk, and now he has a renewed love for others—the older generation, a group of strangers each and every time. "I need to touch their hearts somehow," he says. Every performance is unique, and he always thanks everyone for giving him the opportunity to sing for them. When he thinks back to when he used to be the brooding tortured artist, he feels that life is vastly more fulfilling now. He now smiles and grins ear to ear while he performs. Karl provides a beautiful gift to every life he touches. He is now the fastest-growing entertainer in this industry, with more than 1,400 shows booked in a year since he launched Joyful Noise Music. Unbelievably, some of his clients reserve him three years in advance!

Find Karl at *www.Facebook.com/KaliforniaKarl* and on Instagram as KaliforniaKarlMusic.

My Mom Was My First Superhero

Growing up, I was glued to the TV watching Batman, Batgirl, and Catwoman, but in real life, I saw my own mother as my first superhero. If you are a friend or family member reading this, you might be thinking, "Really?! This is not the mother you described all these years." I am not going to go into detail about my mother, because we had a very tumultuous relationship and that's an entire book right there. I will say this: With time and healing, if we are lucky, we can find the goodness in people we once didn't feel connected to. The advantage of age is developing an analytical mind, wisdom, and forgiveness. She wasn't a loving parent, but when it came to her work and her passions, she was as good as it gets.

Here are some memories of my mother that will stay with me forever, because during these incredible moments, she wasn't trying to be someone amazing or impress anyone; she was simply being a compassionate human. And when I looked at her helping kids with disabilities, the hearing impaired, building a business to help transgender people struggling emotionally and physically, and assisting strangers on the street, I saw someone extraordinary. That's the person I want to remember. She was her most beautiful self without all the heaps of makeup, the perfectly styled hair, and one too many plastic surgeries; those things gave me the heebie-jeebies. I thought she was her most real and beautiful self on Christmas morning in her blue striped footie pajamas with no makeup, opening presents like a child.

One of my earliest memories of living in New York was seeing my mother suddenly turn into a superhero right on the busy streets of Manhattan. She was a full-on superhero minus the cape. If she had seen a supercool cape at Bergdorf Goodman, I am sure she would have owned a few, but her calm and precise thinking was all she needed in what happened.

My mother and I were walking around the streets of New York one afternoon when we witnessed a horrible accident. A car had run into a woman riding her bicycle; it was the early '70s, and people didn't wear helmets and protective gear. I seem to remember the girl was wearing a long, flowing skirt.

We heard a crash, and people huddled around the scene. When we got there, my mother pushed through the crowd and found the twentysomething girl lying on the ground; she had an enormous puncture wound from her kickstand. I will never forget what I saw, and I will stop there with the gory details. Nothing fazed my mother though. She sprang into action, directing someone to call 911 and instructing the crowd to give us space. She commanded the situation with strength and clearheadedness.

By then, a bigger crowd was standing around and staring, and Mom was talking to the very scared and badly injured girl. Mom knew exactly what to do and was incredibly calm under pressure. She was Superwoman, and I was her assistant. "Go across the street to the drugstore; get me gauze, Betadine, and bandages right away!" she told me. Off I ran across traffic, waving my hands to get across the street. I entered the pharmacy and breathlessly told the employee what was going on right outside the window; they could see the large crowd and chaos. No one ever asked me for money. They gave me everything I asked for, and I ran back across the street.

My mother meticulously bandaged the poor girl's badly injured leg. The wound was extremely deep and horrifying. When the ambulance arrived, my mother explained what had happened and she assured the girl she would be okay. The paramedics took over and lifted her into the ambulance by stretcher. I was trembling at what I had just seen. My mother had been the only one with a plan. She was calm, focused, and attentive to the feelings of this scared girl. What she taught me that day stayed with me forever. Most people gawk and do nothing. She was a superhero in my eyes, willing to do whatever she could for a stranger. I grew up believing that this was what I was supposed to do—to help anyone in a time of need. I value this lesson every day.

Syracuse, 1988

I was a senior in college taking a long road trip from Syracuse, New York, to Connecticut when the most unexpected thing happened. A big rig stopped suddenly, and I could see clothing and numerous personal belongings strewn across the highway; it was as if someone had dumped two suitcases all over the roadway. As I drove about five miles per hour, I noticed more and more items, and then I saw what had happened.

On the left side of the road, a car was flipped over on its side. I quickly pulled over and ran towards the car. As I made my way over, so many thoughts ran through my head: "Are you out of your mind?! You hate blood and gore! What if the person is dead or close to death and...." But as I ran closer, the most incredible thing happened. A twentysomething guy was pulling himself out of the car, and as he was almost out, I helped him make the final escape right into my arms.

He was shaking and confused. I grabbed him and held on. "Are you okay?! What happened?" I asked. He told me he had fallen asleep and didn't remember anything else. Another kindhearted person stopped on the other side of the road and ran towards us. He was an off-duty paramedic and took over by calling an ambulance and checking the man's vitals. I tried to gather as much of his stuff as possible before leaving him in good hands. At that moment, I could feel my mother's superhero powers surging through me. How could anyone not stop and help someone in need? I just couldn't.

Fast-Forward to 2017

Over a year ago, an extremely panicked older woman came running into a hardware store and approached me as the checkout guy was ringing up my items. Here's how this played out:

"I need something to open up my car window! We might need to break it! I need *help! Please!*"

"What's wrong?" I asked.

"My newborn granddaughter is locked in the car."

I ran to the car and asked the young guy at the checkout to follow me. When we got there, I could see the driver's-side window was open only about an inch and a half. The grandmother and mother were understandably upset. The baby was asleep, but it was ninety degrees outside.

"Let me see if I can wedge my arm into the car window," I said. I'm a mom, and this is what we do. At least, this is what I do. This was not the first time I had seen a baby locked in the car, and it's terrifying. The other time there had been no open windows, and I just hugged the mom until the fire department came. As far as I am concerned, any kid in trouble could be my kid, so I am going to react as if all kids in locked cars are mine. I would probably be more of a wreck, but I always want a happy ending.

When you are in Supermom mode, you ignore that your arm is so squished in a tiny space and you might not be able to get it out. Whatever. I even thought the window could break. Who cares? In my gut, I knew we would get that car open, and I was determined that this would have a happy ending. There was a beautiful newborn trapped in a car, and nothing was going to keep me from getting in.

I asked the mother to walk around the other side of the car and direct me where my arm should go to reach the lock, because I could not see the lever. She directed me and within a minute, I unlocked the car and the tearful mother and grandmother dove in the car. We all cried. I was shaking and still had my arm stuck in the window. Were there pictures? Friending on Facebook? Instagram? Twitter? Are you kidding?! Who cares? I have no idea what their names were, and it didn't matter. We were all so happy and were hugging.

I had no desire to share what had happened in so much detail, but I felt that the message is clear: We should all help one another whenever possible. That is the happiest part of the story, second to seeing that door open. Sometimes real happiness is unexpected, surprising, and genuine. Have you ever offered to help a homeless person? Given a stranger a compliment? Helped a senior citizen load groceries into the car? Asked someone in an accident if he or she needed help in any way? Have you done a random act of kindness? An act of kindness can cost you nothing, only your time, attention, and open heart. You increase the chance for happiness not just within yourself but in someone else's life. And then that person pays it forward.

Giving 100 Percent of Whatever You Can Give

My stepmother has always given back to our community in Stamford, Connecticut. I was too wrapped up in my own life as a teen to see the magnitude of her compassion and generosity.

In 1972, right before marrying my father, she converted to Judaism. She told the Reform rabbi she would convert just as long as she could continue to believe in all the things she believed in. After she and my father moved to Stamford, they joined a Reform temple and she served on different committees and assisted with Passover Seders, fundraisers, and other events. Eventually, she was elected president of the temple's sisterhood. She spent hours of her time organizing and planning events and making sure each one was an incredible success.

With her passion for helping others who were less fortunate, she spent years volunteering for Meals on Wheels, delivering fresh meals to seniors. As a family, we donated food for Thanksgiving meals and wrapped Christmas presents. Years later, she taught English as a second language, and is still friends with her students. Recently, I asked her if she realized just how many mitzvahs she had done. "I never really thought about it," she said. "I did what I did because I wanted to and knew it was the right thing to do."

Meet Christine Dimmick

Christine Dimmick is a sought-after wellness expert who speaks regularly at Canyon Ranch and the JCC Manhattan. She is the founder and CEO of The Good Home Co., a cancer survivor, and the author of *Detox Your Home: A Guide to Removing Toxins from Your Life and Bringing Health into Your Home*.

Janeane: I remember moving into my house and my daughter getting extremely sick…from our house, but we had no idea that was the source of her ailments.

Christine: Oh gosh! Was it mold?

JB: That came after, but everything started with the carpeting, because she has a bad allergy to dust mites, and then we had a water leak, and then she had asthma, problems with mildew, and on and on. Terrible.

CD: And it was probably the off-gassing from the carpeting. Mold, off-gassing, mildew—we are exposed to chemicals we can't even smell. You have a toxic mess. Ugh! I am so sorry, but I am not surprised. First of all, there is no place that is toxic-free. You go to the mountains in Nepal, and you are still going to find some toxins—it's in our air. As it gets worse, it is coming into our homes and we are experiencing this. A lot of people are asking, "What is going on? I don't understand." It's not you! It's our world. It's our new paradigm, unfortunately.

JB: Now, you are a cancer survivor. What happened that led you to look at your own world differently?

CD: I have always been into natural products, natural ingredients, essential oils. I have a company I started called The Good Home Co., which is a natural cleaning products company. I started it in my kitchen over twenty-four years ago. What happened was, about three and a half years ago, I was diagnosed with breast cancer, and it was the kind that fortunately was stage zero to stage one; it was caught really early, and I only had to have radiation. I was so fortunate, but I also had to stop and say, "What is going on? Why did I get it?"

I lived a natural lifestyle, or what I thought was a natural lifestyle. I went to SoulCycle; I ate my kale! What was going on?! I also had two very close friends die around the same time, within six weeks, of cancer at the same age—in their forties. At that point, I realized there was something going on here. This was not normal. My grandparents and my mother never talked about people in their forties passing from cancer. That's when I really took a deep dive, and what I found was not so pleasant, but the more you know, that's how you change it. You can't just ignore it.

When I got that call that I had cancer, I also knew I was lucky. I was forty-five—young. I took a deep dive and wrote *Detox Your Home*, looking at all of the chemical toxins we are exposed to on a daily basis that contribute to this.

JB: So, what should people do to take a good, hard look at their homes?

CD: The first thing I want people to do is understand there is no toxic-free environment. We all live in it, and we are all exposed to it at some point. What we want to do is, number one, create regulations to avoid it. Number two, we want to minimize it as much as possible, but support people who are creating a new paradigm, so we can live a healthier lifestyle in a toxic-free world.

Just because it is on the shelf doesn't mean it is safe, even if it's at Whole Foods. There is so much "green washing." People see a shampoo that says "vegan," and they think it is okay. Vegan does not mean chemical free and organic—[it] just means no animal was harmed to create the product. *DetoxYour Home* focuses on how to shop and what to stay away from. For starters, stay away from bottled water. Bottled water is coming from your own municipal sources. You don't have to buy bottled water. Get a filter; it's polluting with the plastics, and the majority of the bottles don't get recycled. They go into landfills. You see the oceans off the coast of California; it has gotten out of control. Now we are looking into how we are going to fix it. I have an eleven-year-old. Anyone with kids, they will have jobs in conservation and changing our world.

JB: I think it's ridiculous when I see a product that is labeled "natural." I tell my daughter that means nothing and is just marketing. Natural does not mean organic.

CD: Correct. We have to police them [the products] ourselves, and my book is an effort to help people understand what to look for. I truly believe that if it is on the shelf, it should be good for you. I believe that. I think the manufacturer has a responsibility to the consumers that are paying and buying their products; they should be healthy and consumers should not have to think about it.

My grandmother was a former smoker; she was ninety years old and passed last year. And when she quit, she said, "Christine, they never told us they [cigarettes] were bad for us. We all thought they were fun and healthy. I never would have picked it up if I knew it was that bad!" You can see today in our modern times and see how that translates. For women, too, all the creams we put on and all the beauty products, they are so bad.

JB: And trying to convince teenagers to try and switch to something that is nontoxic is tough, because they are surrounded by all these marketing campaigns.

CD: Right, and I think the important thing to teach them is that marketing isn't everything. My son believes it, too. He has issues with food, and he wants to drink Gatorade and other stuff with food coloring. I look at the label and tell him it's corn syrup and water.

JB: And dyes.

CD: Yes, it's terrible what is in there.

JB: Yes, and the dyes are really toxic. I think if you make small changes, especially with kids, that is good. For instance, we don't have soda in our house. I use seltzer and juices.

CD: Right. We think we are disappointing and upsetting our children, but you have to look at these products. You have to look at the sugars; you have to look at the products that you think are okay to put in your pantry. Just like cigarettes. You wouldn't give your eleven-year-old child cigarettes to smoke, and yes, I am comparing cigarettes to sugar, because it is as addictive; it is shown to be that way. We have to look at obesity and their health. I love to bake! I reduce the sugar, and it is considered a treat; it is not an everyday thing. I remember back in my day we had soda with dinner.

JB: I was totally addicted!

CD: Yes! Don't get me started on Diet Coke! The ingredients and all the diet stuff! My mother finally told me that I had to stop drinking it. I was drinking a liter a day!

JB: Yes, sodium saccharin; it was so addicting. I think it's ridiculous that I used to order a bacon double cheeseburger, large fries, and order a Diet Coke! That made *no sense*!

CD: (*laughs*) Listen, there is a healthy balance. I love French fries, but I will have a kale salad with them.

The more we can buy organic, the more we support that industry, and it is healthier for us. We have to look at everything in and on our body, including our fashion. We have fast food and we have fast fashion. I have a young child, and I want to make my dollar stretch, so I would go to these stores and buy five for a dollar. Once you see and understand the hidden truth why things are so cheap and what they are doing to make products so cheap, you need to avoid them. They have to cut corners, and that means not disposing of the chemicals properly. There are dyes involved in making all of our clothes.

JB: I break out terribly from formaldehyde.

CD: I wanted to break down the parts of a house, from the bathroom with cleaning products, shampoos, and makeup to the kitchen and food. BPA is in plastics, but we are exposed to it in frozen peas and meats. Vegetables are put in plastic in a store.

Even your detergent is leaving a coating on your clothing you are exposed to; this can cause asthma and other skin reactions.

Sunscreen. Every sunscreen except those made from zinc causes coral bleaching in our water. Hawaii has banned it. Climate change and water temperatures are causing a problem. Hawaii is creating a ban on these sunscreens. They should be banned everywhere. Chemicals oxybenzone and octinoxate cause endocrine disruption; it's harmful to you and the environment; it causes children to be susceptible to infertility, weight gain, early development. There is a whole list of things. There has been minimal policing of this, if any.

There is a lot of misrepresentation in the green space.

Vegan doesn't mean organic and natural. You have to research and look at them; it means no animal products are used in the makeup, food, et cetera.

GMO is important. The website *www.justlabelit.org* is pushing to have GMOs labeled; this is important. We don't know if GMOs will cause issues in us. We could find that things cause problems down the road. We need to have everything labeled. Organic is great, but shop with your farmer directly. Brandless is online; everything is three dollars.

JB: Growing up in Manhattan, I used to get sick a lot from colds and bronchitis. I know the pollution bothers me. How do you stay healthy when you are breathing in soot and smog?

CD: We have air monitors. We live downtown, so we have a sea breeze near the water, but there is the Brooklyn Bridge and lots of traffic. Living near the water, the air is constantly circulating. There is a brand called PurpleAir; it's a device that tracks the pollution indoors or outdoors, and it tracks the pollution in your home.

JB: That's good!

CD: You know if you need to change your HEPA filter, if you need more air purifying, etc. There is no place that is toxin-free. You can be on Mount Everest and still breathe in BPAs. They have found plastic bags on Everest and in the deepest depths of our oceans. There are plastic bags found in the Arctic. There is no nontoxic place anymore, and that's from the manufacturing.

JB: Do you have friends who think, "Christine, you need to chill out. You are so intense!"?

(*laughter*)

CD: No! They love it, but they hate it!

JB: Of course!

CD: I try to do it with a positive spin. So, we know this; it's all relative. There are still people out there who smoke, and they know the facts. I honestly don't believe it is our issue to have to worry about it. I think this is why we have governments in place, and we need to have responsible manufacturing. People are taking our money for products that we want to buy, but they need to be responsible in the ingredients that they use. I see the only way to go is up, in a good way, to reverse all of this.

JB: Absolutely.

CD: (*laughs*) Yes, I try and only give people a little bit at a time! (*laughter*) Focus on one; it can truly be overwhelming, but once you have done one [thing], you kind of naturally go to the next. And I think once you realize that your health is important, when you really, truly do that work—and that is also personal inner work in realizing how important you are and your health is—then you don't want to put this stuff in your body, right?

JB: Right.

CD: It's easy.

JB: I grew up having tons of eczema, allergies to dairy, eggs, carpets, everything. Now, I only eat organic and I try and take really good care of myself. I see a huge difference.

CD: Yes, I suffer from eczema, too; it came about four to five years ago. I never had it, and it's an autoimmune disorder. Everyone has these autoimmune disorders going on. Eczema, Crohn's, allergies to all sorts of foods and everything. I have taken out dairy and wheat.

JB: Yes, me too.

CD: Yes, but it is absolutely environmental. You have kids walking around at twenty-three who have rheumatoid arthritis. What is that?

JB: That's terrible!

CD: It is terrible! I am just here to help people wake up and really take a look at what is happening, what is going on. And power to the people! Help is everything. Help is our birthright.

JB: Anything else you would like people to know about your book?

CD: I try and make it easy, so when you are looking at it, it is light and not a difficult read. Don't be afraid of it. Information is power—the more you know!

JB: By the way, one of the reasons I wanted to speak to you is because sometimes we are exposed to different things that can put us in a funk.

CD: Right. So many things, with our depression and what is going on with our kids being diagnosed with ADHD and autism. And people say, "No, no, has nothing to do with that." Come on! Why is there an increase? I have spoken with doctors who won't say it publicly, but there are a lot of people fighting that. Big corporations, for whatever reason, want to fight health and don't want the regulations, but doctors say that they see it. They see it. We may be living longer, but our health is not getting better, but we can change that. And I am trying to help.

Find Christine Dimmick at *ChristineDimmick.com* and *Good-HomeStore.com*.

A Walking Candy Cane

When I was age thirteen, my mother fibbed and told the head of the volunteer department at our local hospital that I was almost fifteen. I was told to lie about my age because I could be a candy striper and fulfill my school requirement for volunteer hours. I had no idea what a candy striper was as I wrestled to put on that tiny pink-and-white apron-like dress that resembled a wrinkled candy cane. At first, I thought I looked ridiculous, but it grew on me, and I was proud to wear my uniform. I just wish someone had told me the gig would not involve candy. I was majorly disappointed.

I did everything from delivering flowers to answering phones at the front desk (with the occasional mishap of connecting someone to the wrong department or hanging up on the person); this was excellent practice in improving my interpersonal skills, and I got to see close up what it was like for the patients. At one point, I was assigned to work in the pharmacy. Sorting pills. Not kidding you. Who thought of that idea? Thankfully, I never considered taking home any samples of who knows what I was sorting. What a recipe for disaster that could have been!

There were highs and lows during my days as a candy striper. Seeing those little kids in barren rooms struggling to defeat cancer was horribly sad. Delivering a card to a really, really old creepy guy who could barely hear me and kept saying, "Come closer! Come closer! *Come closer!*" completely freaked me out. I sprinted from the room, almost knocking over my flower cart; it felt like another *Twilight Zone* episode (I am such a scaredy-cat).

The most rewarding part of being a candy striper was delivering flowers to people and seeing how happy they were. I learned a lot about the power of a smile, giving my time and energy to people who needed to think about something other than a temporary or permanent illness. No matter what kind of mood I was in or what was going on in my life at that age, I left my baggage at the curb and entered that hospital with the goal of being present and attentive. The experience of being a candy striper for two years has stayed with me to this day. I am forever grateful to my mother for arranging this incredible #alittletooyoungbutwhatever volunteer opportunity, and if the Stamford Hospital is reading this, I gave the flowers without the card to someone who looked lonely that day. #sendmethebill

Volunteer Your Time, Talents, and Energy

Share your time and energy with others; it's good for you and it's good for the recipients. Volunteer at a retirement home, a hospital, a school, a food bank, or an animal shelter, foster a pet, help out at a local school, drop off food and clothing to donation centers, offer to deliver meals to the elderly or feed the homeless during the year or the holidays. Start a toy or food drive. Clean out your closet and donate to organizations that help others. Whatever you do, just do something with the experiences, resources, and time you have.

In a Nutshell

Nothing says "mood booster" more than the selfless act of giving. Toss your personal baggage for a few hours and focus on someone or something else for a change. Our wounds can run deep, and redirecting our pain and emotions can be cathartic and healing. Don't be a bystander in life. Help others. Be tuned in to what is happening in your surroundings and see where you can be of service. We get all wrapped up in our own stuff and think some of our problems are monumental, when in fact, they can be minuscule and petty compared to the weight of the world felt by others.

Put your talents, time and kindness to work by helping others. Volunteer at a homeless shelter, soup kitchen, nonprofit, or pediatric cancer center during the holidays. And if your issues are monumental, at least you can take a temporary break from your world and bring some goodness into someone else's life. The mental vacation might be just what you need.

What have you done to help others? If the answer is *nada*, well, what *could* you do? The opportunities are endless. We all have some skills to offer, and giving your time and energy can make a big difference. You just might realize that your own situation is not such a sh*tty mess after all. Gain perspective to shift your focus and develop a compassionate, empathetic heart. It's a win-win.

Your Random Act of Kindness Pledge

I am really good at _____, so I will contact _____ and see if they would like my expertise in

_____.

A total stranger once gave me a _____ for free and it made me feel _____. I should do that for someone else at _____.

When I was younger, I volunteered at a _____, I could do that now or try to _____. My skills that could be helpful include: _____, _____, and _____.

I have thought about volunteering at our local _____, but I am filled with lame excuses. I want to be a good community member and a great role model for my _____. They can come with me and

_____.

There is an older _____ who lives all alone on our street. Maybe I can stop by and see if she/he needs

_____ or _____. I could invite her/him over for _____ sometime.

During the holidays, I always say I am going to volunteer at my local _____. This year it's a plan, and I will sign up by _____ and bring _____, _____, and _____.

If I see a stranger in need, I am going to _____ and _____. I am going to be more open to helping people and doing whatever I can do as a random act of kindness. It could even be: _____, _____, and _____. I know I have a lot of _____, so I think I will donate them to _____. That's a start!

CHAPTER 8

Nurture Your Relationships, but Know When to Boot the Toxic Ones

"It takes a lot of courage to show your dreams to someone else."
—*Erma Bombeck*

Some of the best advice I received on the *Get the Funk Out!* show came from award-winning softball coach Sue Enquist, who said loudly and firmly, "Toxic people will suck the life out of you!" And then she went on to explain how when we share our day with our loved ones, we bring those toxic people to the dinner table, to the bedroom, and wherever else we find ourselves rambling on about them. And for me, I lie awake at three in the morning overanalyzing my conversations with these crazy people that put me in a funk to begin with and wonder why I had anything to do with them in the first place.

I know. I get it. You would rather just stay curled up on your sofa binge-watching your guilty pleasure, but after a while, it is time to smell the roses (and shower) and push yourself to go meet your friends and family or make a new connection. Not much can happen to change your life while you're in your hermit cave. Taking time to be alone is okay, especially for those who are introverts, but after a while, clean yourself up, throw something on that makes you feel great, and get your butt out the door. You will be glad you did.

Wouldn't you rather be alone than be with people who don't support you and believe in you? I know I would. When people criticize you and put you down, it's time to find new friends. Don't believe all the nonsense being thrown your way, because as the saying goes, only you can make you feel bad. Words are just words. If you believe the negative comments people make, you will fall into a victim mentality, and that is not a good place to be. You will never take risks and believe that what you create is worth anything.

True friends support you through everything. They listen, they don't judge or criticize, but they also give you a reality check and honest feedback, which might seem harsh at first, but after all, they have your back and want the best for you. If you find yourself making friends with people who are judgmental and critical of you or others, it might be time to find some new friends. Your posse is out there.

If you find yourself in a relationship filled with negativity spewing in your direction, get out. Use all the bad vibes you feel as fuel for your fire and know that you deserve better and happier times. Believe what you believe, not what someone else says you can achieve. Don't believe the negative toxic sh*t people spew, because they have their own insecurities and unfulfilled dreams. Live your life trying anything and everything you want to, because you have one life to live. Live it the way you want, not following the compass of people who think they know what is best for you. Cheer yourself on through your disappointments and failures, and just keep going. Keep moving, keep believing, and be flexible when things don't work out the way you planned. Improvise when needed, create a new plan, and let your positivity steer the course.

Don't you wish that someone would already have warned you that your reactions and actions towards life's stomach punches are better handled with clarity and rational thinking? But most people are not so rational and clearheaded when they are younger and inexperienced in life's assaults. Wait! We are not always rational and clearheaded when we are grown-ups! If we are lucky, we are more rational and calmer as we age, but I am still working on that one.

A few years ago, at a Los Angeles acting event, I had a surprising experience, which had nothing to do with acting and everything to do with my self-esteem and letting a toxic stranger annihilate me. A casting director was holding a workshop to analyze our headshots. I attended because I thought he was a big deal and his opinions mattered. I soon learned that wasn't the case.

There I was, almost in the back of the room, when he held up my headshot, mispronounced my name, and began to skewer me in front of everyone. He laughed and mocked me about everything, and I just took it. Some people laughed, while others just cringed. When I left the room, I felt like I wanted to never return to acting. And then I met someone representing a casting company. I told her what had happened, and she laughed because she knew whom I was talking about. I guess he had a reputation for meanness. He was known for his mouth and his inflated ego.

She looked me right in the eyes and said, "Never worry about getting older, because when you have wrinkles, they are a sign you have lived life, and they represent your journey. And smile lines? They are the best lines to have! So, embrace everything about you, because that is what makes you *you!*" For an LA event, this was not what I expected. I thought I was supposed to defy my age and look younger than my years. A total stranger with heaps of kindness had given me a reality check. She sent me off with the best parting gift—a hug and great advice to not "take anyone's sh*t."

That casting director gave me some essential armor as I moved forward. I am actually thankful for that experience, and I feel sorry for him, because we always remember how someone made us feel. I decided to never sit back and let anyone skewer me. No one has a right to belittle anyone for entertainment purposes. Besides, what he had to dish out was nothing compared to my backstory, which left a few scars, but here I am. His words stung, but they are just words, and I chose to flick them off and take my father's advice: "Just keep going" with whatever I choose to pursue.

I have lost both parents. Well, I didn't technically *lose* them, like in a mall or on an overseas trip. They both passed away. The dynamics of relationships and the depth of one's love is always an issue with death. You begin to see the person differently, and of course you have a boatload of questions that he or she cannot answer anymore. Most times, if you have pent-up anger, you might find forgiveness in your heart and some level of understanding. Those last two things will enable you to move on peacefully and heal your wounds that are still raw. Forgiveness is a powerful thing, and so is gratitude.

Of course, there are other people in this world who have a life that is a gazillion times worse than ours. I learned that from chatting with hundreds of guests on my show over the past ten years. I am constantly humbled to hear people share their stories and strategies for powering through the worst of times. They have a mindset that can help almost anyone stop funking around.

Nurture the Relationships That Matter

A great way to nurture relationships with family and friends is to tell them how you are feeling, apologize to heal wounds, or share that you are thinking of them by picking up the phone or sending a text or an email. I personally think phone calls are the best way to connect, because hearing someone's voice provides a deeper connection. My second choice is writing a letter. I know. I am so old school, but handwriting a thank-you note or just something that says you are thinking of someone is very meaningful. Fine, you can also text, but letter writing was big back in the day. Now I sound like a dinosaur.

When someone receives a handwritten letter, it creates a meaningful moment for the person. You can't get that kind of feeling from a text or an email. Writing a letter allows you to use a pen, convey your thoughts, maybe elaborate more than you would in a text, and send something special. The note could be written to thank someone for calling, visiting, caring, helping, or being supportive, but it could also be just a few words of thanks or "I am sorry, I was wrong, I love you, I screwed up big-time. I am an idiot but please forgive me, and I am thinking of you." Can't go wrong with old-school.

My loving stepmother sends the most beautiful cards and thank-you notes, and so does my thoughtful and endlessly kind mother-in-law. I learned as a kid that when someone gives you a gift, you send a note. I used to write letters to my dad and grandmothers all the time. I even wrote a letter to my high school writing teacher thanking her for being so inspiring and supportive. She told me there are no wrong answers when it comes to creative writing; it's all about what you feel in the moment.

The one person I write cards to and send an occasional package to is my stepmother. Care packages and cards are loving surprises; they remind me of the summer I went to sleepaway camp at eight years old and my grandmother sent me candy, Hostess cupcakes, Cheez Whiz, and more junk. "Happy" doesn't even begin to describe my eight-year-old self. Sugar high, junk food buzz. Was I homesick? Not for a minute.

My love and respect for my stepmother grew immensely after Dad died. I could see and feel the cavernous void he had left in her life, and her pain made me extremely sad and empathetic. With Dad gone, she was my responsibility now. Period. I would take over where Dad left off, or at least I would try. I was going to be there for her every day, even if only by phone, and would do what I know my father would have wanted. Besides, the void my dad left in her heart was massive, and if I could just do a little something to help her through the worst time of her life, then her life would be a little less dark and there would be a glimmer of light.

In a time of loss, no one should feel alone and abandoned. The danger of lack of connection and purpose can drive people to have negative thoughts, and despair worsens. All we need in those dark times is a glimpse of the light, and then as time goes by, the darkness lessens and the light shines brighter. However, you must want to see that light grow. If anything positive came as a result of my dad's death, I would say it was a deeper connection with my stepmother. Never would I have imagined this happening, but life can be remarkable and surprising at times.

My stepmother lives in a place that she never really wanted to move to in the first place. The move would have been a heck of a lot better if my dad had been along on this new adventure, but his time in Florida was cut short. She left Connecticut for Florida in August 2015, because the cost of living was skyrocketing and financially there was no sense in staying. They put their house on the market just a few months before dad was diagnosed with metastasized stage four cancer on August 4, 2015.

Dad passed away four months later. I never imagined I would be her confidante, her friend, and the person whom she opens up to almost every day. We have the most amazing relationship, and I never thought I would say that. Through death came something wonderful, something we never had before. What we have now is beautiful and hilarious at times. On a recent visit, we were talking so much, I charred a sweet potato in her microwave and was wondering why smoke was filling her condo and billowing across the kitchen. We were probably in the midst of a deep conversation, like some of the many over the past three years, and they keep getting better.

When I decided to spend Mother's Day with her, instead of with my kids and husband, my family knew that my decision was the right one. Dad had just passed away five months earlier, and she was still residing in the depressing rental house. I did not want her to spend Mother's Day alone. She had put up with a lot over the years—my blaring music, horrible grades, off-the-wall mother, loud electric guitar playing, eclectic summer jobs, and my adventurous side. When Dad passed away, she went through the worst emotional roller coaster of her life. She said she lies in bed at night talking to him, but he never talks back. "That's a first," I said. She giggles, which is really nice, considering I hadn't heard her laugh in ages. I love making her laugh, and we hug more lovingly than we used to. If I can get a smile or a giggle out of her, I know her day is a drop better.

I have great respect for my stepmother of more than forty-three years, and such sadness at the same time. We never really knew each other until now. I lived with my dad and stepmother for only a year and a half before college. They were going through the worst financial rough patch, but they warmly accepted me. I am forever grateful that they turned my life around.

When I moved in, I wasn't sure if she was *really* as nice as she seemed. "Could it be an act?" I thought. She was just so consistently kind, hardworking, and thoughtful, and she loved to cook. All I knew was, she was definitely *not* my mother. When I was six, my mother rudely said of my stepmother, "She is nothing but a cheap waitress." I imagined she waited tables at a cute little diner, or maybe Dad had met her at the Howard Johnson's he took me to so often. One day, I asked her if she really was a waitress, and it turns out she never waitressed at all; this opened a conversation about her entire backstory involving interesting careers and creative pursuits.

When we reflected on my father's life, we agreed he had at least nine lives. He experienced horrible marriages (yes, Dad was married a few times), deceptive business partners, heart attacks, failed businesses, quadruple bypass surgery, extreme weight gain, emergency valve replacement surgery, knee replacement, emergency surgery to reconnect four fingers, and the cancellation of a meeting at the World Trade Center the morning of 9/11. She was with him every step of the way.

As we packed up my father's clothes and memorabilia that Mother's Day weekend, she shared her hesitation when he had proposed in 1972. She carefully unfolded a very tattered letter she wrote to him from the Mandarin hotel in Hong Kong, where she was staying for work. We could barely make out the faded blue ink, but when I read her letter, the words began to come together. Tearfully, she had me flatten the wrinkled pages and tape them back together. She asked me to read the letter aloud. I could not imagine how she could withstand the emotions flooding back. When I heard her whimper, I felt horrible inflicting more pain. The words were a searing reminder he was no longer here.

To my surprise, she smiled through her painful tears and asked me to continue. She was the happiest I had seen her in months. She relived that night in Hong Kong, when she had fumbled towards taking another terrifying leap towards love. Upon her return from Hong Kong, my father was there at the airport, ecstatic to see his girl. They married on November 19, 1973, in Florida, among family and friends. Her letter stayed in his wallet for years; this was the first time I had heard this story and seen the beautiful letter.

When we were told in August 2015 that my father had stage four cancer, it was not earth-shattering news. His pale skin and constant pains already had made me think something was wrong. By the time the doctors figured out that Dad had metastasized colon cancer, there were no options. "Why can't they just cut it out?" he would ask in disbelief. His heart was barely functioning due to advanced heart disease, and surgery would have been too risky.

On December 4, 2015, Dad passed away peacefully. We spoke four times that day, and he was still cracking jokes. Our "verbal volleyball," making each other laugh with improv and jokes, was the best. But the days had grown more stressful, because of the ominous weight of my "any day now" feeling. When he called at five in the morning in a morphine stupor asking, "Where are you?!" the drugs and cancer were taking over. I knew someday I would miss the sound of his warm, loving voice. He was my biggest cheerleader.

The idea of boxing up my father's life seemed so strange. A total stranger would be sorting through his possessions at a thrift store. His keepsakes hold so many stories that define him as a man and as a father. Those suits he wore into Manhattan, gorgeous caramel-colored cowboy boots so meticulously cared for, camel-colored Stetson hats, soft flannel shirts and sweaters. He was a workaholic, a man with a mission, dedicated to all his pursuits and the people he met along the way.

Now, as I face the woman he adored, the woman he knew would be a great stepmother and partner, I am so thankful she took a chance on him. If there is one thing I have learned, there is no time frame for grief; this is a very personal journey, and it's a bumpy ride. If I can somehow help her build a new life, crack a few of my father's stale jokes, and help her though this storm, I will have done my job.

Meet Sue Enquist

I met Sue Enquist, former UCLA softball coach and founder of ONE Softball, several years ago when she spoke at a TEDx event (an independent TED Talk-like event) in Orange County, California. Her words were so powerful and relevant to people in any occupation and of any age. Her tremendous experiences as an athlete and a coach inspire and illuminate what it means to build healthy habits, how toxic people can inundate our lives when we don't even realize it, and why failure is key to success and long-term grit. And nervousness, well that's just fear turned inside out.

Sue grew up in San Clemente, California, with a military father and a mother who said she could achieve whatever she wanted. Her brother taught her how to compete, and her sister instilled in her the idea of having a lot of faith. She attended San Clemente High School and played boys' baseball, which got her into UCLA. Sue developed a passion for baseball at an early age. She played all sports in high school, and especially loved surfing and softball. She played nationally and later became part of the Olympic program, traveling the world and coaching fifteen UCLA Bruin Olympians. Her athletic achievements drew a lot of attention when Title IX became law. By 2012, it had been over forty years since Title IX had taken effect. She had planned to become a respiratory therapist with a BS in kinesiology, but her head coach at the time asked her if she would help for one quarter before she finished her degree. She agreed but said she would never coach! Sure. She got bit by the coaching bug. Sue loves sharing information, watching how other people strive toward success, and helping others achieve their goals. During her years as a player and coach, the UCLA Bruins won eleven national championships.

I asked Sue to share advice for parents who want their kids to get involved in sports.

She said parents should encourage movement and performance. Students need to love the struggle of competition, and "the game doesn't have a memory, so you need to start over every day." She believes that kids need to be active and spend time outside; this promotes a healthier lifestyle long-term. And her views about phones are similar to mine. She adds, "Set controls around the use of the phone."

Agreed.

Sue believes that sports give kids an opportunity to develop discipline and structure and to set priorities. The habits of student athletes have a long-term impact in the workplace. Prioritizing and being disciplined are keys to success. Sue pointed out that some of the benefits of sports for girls include greater self-confidence, a decline in teen pregnancies, and more emotional stability.

After Sue became a coach, she met some incredible influencers who told her, "Give one hundred percent of what you have and stay positive in your thoughts, even though we all have a strong voice and a weak voice. You have to stay in your strong voice but be aware when you get in your negative voice."

Sue's years attending UCLA were invaluable. Her professors taught her how to learn and gave her the tools to be successful in other environments, whether she was starting her own business or doing something outside of her comfort zone. When she got into coaching, she started her own business and created and invented her own products. Her softball coach, Sharron Backus, taught her that "wins and losses come and go, but how you treat people and how you affect people have a lasting impact." Sue knew she wanted to continue to have a lasting impact on people's lives. She traveled the country and taught about "how to be competitively excellent in terms of your personal best." She shared that one of her greatest coaches was John Wooden, who taught her how to be her very best in softball.

When it comes to failure, Sue offered important advice that applies to anyone at any age: "If you can teach parents to go out and let your kids fail, failure teaches us. You can hold hands with failure, and don't be afraid of it."

Sue shared her thoughts on sustainable champions. "People who are champions might get to the top and disappear, but sustainable champions show up in their workplace or in the community and have the ability to master awareness when they are in their good or bad thoughts. When student athletes develop awareness, they learn to show up all the time, respect their elders, treat their teammates with respect consistently, and at the end of the day, people will say they love competing with her. She showed up on good days and bad days."

Sue shared her talk at TEDx in Orange County about "bottom feeders."

"We go through life so quickly and lose awareness," she said. She learned the 33 percent rule—it is like armor, something that will protect you and your greatness. "If you have this awareness in your family, community, on your teams, in your workplace, these people won't affect you negatively. But you need to understand that one-third of the people you meet will *suck the life out of you!* [*Yes!* This hit home for me!] They never put a filter on it. Then the middle third, [when things are good], they are great, but when things are bad, they turn into the bottom third."

She continued, "The top third understand the conversations in their head; they have negative thoughts, but they don't let it affect their behavior or their outward words. The top third is what you want to be." Here's what also resonated for me: Sue explained that we tend to "bring home the bottom third. We have a bad day and drive home and spew the bottom third at the dinner table! And now you have the bottom third sitting down at your table. It's about awareness of what you are doing at any age. If you can build the awareness component, you can self-regulate and not bring home these bottom-third people."

Sue said it's important not to worry about giving 100 percent each day. "Surrender to not being one hundred percent. Stay positive in your words with your children." She said, "The parent role is getting lost. You don't need to be your kids' Facebook friend. You need to be a leader; give structure, discipline, and a strong voice. You don't have to be her best friend right now. You can do that when she is twenty-five and done with college." One pattern she has seen over the past twenty-seven years at UCLA: "The athlete that came in balanced and had a healthy sense of self, she had a mom who was a mom. Not a best friend in her mom. You don't party with your mom. Your mom is supposed to be your mom. Parents need to have a specific place for their daughter—they have less than five core friends; they need a mom."

Kids need to have respect for their parents, their teachers, and their coaches. If you are a parent, creating respect means guiding your kids consistently with a positive message. Around ages twelve to eighteen, and twenty-two and up, they have conflicts with their moms. Just keep sending a "strong consistent message, and they circle back around to you and realize how great they had it with you," Sue said.

Sue believes parents need to find a niche that kids like and support their interests. Activities such as painting, ceramics, building video games, or any outlet can nurture and grow their passion at an early age, "which builds self-confidence, and that puts you in a community of like-minded people. Being detached and not having purpose puts them in a dark place."

When kids are angry, try to get to the root cause of their anger. Establish that they need to speak calmly. Let them speak at least three times more than you. Your role is to listen actively and speak less.

Sue shared that you just "have to be okay with your kid just being average at math." Some parents would probably flip at this statement, but not me. I know there are so many different intelligences kids have. Just because they might not be great at one thing doesn't mean they aren't brilliant in another area. I value mental, physical, and emotional health above anything else. Sue suggested parents hone in on what their kids are good at and enable them to solve their own problems at times. She suggested asking them what they think will help them in any given situation and emphasizing that it is okay to fail; this is how we all learn. "They should not have the easiest path," Sue said. "Getting up after failure is a lifelong lesson. Coach Wooden said not every kid will be the best at math and English. Don't pressure them to be an A math student when it's not their ability. Give them the discipline to achieve and do their best." In some subject areas, they might be just average, and you need to be okay with that.

Sue and I discussed fear and failure, and the impact they have on kids' lives.

"You don't find a lot of people talking a lot about fear. There is so much science on how the brain works. We do know that we need to make people feel better by getting them to talk about fear. The thing that is impressive about my career is, I have to come to find a common theme despite the gender, sport, and school." She said athletes she meets speak "freely and embrace fear so it no longer becomes the dirty little secret. When you think about all the great athletes out there, there is a sense that they have been blessed with the warrior gene and they never let fear capture them; that is just not true. The one that is expected to win has to master the fear and the fear of failure the most because everyone is expecting that person to be successful." She knows firsthand thanks to her experiences with student athletes that they were able to become great because they overcame and avoided negative self-talk.

Here's how Sue sees the two voices in our brains: "There is the positive voice and the negative voice that projects ahead the fear of failure, saying, 'I'm going to fail,' and it projects behind with 'I am not worth it. I am never going to be good at this, because I never have been.'"

Sue explained that the sustainable champion has the ability to say, "I've got you, weak voice. I see what you are doing." She added that he or she has "the ability to capture all of the positive trigger words and take over that conversation; then when fear happens, they are very objective about it, and there is a learning opportunity." She mentioned Billie Jean King, "one of our greatest role models, who said that pressure is a privilege. The ability to be in a moment where there is so much at stake—that is a privilege." Sue pointed out that "students are not idiots if they lose the game. These sustainable programs let the athlete off the hook." Athletes can talk about their fears in a way that is healthy and constructive.

I think being nervous makes you prepare more, and over time, the nervousness dissipates.

What Sue said next really resonated with me: "Nervousness is excitement turned inside out. Your body doesn't know if you are in the finals of the World Series or the Super Bowl, a geometry test, or a wedding. It's your brain that puts the label on that energy." She explained that at UCLA, sustainable champions never say, "I am so nervous." They say they are excited. Sue pointed out that this is a different way to teach your body how to look forward to and love the anticipation. "The day to celebrate is the day you get tested. You get to celebrate all of the hard work you put in." She said athletes can spend nine months getting ready for a single moment, so they need to love the anticipation, because "that's ninety percent of our life."

We took a slight but relevant diversion to discuss the role of teachers and how not to be "Captain Obvious." Teachers will surely see areas of weakness in their students, but they can't be Captain Obvious, because words have an impact. Students should be told how to do something. "State the situation, and if you are a good coach or a good teacher, always—after you state the obvious—give the how-tos. Teach them how to cross the bridge over to success as they sit in that failure moment. They need to be okay with failure."

Sue's analogies apply not just to sports but to life.

She shared that her dad was a World War II veteran and her mom was a very positive person; they instilled values with no boundaries. "You didn't turn certain things off in the classroom or [on] the ball field. These lessons must be present everywhere," she said. She just wishes there would be changes in sports standards. I could not agree more. "If you are a coach, it should be unacceptable to yell across the field at a nine-year-old. If you are parent, yelling at your kid should be unacceptable during a game, and if you are a student athlete, it is unacceptable to throw your helmet. I wish those standards were as high as they are in the classroom," she said.

If you're a parent, don't break the game down after the game. Kids should have an engaging conversation for a few minutes, but don't talk about the game unless the kids agree. Daughters especially don't want their dads "breaking the game down and dissecting everything," Sue said. "If they don't want to talk about it, don't push it." She said usually they just want to know what's for dinner.

Sue sees a long-term impact of fathers on female athletes. "Their intentions are great, but their words are indelible on the brains of their daughters." And what about her experience with UCLA athletes? "For girls who are student athletes at UCLA, she has a strong sense of confidence. She has a dad who let her manage the game before and after, win and lose. He wasn't under her skin 24/7." When dads attempt to make girls better, the girls take the feedback personally, and these words impact their strength outside the ball field long-term. "Inside, you are not happy and don't believe in yourself. I warn the dads, 'Have positive, constructive, then positive feedback,'" She said. She calls it the "constructive sandwich." Girls remember strong words when they are young. "Be a dad first," she added. "Catch your daughter doing things right and talk about that. Words are indelible on their brain."

I asked Sue, could she share advice for women who are in a funk and say they don't have time to work out?

"Start with one minute today. Do twenty-five leg extensions, then thirty-five tomorrow. Then park your car and lap the school one to three times. Do the toe test and check yourself. You are at seventy percent, so give one hundred percent of seventy percent or whatever you have. Be aware of your strong and weak voices. If you ever listen to how you talk to yourself, you would never let anyone else talk to you that way. Why do you talk to yourself that way? We are our own worst critics. Would you date your inner voice?"

Sue was once a professional surfer. She was an amateur in junior high school and high school, then turned pro towards the end of her career. She recalled a wonderful upbringing in San Clemente with great influences. Sue grew up surfing and competing and loved it. Surfing is her passion to this day and her go-to outlet. She surfs, paddles, and runs every day. She does a few things consistently, and she told me that Coach Wooden said, "Make every day your masterpiece. It's your masterpiece. You don't have to perfect. Just perfectly try at being perfect."

Her motto on her website: Prepare, Love, Honor the Game. These three principles apply to life, the workplace, and sports.

"This is a life model in everything we do—a model that crosses all genders, all sports, all workplaces," she said.

> "Everything you do, you have to love what you do and love the preparation. Preparation is the first principle in our life model. If you want to be a sustainable champion, meaning the best you are capable of being, you have to focus on getting one percent better. You have to love the anticipation. You have to be able to take the baby steps every day. The second thing that makes a sustainable champion and your ability to reach competitive greatness—Coach Wooden's pyramid of success—is to be able to love and be committed to the struggle. Being great on good days and bad on the tough days. Be the person to love the struggle. Honor the game. The game doesn't know your history. The game doesn't know your background. When we look at athletic greatness, what makes [the athletes] great is that they truly believe that today is a new day to be great all over again. Master the fundamentals of the game and you'll play some pretty good ball."

Find Sue Enquist at *www.onesoftball.com* and on Twitter @sueenquist.

At some point in your life, you will come across all types of toxic people. You know whom I am talking about. We all know these people; they wear us out and leave us wondering why we bother. Hopefully, you will wise up and decide you have had enough of them and stop investing your time and energy in them.

Unfortunately, you might not be able to follow through with your smart decision, and they will slowly creep back into your life like a rash you just can't get rid of.

You'll change your tune, rationalize having them back in your life, and there you are again—a glutton for punishment. Why do we spend time with people who pick us apart, lower our self-esteem, bad-mouth others, and leave us feeling worn out and exhausted? We become used to the verbal noxious stuff they spew, and instead of finding healthier relationships, we are complacent and do nothing. Hopefully, you will realize that the stress and anxiety you feel is most likely enhanced by these toxic dependencies, and it's time to cut your ties and *wake up!* There is no need to agonize over ending relationships that make you physically and mentally sick and wear you out. Save yourself, be bold, and have some pride! Life is filled with tough choices, and sometimes we must put some distance between us and other people, even if we are related to them.

"You can pick your friends, but you can't pick your family," a wisecracking old man once told me. He was right, and the truth is, you don't even have to like your family. Yes, I went there. You don't have to. You should try to respect your family members if possible, but if the time spent away from them is happier than time spent with them, please choose a sane, happy life. We don't need to let our family suck the life out of us. Why do you think people dread the holidays? We see people during the holidays whom we see perhaps only a few times a year, and as soon as we enter the room and come face-to-face, it's hard to believe a year has flown by! Breathe and take care of yourself. Your sanity is your number-one priority.

We have choices and as we get older, we make big choices that aren't always easy and are not always accepted by others. You might be criticized for your bold choices, but these choices are necessary, and they are yours. Always look after *yourself*, because living a life based on guilt and emotional pain is no life at all. To test my theory, take a break from someone who creates a knot in your stomach and causes duress in your life. Walk out of the room when you feel that stress knot in your stomach and feelings of anxiety and discomfort. Shut the door and lie down. If you are at someone else's house, take a break and get some air. Assess your physical and mental state. Write down how you feel, how you live your life differently because of this person, and ways you can handle your interactions in a healthier way, or at least ways that work for you.

If you are brave enough, start a conversation with that antagonist or annoying person another time (not at the Thanksgiving table), and see if you can gently express how you feel. If you think I have lost my marbles and that change is absolutely impossible, try to play nice and stay positive in your own life. You (hopefully) don't have to spend endless amounts of time with people who aggravate you. Find a way to interact peacefully while saving your soul.

You might be someone who has a conflict with a friend or family member. You might not be speaking to each other, and a lot of time has gone by. Been there. When you really consider the reason behind your separation, think about whether your relationship is important enough to salvage. Be the bigger person. Conflict can eat you up inside. People don't know where to start, so they do nothing; they are angry, hurt, and fearful. I once had a phone call with my dad that didn't end well. We didn't speak for months. Then Hanukkah came around, and I picked up the phone and simply said, "Happy Hanukkah, Dad." He was shocked, tearful, and embarrassed that so much time had gone by. I valued our relationship and was tired of the distance between us. More important, what separated us for so long was stupid and not worth the division. From then on, our relationship improved and we spoke often; it pained me that we had not been speaking all those months, but I hadn't known what to do, so I had chosen to do nothing. Dumb move.

It is very easy to form an opinion about someone who is a crabby, difficult person. If you are related and you must spend time with that person around the holidays, try to understand that this pain-in-the-butt person might be bitter and angry for reasons completely unrelated to his or her relationship with you or anyone in the room. Maybe he or she has lost a loved one, gotten screwed over, or is experiencing a devastating health crisis. A fearful or upset person may initially show anger when really this person is scared and sad deep down. Always give people the benefit of the doubt and try to discover who they are at their core.

When I turned sixteen, I hit a crossroads. My mother and I were not close at all, and my weekend visits with my father were making her increasingly bitchy and critical. When I was home, I spent my time in my safe space—my room. The day after my birthday, she asked me to leave and live with my father. She instructed me to return her birthday present, which I had no interest in anyway (it was a fancy watch I didn't want), and off I went to my room with a confident swagger that I had never known existed. Packing had never been more exciting.

Dad had been asking me to consider moving in with him and my stepmother, but now the decision was being made for me. Right in the middle of finals, I packed up my things and was told I had to stay in my room and was not allowed to leave the house until my father came to get me. She hired a friend who was a security guard to make sure I didn't run away. I had visions of tying my sheets together and hoisting myself out the window. Clearly, I watched way too much TV. In hindsight, I am so thankful I chose to wait for Dad and not risk losing any limbs.

January was Fashion Week in New York City, and because Dad owned a women's sportswear company, this was his huge yearly event. He also wanted to make sure I clearly wanted to live with him. "Where else would I go?" I thought, because there were no other options, except for maybe a chance to stay at my best friend's house. Dad seemed to legitimately love me, so I agreed to his offer that he had been hoping I would accept; he had been trying to get custody of me since I was a little girl, and up until now there had been no way my mother was going to let him win the power play.

Before I was asked to leave, Dad and I had finally started to spend time together over the weekends, and we barely knew each other. At one point, five years had gone by since I had seen him. Moving out of my mother's house turned out to be one of the best and bravest moments of my life. I am thankful she asked me to leave, because my living situation was toxic and emotionally wacko. I was always respectful, but was tired of being fearful and uneasy around her. Fast-forward to about ten years later. I was living in Boston, and Mom called me from her home in Tortola, one of the British Virgin Islands, wanting to connect. "I don't hate you," I said. "I just can't have anything to do with you." I spent my childhood emotionally and physically abused, and finally was brave enough to speak my mind in a calm manner. I felt safe and secure in my decisions. I had seen her only twice since she asked me to move out, and both times reaffirmed how disconnected we were. The distance between my mother and me saved my life. I was able to learn who I was and begin healing. How I saw myself was not who I really was. I had a warped sense of body image and very low self-esteem. When she said, "You will regret not knowing me," I knew enough to know I was severely emotionally scarred and trying my best to recover academically and emotionally. College was a few years away, and I needed to change my perception of myself and what I was capable of.

I kept the conversation very civilized and wished her well. The truth is, my mother was toxic and unhealthy for my mental and emotional well-being. We were never going to have a relationship, and I was okay with that. I chose my mental health over a relationship with my mother, and I had a limited emotional connection to her and longed for what I could never have—a real relationship. Everything I ever wanted in a mother was fantasy and not my reality. My father used to say when I was younger, "I wish your mother had been the woman she should have been." My response? "Dad, she would have been a completely different person and not the person you married." He was fortunate to have met my stepmother when I was five, and she became his devoted life partner.

We are all a work in progress; it is up to us to make the decision as to whether our family and friends are with us or against us. We make tough choices out of necessity. Surround yourself with people who adore you, support you, and have your back. Your inner circle should love your every scar and imperfection and cheer you on throughout life's bumpy ride.

CHAPTER 9

Tweens and Teens and
In-Betweens! Holy Sh*t!

"I hated high school. I don't trust anybody who looks back on the years from fourteen to eighteen with any enjoyment. If you liked being a teenager, there's something wrong with you."—Stephen King

Tweens and teens, and young adults, can easily experience funks. For everything from hormonal and social changes to the stress of everyday life and relationships, they need coping mechanisms and routines to keep them mentally and physically resilient. Health and wellness experts and psychologists have a slew of advice on how to pinpoint signs that kids are experiencing a funk, and why sleep, proper diet, and exercise are critical for maintaining health and well-being. If you have tweens, teens, or in-betweens, this chapter is loaded with funk-proof strategies for you. I am a mother. I feel your pain. Hang in there.

With topics including mood swings, raging hormones, and daily stressors, this chapter covers the rocky waters of tweens, teens, and young adults, and why these years can be extremely challenging and rewarding at the same time. If you have kids in any of these age groups, you already know that communicating with your kids can be a tough nut to crack; they can spend way too much time in their online worlds and less time focusing on what is right in front of them. They are growing and changing while being caught up in technology and online behavior that can be detrimental to their self-esteem, psychological development, and relationship building. There are certainly many benefits of using technology for meaningful purposes (for instance, using FaceTime for studying, connecting with people who are far away or not feeling well, keeping communication open, and so on). However, technology can suck kids into a vortex that is hard to get them out of and creates a barrier between you and them. The relationship you once knew can feel like a distant memory, and you will long for those younger years.

Knowing how to carve out quality time with teens is critical to building and maintaining healthy relationships and ongoing communication. Get to know their needs, interests, aspirations, and social circles (easier said than done). You may not love what they find intriguing as a hobby, but keep an open mind; they need to feel they can share their life with you and not feel judged. For example, your child might be a young slime entrepreneur and slime is not your cup of tea; that's fine but let your child share the new venture and excitement with you. You were a kid once, too.

Set ground rules and boundaries regarding phones. Be present and expect them to be present, too. No one should be texting at the dinner table or during a family outing when the point is to spend quality time together. There should also be "power down" time that everyone adheres to. Be firm and loving, so they understand there is no wiggle room with your phone policy. Technology serves a purpose, but overuse can be a detriment.

Maintain balance and enable your kids to grow and make some of their own decisions. (I say "some" because using their savings for a $1,500 iPhone is a bad choice.) Parents can feel shut out of a teen's life, and sadly, some might not even know their kids at all. It is critical that parents make time to connect, love unconditionally, and be a good listener when teens are ready to share; it might be tempting to lecture them and share "back in my day" stories, but you will lose their attention really quickly due to boredom and lack of interest. The eye roll is your blatant cue to put a sock in it.

If you're a parent, don't try to be your kids' best friend and solve their every problem. Ask your kids if they would like your advice or help with a situation; they may not want your input at all or, better yet, they might welcome what you have to say. Be open-minded and don't take it personally if they don't want your help. Be their mentor and confidant. Let them vent and feel that they can come to you with anything that is weighing them down. You want to teach them how to be a problem solver, figuring things out carefully, not impulsively, because after all, they will have plenty of problems to resolve throughout their lifetime.

Providing support, encouragement, and guidance is critical in these bumpy tween, teen, and college years. Let them do the talking and don't try to fix everything; it is important that they develop lifelong skills such as decision-making, time management, coping, and resilience, as well as strong moral values. Self-esteem, drive, and motivation can be influenced strongly by outside sources, and parents need to be the driving force in their child's mental and physical well-being. The teen years are challenging, which is why staying in communication and having a healthy relationship are beneficial to kids' long-term development. Yes, I know! Easier said than done. Just remember, you can't hold their hand every step of the way. Kids learn important lessons from their mistakes; they should never feel they are being criticized and put down when they mess up. Forget about being a helicopter parent or providing an overly protective bubble for your kids to inhabit. Our fears as parents can rub off on our kids so that we create these phobic little people who never want to leave the nest. Prepare them for the real world by letting them learn from failure and mishaps; this is how they learn and grow.

At one point or another, you may notice your kid is shutting you out. You get one- word answers when you ask, "How are you?" or, "How was your day?" "Fine...good," they respond flatly; they appear closed off and you don't know how to get through. You may feel like you are prying open a locked door, but don't give up. Try to spend as much quality time together as possible. Emphasize to your kids that they can come to you with any problem, at any time. Don't be a helicopter parent or the complete opposite, thinking they don't need any guidance or parameters. If you feel like you are having trust issues, and your intuition tells you something is wrong, trust your gut. You just might be right, but back up your feelings with facts. You don't want to come off as distrusting and accusatory. Kids have bad days, just like you and I. Be compassionate and empathetic. You were their age once. Make sure you have the facts, Jack.

If you never seem to be able to get your kids to open up, suggest talking with a therapist or a family member they are close to; there might be things they don't feel comfortable sharing with you, and that's okay. Help them help themselves, and do this in a very loving and supportive way. What are a few things you can do? Listen. Empathize. Show compassion. Ask if they would like your input and keep listening. Listen to what they say, how they say it, and why. Pay attention to their nonverbal cues, such as behavior. Do less talking and more listening. Try not to solve everything quickly and easily. There may be something deeper going on and they just need to know they can confide in you and share what they are going through.

A lot of times, if you ask your teen to try something new and different, you might receive pushback, excuses, and maybe a firm *no*. Sometimes kids are insecure and afraid to move outside of their comfort zones. Haven't we all felt that way at one time or another? I know I have! Think of all the things you fear the most and how you felt as a tween and teen. Some memories might be uncomfortable, right? Public speaking? Eeek! I would shake and stutter. Singing? Are you kidding?! I used to pretend to sing in high school while onstage with my classmates. I moved my mouth and nothing came out. Lip-synching queen! School dances? Major stress and discomfort. The list could go on.

The following techniques come in handy at any age; they will help your kids manage their daily struggles and encourage self-care routines and creative diversions. These suggestions promote mental health and wellness, while easing stress, anxiety, and depression. Offer to join them in these activities or encourage them to invite a friend (hopefully, you won't get any eye rolls). Do your best to encourage these practices on a daily or weekly basis; these routines and creative distractions can pave the way to adulthood.

Exercise

Exercise can be as simple as dancing to music, walking the dog, or taking a walk with a fun destination in mind. Some kids enjoy being part of a sports team in middle school and throughout high school. If joining a team is too competitive and not an option, find club sports outside of school; this is a great way to stay active, continue learning, and create new friendships. Daily exercise can improve sleep and can contribute to a healthier mood and metabolism. Find something you can do together or start a conversation to discover what they would like to do. Self-defense, rock climbing, tennis, skating, skiing, hiking, biking, running, and snowboarding are just a few ideas to get you started. The list is endless.

Some teens participate in after-school sports, while others only spend time on their phones and other electronic devices. We all need exercise to decompress, especially tweens and teens. It helps them sleep better and perform better in school, and their moods improve while their stress and anxiety decrease. On the weekends, consider creating a routine of walking, swimming, biking, hiking or doing any other activity together. Then grab a bite to eat to continue your quality time. Take turns choosing the activity and a meal you will both enjoy.

Meditation

Teen stress and anxiety can be just as bad as adults. In an article on psycom.net entitled "6 Common Triggers of Teen Stress," Kathleen Smith, PhD, points out that, "According to data collected by the American Psychological Association for the Stress in America Survey, teen stress rivals that of adults. Results of the survey show that not only do teens identify that their stress levels are not healthy, but they also underestimate the impact stress has on their mental and physical health," which is why kids need coping skills. Meditation can play an essential role in decreasing stress and depression. Meditation helps slow down impulsive and reactionary young brains and gets teens to think first about consequences and outcomes. Teenagers lack impulse control because there are biological issues at work. Meditation quiets the mind; improves focus, concentration, and memory; and increases self-esteem.

There are numerous types of meditation, such as breathing meditation, mindfulness meditation, and mantra meditation. Do your homework and find courses that meet your kids' needs and address their wellness issues. There are also online courses and meditation apps available. Apps are designed to help ease anxiety, depression, and stress. Meditation improves sleep, reduces trauma and PTSD, decreases anxiety when someone is in a stressful situation (for example, a test or surgery), and promotes healing from illness or a bad experience.

Kids can meditate while sitting in bed in the morning or in a quiet place during the day, or while walking or listening to music. Meditation can also be done while creating something, such as a drawing, painting, or a ceramic piece; it is not about the outcome but the process of creating art and how it makes someone feel. Meditation helps the mind focus, unwind, and clear the clutter.

Mindfulness

Mindfulness is a psychological process that focuses your attention on whatever is happening at this very moment. Meditation brings this awareness to the forefront and provides several benefits, such as promoting healthier sleep and improving creative thinking, which applies in and out of the classroom. When kids are creative and their ideas are flowing, they are less likely to be stuck in negative self-talk. Mindfulness promotes an increase in self-awareness, helping kids tune in to who they are and how they feel at that very moment, and focus less on the past and future.

Yoga

You might think that not very many kids would be interested in yoga classes, but kids of all ages practice yoga. Some schools offer yoga classes, which is a great outlet for stressed students. If you attend a weekly yoga class that is not too challenging, consider inviting your tween or teen along. If you get an immediate refusal, suggest getting a meal or snack afterward at your child's favorite place. Yes, I know. It's a bribe. Hey, sometimes bribes work, and then kids discover that yoga is pretty cool after all. They might see a familiar face in class or invite a friend. You just might create a weekly routine for the two of you...until all their friends come along and you are left in the dust, but hey. They now like yoga, so mission accomplished.

Create Your Own Routines

Weekly routines can be as simple as weekday meals, treats, pampering (facials, manicures, pedicures, and the like), weekend outings and activities (such as movie night, outdoor activities, trying new restaurants, or any activity that can be uplifting and something to look forward to). It's so easy to get wrapped up in "we're all so busy," but we all need to reconnect and slow down our pace from time to time. Ask for your kids' input and make sure to follow through on their suggestions.

Share your life with your kids. If you read something interesting, meet someone intriguing or start a new project or job, share all of that. Let your kids see that you have a life of your own, that you are a lifelong learner, and what you value in life. If nothing else, this will be a way for you to connect with your kids and have more meaningful conversations. Sharing your values and interests creates a deeper connection between you and your kids; what you do and say will be emulated, and they just might do the same for their kids someday.

Volunteering

Volunteering can turn into a lifelong passion. Of course, they might not want to explore this option at first, but there's a plethora of ideas out there. My earlier experience as a candy striper led me to an internship at a local hospital for three years during college, and then another internship at Tufts Medical Center after college. There are so many wonderful ways for tweens and teens to learn to love volunteering; they can find enjoyment doing something meaningful in their community, whether at a food bank, an animal shelter, a retirement center, or a community radio station.

Do the Unexpected and Find your Fun!

Surprising your young or older kids with a fun activity will do wonders for their mood and your relationship. Keep in mind that your "great" idea might be boring and mortifying to them. Make a conscious effort to not embarrass them and look like you have no clue. Trust me. Your efforts will be worth it, but just don't choose something radical that you think they might like. Find things that you know will perk up their mood and form a bond between you. If you have no idea, ask them. Maybe they just want a day off with a friend to go hit the mall or a local eatery. We all need downtime, and the unexpected breaks can be the best.

Create a Clean, Chill Space

Some men have man caves and women do, too, but what about tweens, teens, and in-betweens? Everyone needs a place that helps them unwind and enables them to take a deep breath from their nonstop busy life. It doesn't have to be a huge space, and your kids might choose an area you would never have thought of, like the garage. Let them decide. Declutter an unused spare bedroom and let them decorate the area according to their tastes and interests. Even a little nook near a window with a great view can work the same magic. Having a chill space is great for anyone, because it's a place to unwind, reflect, and find clarity in the stillness.

Be a Role Model

Your verbal and nonverbal behaviors make a big impression on how your tweens or teens perceive their world. To this day, I can hear my father yelling at someone as he drove too close to the person's bumper. He was constantly swearing and berating people as they drove, and I never wanted to emulate his behavior. Until one day...I was driving with my younger infant daughter and someone cut me off. I yelled, "A**hole!" very loudly...but I forgot my infant was in the backseat. All of a sudden, I heard a very young voice shouting, "Aah-hole!" OMG! Panic set in. Worst Mom Award goes to...*me!* I quickly yelled out, "Applesauce!" She liked that word a lot better, and we yelled it all the way home. Nothing like a little reality slap from your child to set you straight.

How you treat your kids will come back and bite you in the ass one day, so behave. Kids who are mistreated are more likely to take out their baggage on someone else or their future kids, and there will be long-term emotional repercussions. Everything you say and do, the behavior you model, can be mirrored in your kids. If you need help in parenting (no one ever said it was easy), get help. You will become a better parent and a better person. You can break the cycle of bad behavior. Kids are precious, innocent little beings who should never be mistreated or abused emotionally or physically. If this speaks to you, please get help for your sake and theirs.

The Power of Sleep

We can't cheat our bodies of sleep. Sleep impacts everything, including our mental, physical, and emotional states. Without sleep, we lose focus, throw off our metabolism, gain weight, become moody and anxious, feel off-kilter, and develop unhealthy habits (such as consuming too much caffeine and eating poorly). In college, I once tried staying up cramming for an exam, and by four thirty in the morning I thought, "I'll just take a little nap...zzzzzz." Ha! I woke up and realized I overslept and missed the exam. When I sprinted to the classroom, there was no one there. Cheating your body of sleep doesn't work.

What happens when *you* don't get enough sleep? Do you feel a little bitchy? Exhausted? Dizzy? Have a lack of focus? Feel out of sorts? Crave sweets and caffeine? How about feeling anxious and depressed? If you're a parent, you remember those newborn days when you were up at all hours of the night and you felt like a train wreck the next day, because you saw the sunrise and wish you hadn't. And if you didn't get enough sleep, depression might rear its ugly head. Well, the same things happen to teens. They have problems staying focused and regulating their emotions and impulses. Emotions are very affected by lack of sleep, and teens' brains are still developing; they need sleep to continue growing and performing effectively. When they stay up late on their phone or tackling heaps of homework, they will not feel and perform their best the next day. Students who don't get proper rest and try to compensate with caffeine and energy drinks are kidding themselves; they might even fall asleep in class. Sleep is key for proper health and wellness and affects mood, metabolism, the nervous system, and more.

The National Sleep Foundation (www.sleepfoundation.org) reported that lack of sleep affects us physically, mentally and emotionally. In their article entitled "The Complex Relationship Between Sleep, Depression & Anxiety," they point out the correlation between sleep and mood. "If you're feeling low, you may not realize that lack of sleep is the culprit. But even small levels of sleep deprivation over time can chip away at your happiness. You might see that you're less enthusiastic, more irritable, or even have some of the symptoms of clinical depression, such as feeling persistently sad or empty. All these alterations to your mood can affect not only your individual mental health, but your relationships and family dynamics as well."

If your kid looks exhausted or seems to be getting sick, insist on a nap. Yes, I know. Some people don't like how they are in a foggy haze when they awaken. However, a twenty- to thirty-minute nap will recharge the mind. If there is a bigger sleep debt or illness, consider a longer nap. Our bodies usually tell us what we need. You can't fight sleep debt, especially when you are struggling to keep your eyes open; it's a losing battle.

Create Sleep Routines

I believe in routines, because I know what happens when kids have bad nighttime rituals or none at all. The habits they start at a young age will be ingrained and carry on through adulthood.

Try some of these nighttime policies:

- No TV in the bedroom
- No phones or technology in the bedroom, and devices turned off at least an hour before bedtime
- Dim the lights (create a wind-down ambiance)
- Avoid unpleasant people and conversations that would keep your kids from winding down
- Encourage kids to listen to music that relaxes them
- Recommend some books or "fluff" reading (such as magazines) to calm the mind
- Suggest a shower or bath
- Encourage them to have a clean, relaxing bed waiting for slumber

Teach your tweens and teens to free themselves of distractions as they wind down; it is always a good idea to tune out the world at a certain hour. Everything will be there the next day. You might feel like you are talking to a wall trying to convince your kid that sleep routines matter. Don't resort to nagging—or worse, yelling.

Kids do come around sooner or later. They need us more than they want to admit.

Establish a bedtime routine; this is good for your kids and you (who doesn't like downtime?). Being overscheduled and glued to a phone late at night can and will cause numerous problems. Social media is an addiction that is detrimental mentally and emotionally. Remember—whatever they have is yours. A phone is a privilege that you own; you pay the bill, and therefore it is your phone. You set the ground rules. Think about the expense of that hypnotic, tethered device—the phone itself and then the monthly fee. Reeling in screen time will be a battle at times, but be vigilant.

Sugary foods before bed also affect quality of sleep and performance the next day. Kids need to learn what foods work best for their bodies, and when they are hungry late at night what choices to make. Clean out your junk food pantry; it is harder to eat poorly if you don't have crappy food in the house. I am not saying load your refrigerator with tofu and broccoli for their late-night snacks. Have better choices than traditional processed junk food. Your kids won't think you are from another planet if you teach them about health and nutrition at a young age and make changes they can understand and live by.

The Ripple Effect of Food and Diet

Many kids start their day with a trip to their local Starbucks or other coffeehouse. Some choose drinks amped up with so much sugar, while others opt for coffee concoctions. Sugar and caffeine—not a great way for anyone to start the day. I admit to drinking coffee, but my days of drinking a sugary hot chocolate and scarfing down a glazed doughnut for breakfast are in my rearview mirror. By lunchtime, I was exhausted from the crash of the sugar high. I had zero energy and no attention span in school.

If you have tweens and teens, try to keep tabs on what foods and drinks they start their day with. Sometimes it is impossible to know what goes on at school with your kid's diet. Just know that there can be a domino effect with everything they put in their body. If your kid gets sick easily, keep tabs on foods that impact their immune system. For me, sugar, gluten, and dairy are no-nos. And I was the queen of dairy and chocolate as a kid—with a side of eczema and other issues. No one was going to come between me and my M&Ms or bacon double cheeseburgers. Not even my chronic immune issues.

Massage

Massages are a great way to ease teenage stress and anxiety. Choose a female masseuse and sit in the room while your tween or teen gets the massage; it also helps to have an experienced masseuse who has worked with kids before. For teens who compete in sports, getting a massage eases sore muscles and alleviates anxiety. Kids have more stress than most adults realize, and treating them to a massage improves their mood, reduces stress and anxiety, and improves sleep and overall mental and physical well-being. They have their own smorgasbord of stress, and we need to be compassionate and understanding. A massage is a great mental and physical de-stressor at any age. Treating your kid to a massage can bring about a completely different mindset and mood change in your home and at school.

Staycations

Encourage your kids to take a staycation and explore your local surroundings, checking out events, restaurants, and other seasonal happenings together. You can also have a staycation without leaving the house. Ideas include a spa day, a movie night, hanging out in a tent in the backyard, catching up on reading or favorite shows, taking a break from technology and disconnecting from the world, cooking, crafting, or whatever else your tween or teen is into. Sometimes wearing pajamas all day and having a low-key, no-plans day is just what we all need.

Journaling

Expressing what they are feeling is an important lifelong tool for kids. Many kids feel comfortable sharing their feelings and experiences in a personal journal. Writing is a wonderful way to dump out everything that is going on without feeling judged and worried someone will read what was written; it also helps people process whatever it is they are going through and work through issues.

Group and Individual Therapy

Kids won't always talk to adults, but they will open up to their peers, especially when they feel kids their age are going through similar stuff. Some of the greatest breakthroughs with kids happen in group therapy, when tweens and teens are aligned with kids facing similar issues. When kids have a safe space, filled with activities, trained facilitators, and strategies designed to foster openness, creativity, and the safe expression of pent-up feelings and experiences, they can begin to heal and work through their issues. No one should suffer in silence. There are numerous helpful resources out there. Sometimes there is only so much you can do as a parent and outside help is needed.

Individualized therapy can help kids get back on track and express things they don't want to share with anyone else. When they connect with a therapist, they have an opportunity to express what they otherwise keep trapped inside. Listen up: That is okay. Don't try to pry whatever it is out of them if they don't want to share right now. Everyone needs to have a safe space and a confidant. The world is a very complicated, anxious place at the moment. Many kids are dealing with high levels of stress, PTSD, anxiety, and depression. If you suspect your kids are struggling, encourage them to see a therapist and work out whatever is troubling them. It's not a sign of failure that you can't help your kids through a rough patch. You are helping them by getting them help. Therapy is a smart move, because doing nothing can be detrimental; it's not healthy for anyone to feel that he or she is alone with no one to help in a time of crisis.

Positive Self-Talk and Affirmations

Think about all the self-hatred and loathing many of us have for ourselves, such as poor body image, a warped sense of self, negative self-talk, and feelings of inadequacy and self-doubt. Well, tweens and teens and in-betweens go through the same exact thing. What if we flipped those internal conversations and negative self-talks and focused on the positive narrative? Kids are so tough on themselves, and for many, their world is wrapped up in how many likes and comments they receive after posting a picture of their new haircut, slimmer body, or outfit. Why do we define ourselves by what others think? What matters is how we feel in our own skin. Encourage your kids to be unique and brave and to pursue what they want in their lifetime, not what they think is expected of them. Never forget to tell your kids or others you know that they are doing well, and you are proud of them. Encourage them to focus on the present, not dwell in the past or worry about the future.

The Power of Pets

Consider adopting a dog or cat from a shelter, but only if you and your kids decide you all have the time, energy, and dedication to care for a pet; it's a big commitment and should be a team effort. Like to travel? You won't be doing much if you commit to a big dog at home and don't have backup doggie care. Think realistically and honestly, because these decisions should not be made impulsively and selfishly. With the right mindset, having a pet can be wonderful and give you years of companionship. Can't commit to a dog? Consider getting some fish or another animal that needs less attention. Your home will feel a little less lonely when you have another creature to care for.

ASMR

Have you heard of ASMR (autonomous sensory meridian response)? I had not either until my teenage daughter showed me some videos that she was watching to relax at night. ASMR videos have become a visual and auditory sensation on-line, because viewers love seeing and hearing sounds that relax and sooth them. According to *www.theasmr.com*, "ASMR refers to the Autonomous Sensory Meridian Response and it is a physical tingling sensation that begins in your scalp and moves down through the spine to the limbs." The website, theasmr.com, indicates that it is usually triggered by audible stimulus such as "whispering or scratching, though it can also be triggered through physical touch. ASMR is also referred to as Attention Induced Head Orgasm (AIHO) or Attention Induced Euphoria (AIE)."

If you look up ASMR on Instagram, you will find over five million posts that show everything from eating, whispering, tapping, cutting soap, playing with slime, and more. YouTube is loaded with an assortment of ASMR videos, too. Some people (not me) find the sounds of people eating a honeycomb close to a microphone soothing, but you might as well scratch your nails on a blackboard if I have to listen to someone munching away. I tried to be open-minded while watching someone assemble their fast-food double decker piled high with everything, including fries squished into the heap, but as soon as I heard him chomping away, I was done. There are plenty of other sounds that are calming, induce sleep, reduce anxiety, and might give you a "tingling sensation" in response to certain sounds; this experience has also been described as a head orgasm, because it can give you the chills from head to toe. Certain stimuli can cause ASMR, and what is soothing for one person may be irritating to others. Some people watch the videos to help them sleep or relax, and the videos might even help with anxiety and depression.

Find Your Creative Jam—Coloring, Drawing, and Other Creative Pursuits

Coloring is not just for young kids. Anyone at any age can find enjoyment in coloring books; this creative outlet is calming and feels like a meditative experience. Coloring benefits our minds, bodies, and mental well-being. When we color, we experience stillness, calm, and less stress; it may also reduce anxiety and depression. Spark your kids' coloring interests by giving them a creative gift bag that includes a notebook or journal with a cover design that they would like, markers, pens, coloring books that reflect their interests, and other crafty items to spark creativity.

There is another activity that has become wildly popularly with kids and adults. If you haven't already noticed, slime has made a huge comeback, but it's a completely different amped-up version of the gooey, sticky green substance introduced by Mattel in 1976 and featured in movies and TV shows. DIY slime making has exploded, and it's not just tweens and teens making their own unique slime creations. Adults are developing and marketing their own slimes with textures and aromas as diverse as the creators. Playing with slime is relaxing because of the tactile sensations and the wide variety of aromas that slime creators develop. Just closing your eyes and smelling one of these slimes can be soothing and relaxing, like smelling a freshly baked cookie or fruity cereal. People also enjoy the sound slime makes when they press their fingers into it. Slime creation has become a wildly popular creative science experiment amped up to a whole other level of fun and self-expression.

The textures, smells, and marketing of slime have become extremely expansive. Slime types include clear, fluffy, thick, glossy, crunchy, buttery, snow butter, and cloud. Some slimes smell just like cherry Coke, Oreos and milk, a piña colada, bubble gum, pumpkin pie, and popular kids' cereals from the 1960s (Froot Loops and Captain Crunch). There are even glow-in-the-dark slimes, slimes that self-inflate, and slimes with Floam beads or other clever add-ons and accents. The colors and consistencies of slimes have no limit.

The marketing of slimes, creative packaging, and slime videos promoted on Instagram, YouTube, and other social networks have enthralled a growing online audience. As the slime community continues to expand, parents are seeing slime creation as a great outlet for old-school fun, and a way for kids to go from slime amateurs to slime entrepreneurs. Successful "slimers" can attract huge followings on Instagram and land sponsorships on YouTube. Some kids send handwritten letters with their slime orders and meet up at slime conventions and events around the country.

Slime events are a healthy social outlet for kids to meet other like-minded slimers all over the world, grow a slime business, and have some fun in the process. Some slimers become so famous on Instagram that devoted, adoring fans come from all over to meet them. There is no limit to what slimers can create and market, so before you say no based on the messiness or expense of making slime, consider the positive outcomes as well. Special thanks to @ sslimegirls on Instagram for sharing her expertise and helping craft this section.

Art Therapy

Creativity is like medicine—or better yet, like a mental vacation. You immerse yourself in something that takes you away mentally and brings a smile or a new feeling to your day. The experience of creative expression has been shown to have a positive impact on emotions, mental and physical health, and overall well-being. Moods are lifted and creative inspiration flows. There is nothing like expressing thoughts and emotions in a piece of art, either in a solo or group experience.

Wellness Retreats and Specialized Teen Therapy Groups

If your tween or teen is suffering emotionally, consider a wellness retreat or an outpatient teen group specifically designed for kids with anxiety, depression, and PTSD. Ask your health-care provider to assess your child's needs and recommend a group therapy program. Classroom activities are designed to relax kids, help release suppressed thoughts and feelings, and help heal depression, anxiety, and self-destructive behavior. An effective program will meet your kids' needs and provide an experience that teaches coping skills, relaxation techniques, and self-care, while enabling them to make new connections and finish the program with a brighter outlook. If your kid needs more intensive therapy, consider a wellness retreat for teens. Do your homework and find highly rated wellness programs; these include mindfulness retreats that incorporate emotional support animals, such as horses and dogs. Find programs that fit your child's emotional needs and interests. Keep in mind that your kid might not support the idea of going away to a retreat, but in the long run these programs have been shown to make a difference in kids' lives.

Self-Care for Tweens, Teens and Young Adults— Why It Matters

Take a close look at your kids' daily eating, sleeping, and self-care routines. For example, do they bathe regularly? Do they forget or not care about showering and need reminding? Sometimes when people do not bathe regularly, this is a sign that they are wrapped up in their inner world and that taking care of themselves is the last thing on their mind. Pay attention to the nonverbal cues and behaviors. You might think your kids don't need your advice and guidance about basic self-care routines, but if you suspect something is wrong, you have the right to be concerned and guide them. After all, once they leave the nest, they need to know about the proper care and maintenance of their grown-up selves. Now is the time to teach them.

Do you allow phones in their rooms? Do you have a cutoff time and monitor their screen time? Again, some parents are very lenient and think a junior in high school can be left alone to decide, but not where I live. The first thing to be compromised is their sleep, then their health and academic success. After a certain hour in my house, phones are turned off and kept downstairs; this rule has been in place for years.

There is no reason for tweens or teens to have a phone in their room at night. Sleep is critical for physical, mental, and emotional development, and phones are a detriment to your kids' well-being; they are even a detriment to adults! We are just as guilty of tech addiction, and we pay the price in our relationships and physical and mental states. Think I am wrong? One of my show guests, Catherine Price, wrote a great book called *How to Break Up with Your Phone: The 30-Day Plan to Take Back Your Life*. Detaching yourself from your phone can be freeing, and you will be amazed by how much newfound time you have and how much time you've been wasting, and your kids might actually talk to you if you all do a tech cleanse. Break up with your phone and see what happens. Encourage your tweens or teens to keep their phones tucked away when you are spending time together. Keep yours tucked away, too. Set yourself up for quality one-on-one time. You'll begin to realize how obsessed you are with checking your phone way too often, and the extra phone-free time will open up your mind to other activities that don't involve a phone.

You Are What You Eat

Snack monster. Junk food junkie. Chocoholic. You know the labels. There are plenty of others. You might have even worn one of these labels when you were younger. Take a close look at what you and your kids are eating. The following is a list of ingredients that are known to be detrimental to health; this is not a complete list. Do your homework and read labels before you make purchases. If you are not familiar with the following food additives and artificial ingredients, look them up. You will be glad you did. Be an educated shopper, not a passive consumer. What we eat affects our health and wellness long-term. If you notice a change in your kid's immune system, it might be due to eating something that is inflammatory to his or her system. Here is a list of ingredients to avoid completely:

- Monosodium glutamate (MSG)
- Butylated hydroxyanisole (BHA)
- Butylated hydroxytoluene (BHT)
- Artificial food coloring, such as Red # 2, #3, and #40; Blue #1 and #2; Green #3; and Yellow #5 and #6
- Nitrite (sodium nitrate)
- Carrageenan

- Olestra
- Artificial sweeteners
- Partially hydrogenated oil
- High-fructose corn syrup
- Recombinant bovine growth hormone (rBGH)
- Polysorbate 60
- Parabens

Processed foods include many unhealthy ingredients; they might be fast and convenient, but there is a negative backlash to these choices. Kids pay the price by having poor health, an inability to concentrate at school, and sicknesses from a weak immune system. For kids who have immune disorders, especially skin and asthma conditions, real food is always a better choice, especially organic fruits and vegetables that have no pesticides or synthetic fertilizers and are not genetically modified organisms (GMOs).

Academic Funks Can Be a Nightmare

I was a nightmare student when I was younger. I didn't think it was possible, but I received the lowest grade in my seventh-grade language class, an F minus. Talk about being *ferblunjit* (confused/ mixed up)! Getting an F minus lowered my self-esteem and left me in a perpetual funk. I was intimidated by my classmates and thought I was the stupidest student in the school. Even when I did try to study subjects that challenged me, such as science and math, I could never achieve more than a passing grade. I did create a kick-ass dirty limerick to help me memorize the parts of a cell in biology. Epic fail.

I had the attention span of an ant, no focus when it came to reading, and zero time management skills. Was it my diet, lack of sleep, and home life? Probably a combination of all three, but I also had no idea how to learn, focus, study, and stay on top of my work. On more than one occasion, there I was the night before a big project, trying to create something I should have started weeks ago. One evening, I casually asked my mother and stepfather if they knew how to build a Sumerian temple; it was due the next day. They looked at me in shock. At three in the morning, I was exhausted and upset, because I had accidently glued my fingers together with Krazy Glue. By the next morning, I was horrified to see my Sumerian project sunken down into a melted clay mess. I quietly placed my disaster project down on the display table next to the perfectly crafted Parthenon and Egyptian artwork (maybe their makers had mostly been assisted by parents); they were clearly getting an A. At least it was obvious I had done my project by myself. Unfortunately, I was the only one in the room who knew what my project was. I am lucky no one tried to eat it, because it resembled an undercooked lumpy vanilla sheet cake.

My academic flops didn't stop there. I went through a really dumb cheating phase, but I was a very bad cheater, so it was an epic fail (a great lesson). I attempted to cram for a science test I had missed by asking a fellow classmate to look at her exam. My lack of preparation was blatantly obvious, and I thought I could wing it and take a shortcut…the morning of the test. Within seconds, my science teacher, who was also my basketball coach, caught me. I was such a bad cheater. I looked like a deer in the headlights of a Mack truck.

Let's just say that being suspended from my new school in eighth grade was so humiliating, but it was an important painful lesson. There was the tearful meeting with the principal and my dad, who had to take time away from his Manhattan business for my stupid antics that ruined his day. I was mortified and ashamed. He was so understanding and could see I was devastated by my dumbass mistake. Karma is a bitch, but I needed to get busted. The best thing I did was attend summer school that year to repeat English and math class. With a lot of hard work, I shocked myself and my father. I got As in both classes and learned how to be a much better student; this was just what I needed. Previously I had never believed I was capable of good grades, but with Dad's direction I could see anything was possible. I managed to stay out of trouble for at least two years before I was busted by karma once again; this time hit me hard because I thought I could cut corners on a midterm paper about Macbeth. The problem was, I could not comprehend the text, so I was incredibly lost and never asked for help.

My stupidity this time was using Monarch notes (now SparkNotes are popular) to write my paper on Macbeth. I could not get through the actual book, because my eyes would cross at every attempt and nothing would sink in. So, I had another (dumb) plan. The problem was, several other classmates in a class of fifteen chose the same sophisticated descriptions to include in their papers, too. We were all suspended and sobbing. From that point on, I never, ever, took another shortcut; it wasn't worth cheating the system, and I certainly never learned a thing by skirting the issue when the subject matter was hard. I needed to own up to my sneaky attempts and just "learn the damn material," as Dad would say. I was fortunate that each time I screwed up, he knew that the humiliation and embarrassment were enough punishment; he didn't need to lay into me more and cause additional hurt. Did I ever learn to love Shakespeare? Not a chance. I attended the play in New York City with my classmates and fell asleep. I thought I would die of boredom and had no clue what anyone was saying, but I had the best nap.

When I moved in with my dad at age sixteen, I was on the road to some miraculous achievements, but there would be a lot of hard work to get there. He didn't waste any time sitting me down and asking me whether I had ever asked the teachers for help. I always thought I could get out of my academic quicksand myself, but that was obviously not working. With tears in my eyes, I admitted that I had never once asked my teachers for help, and he strongly suggested I give it a try. Without fail, he could tell that when my grades did not improve, I had not heeded his advice. The reason was, I felt stupid and did not think I could grasp the information. I thought it was impossible for me, a girl with poor study habits and very little prerequisite math skills, to ever pull off an A in math. When I moved in at the start of my second semester of tenth grade, I was an academic disaster; this was unacceptable. I needed a miracle to pull my grades up.

My successes after moving in with my father are nothing short of that miracle. I became a varsity athlete, because he believed I could make the basketball team. I was certainly not one of the best players. I could barely keep track of all the rules and strategic moves. I just tried my best, showed up, and tried not to get pummeled.

The one sport that I loved from the start was lacrosse. Dad would cheer me on when I started as goalie (I looked like a giant marshmallow in head-to-toe padding—a female version of the Pillsbury Doughboy), and he attended numerous games when I became co-captain and a much stronger player. He would miss work in Manhattan and stand in the rain and watch every minute of the game. Dad's support academically and athletically reversed years of mental anguish and verbal and physical abuse. He taught me the power of humor, hard work, a quick wit, and the confidence to speak my mind; these have been invaluable life skills.

One by one, I hesitantly approached my teachers, and they were more than happy to assist me on my academic road to recovery. I met with them routinely after school and before school, and my whole life changed. I was no longer afraid to admit failure. I would raise my hand and often be the only student to say, "I am lost. I don't get it." When teachers would ask the class whether anyone was confused by what had just been explained, I was the first to raise my hand. Over time, I got used to being very blunt about my inability to grasp specific information. I am pretty sure my classmates were equally lost at times but didn't have the nerve to admit it. I would boldly go where no classmate would go, as I raised my hand proudly, with a smile and often a laugh. "Yup! I'm lost! No idea what you just said," I would say. Nothing awful happened when I admitted my confusion. The world never ended. No one judged me. And my teachers worked so hard to help me understand what I was missing. By the end of the year, I was an A student in math. I had just needed to take that first step and admit my brain was mush, and fully commit to putting in the work; it all paid off, and soon I wasn't feeling so dumb after all. I was ready for college, or so I thought.

I carried this new mindset with me throughout college. When my statistics teacher asked us what the answer to a complicated equation was, almost everyone blurted out the correct answer... except me. I smiled and continued to try my best. When they were all shouting, "Eight!" I was yelling, "Twenty-one!" But I was no longer embarrassed; I was trying my best, failing miserably, and smiling though my blunders. But there I was after class, running up to the teacher to see when he would be holding extra-help sessions. With lots of effort, I got an A in that class, too. I no longer felt shy and stupid. I also never felt stressed when my grades were not as good as I'd hoped for. I felt confident that things would always get better and any negative setbacks would be temporary. I knew that if I didn't speak up right away at the beginning that the subject matter would only become more difficult, and my lack of understanding would continue to escalate. I knew I needed to master each step in order to comprehend the entire course, instead of pretending to understand areas that confused me.

During college orientation at Syracuse University, I didn't realize that Dad was chatting with the crew team coach. Apparently, he mentioned that I would try out for the team, but I had zero experience. "What did you do?!" I barked at Dad (half laughing and half shocked), but he smiled and said it would be fun and a new experience. I had no idea what this all meant, but I showed up at tryouts and made the team. Clueless but willing.

I learned not to say no to new things, whether they were new sports or summer jobs. I was recruited to paint houses, and I thought that sounded better than working at the dry cleaner for a fourth summer. When selling ice cream in a truck proved to be a bad financial undertaking, I took the painting job, and by the end of the summer, my manager made me foreperson. I had the best tanned legs and overcame my fear of heights on forty-foot ladders, but I had so much paint in my hair; it was impossible to get out.

The summer of my junior year of college, I was supposed to waitress at a campus restaurant where I worked during the year. Days before graduation, we watched as a fire engulfed our family-owned restaurant. Many of us had been there when it opened, struggling to pronounce new words like "hummus" and "baba ghanoush." Since I had already paid my summer rent, I convinced Dad to let me stay in Syracuse and waitress at another local restaurant; it was really a bartending and waitress job, but it sounded better to leave that out. I had zero experience bartending, but I was highly praised by very old and gregariously friendly, drunk men ordering ten-cent beers at nine in the morning on a Sunday, laughing uproariously at the Three Stooges. The tips were barely enough to buy groceries for the week, so I tried to sell water filtration systems with a free set of steak knives (another epic fail). I finally fessed up and told Dad I was a bartender, and the pay was close to nothing; he was shocked but praised me for trying anything to make my rent payments. Not my proudest moment, but I learned a lot about myself, my perseverance, and two important lessons: never get a summer job where you go to school, because it's probably a ghost town, and the beer tastes like skunk water.

Dad constantly kept me open to change and newness. There was never failure. When I felt lost in my career and my personal life flopped, he simply said, "Well, I guess it's time to get your doctorate." His philosophy was simple: never stop learning, growing, and moving forward. It wasn't until my father passed away that I realized he'd had about nine careers and there wasn't a moment he wallowed in failure. He just kept going and kept his optimistic path open to new opportunities. Nothing he did was a waste of time. There were only steppingstones to something else. These lessons have become my armor through life to face funks head-on.

My father's words prepared me for any challenges that came my way. My high school guidance counselor once told me I would never get into college. That made me work even harder to prove her wrong. Criticism can be great fuel for your fire. Determination and perseverance are unshakeable once you find your focus and path and learn how to learn. Finding mentors who guide you and believe in you is everything, but you must also want to do the work. In life, you have to put in the work and give 100 percent of whatever you can.

Yeah, College! Woo-Hoo! Uh, Now What?

When kids go off to college, they are not automatically adults. They still have a lot to learn. Not all students are ready for their newfound independence; some lack self-care knowledge and the skills needed for college life. The focus in high school (a cause of stress) is on getting into college, which involves achieving high SAT and ACT scores, prepping for AP tests, and getting "good" grades. No one prepares students for what to expect in college. Most of us wing it; that's part of growing up. Here are some key skills and knowledge students need to have in order to be self-sufficient and stay mentally and physically healthy.

College students need to learn:

- Effective study strategies and how to create routines (where and when they will study and get work done; how to manage their time, distractions, and peer pressure; when to "blow it off and go party" or do something else that seems a lot more fun than schoolwork)

- How to network on campus, including joining clubs and organizations that expand their social life, build relationships, and create new experiences

- What sorority or fraternity life is like and why it can be a great decision for some to be part of it, especially in freshman year when they know very few people and want to feel part of something meaningful, feel less alone, and create close personal relationships

- How to be self-sufficient. For some students, this is the first time they have been away from home. Going to college is the first step towards adulthood, and they are responsible for their mental, physical, and emotional well-being. They need to know what to do when they get sick, whom they can reach out to, where the health center is, and what procedures are in place if the illness requires them to miss classes and meals. For example, students would head to the health center, inform their resident advisor (RA), and they see if a roommate or friend can get food for them if they are too sick to leave their room. Most schools have a plan in place for when illness strikes.

- How to handle loneliness; this can be a terrible experience for freshmen. Keep tabs on your college student so he or she can maintain mental and emotional health throughout the college years.

- How to deal with conflict (such as with their roommates, teachers, or fellow students)

- How to make decisions that positively impact their physical, emotional, and mental well-being

- What to do if they become homesick

- What to do if there is a campus emergency due to an unforeseen circumstance (such as a local fire); whom they can turn to for help and a place to stay

- If there is a class specifically for freshmen, they should sign up! Being with other newbies is a great way to learn more about the freshman experience at school and connect with kids the same age, who are probably having the same feelings.

- Whom they can talk to and share their concerns with

- How to avoid the "freshman fifteen"

- Stress reduction strategies (mindfulness, meditation, yoga, exercise)

- The power of sleep

- Personality theory and how to find out who they are and directions they should explore

- How to handle stressful situations and use coping strategies

- The difference between being alone and loneliness

- Pushing themselves outside their comfort zone

- Finding mentors and counselors for a support team

- Taking on leadership roles

- Building healthy relationships

- Strategies to get over public speaking jitters

- School resources to help them succeed

- Extracurricular activities offered at their school

- School strategies for managing stress, anxiety, and depression

The tough moments students face in college are learning moments that teach them something about themselves—their resilience and grit. This is why self-care is critical throughout college, especially in freshman year.

When All I Had to Worry About Was Dog Sh*t!

Occasionally, I reflect on my childhood, playing and roller skating on the sidewalks of New York City. Fearless and oblivious. The only thing I worried about was wiping out in dog doo (really happened). I had no worries about my safety and well-being. There were no thoughts of being taken or hurt. Well, my mother did tell me that if someone tried to kidnap me, I should fall to the ground and scream, "I need my medication!" at the top of my lungs; this was the scariest scenario and one I hoped would never happen, and besides, what medication would I say I needed? My Luden's cherry cough drops?

Life was easier when I couldn't call home, text, and obsessively use antibacterial wipes. New York was messy and smelly from the garbage strikes, noise, and city pollution, but I loved the busy, chaotic flow of the city. I walked everywhere, took cabs and buses at all hours of the day. There was never a moment of fear, only of adventure, even when a cab driver picked me up with an entire marijuana bush in his front seat and a big lit joint dangling from his lips. My eleven-year-old self was clueless.

I could be gone for hours and not communicate with anyone, and no one worried. Yes, I was depressed because I hated school, my home life was a train wreck, and strangers creeped me out at times, but New York was my playground and my home. I never hesitated at nine years old on a Sunday to walk the empty streets and go to a PG movie alone. I had my two boxes of candy, and there wasn't much more I needed. People-watching was a favorite pastime, and I became an expert in how to divert attention if someone creepy stared too long.

Sure, New York was filled with chaos, seedy Times Square businesses, muggings, and graffiti-filled subways, and there was one scary news story I remember—about Son of Sam. But we didn't have teenagers toting assault rifles, active shooter drills, discussions about teachers carrying weapons, teen suicides due to bullying, and shootings in movie theaters, concerts, churches, and schools. What happened to our world, our sense of well-being and safety? The kids today are scared to do the simplest things, like go to school and get the mail. And when they are not worried about their safety, their concerns turn to academic pressure and expectations that have escalated to an all-time high.

The technology they hold in the palm of their hands has created a world where teens experience enormous amounts of stress, anxiety, and depression. They can see and hear the most gruesome details 24/7. Many are losing sleep and spending hours immersed in their online worlds, looking for acceptance, praise, and connection on social media and in chat rooms. Phones are the first and last thing they reach for. They are stress cases who are trying to balance academic achievement, athletics, SAT scores, and the end game: landing in a "great" school.

What happens when teens can't handle the pressure? They feel overwhelmed by the stress of school, family, their peers, and society. They implode. They hide in their inner worlds and desire to escape the stress of their daily lives. We need to make mental health a number-one priority, because somewhere along the way our priorities got all screwed up. Kids are the future, and their mental health must come first. We can't make them live a life that we once had or wanted to achieve. They have one life to live and it's their own, filled with their own choices. Some will be good choices and some will be bad, but that's how they learn. Isn't that how we all learn? We fall down and we find ourselves in the messiness of life, and then we put ourselves back together and figure it all out.

Mental health must be more important than grades. As a parent, you can push and encourage your kids to believe that grades are everything because the reward is getting into a "great" school, but what happens when, after all their efforts, they don't get into the school they wanted? The same thing happens when you push them to be a varsity athlete and unfortunately, they get an injury that changes their trajectory; they might be sidelined and not able to play after years of training and pressure to succeed. What happens to their self-esteem then? They experience a huge letdown, depression, low self-esteem, and a domino effect of negative consequences. Athletic and academic rejections sting, especially around the time students find out what schools they did not get into; this is why we need to prioritize mental health and how they handle rejection, disappointment, and life after high school. Even the kids who land in their dream school experience stress and question their decision when life gets overwhelming socially and academically.

We need to focus on the mental and physical well-being of our kids, because the Bs they get in math class today have nothing to do with their future success. If they bomb their SATs, that doesn't mean they won't earn a PhD later in life, create an award-winning film, write an emotionally moving book, or live their dream of being a successful entrepreneur. If they are riddled with anxiety and stressed out, kids miss out on having a healthy, balanced life, being present in their everyday activities, and living a life in which their happiness and mental health are top priorities. Kids need balance in their lives and a sounding board for their problems and concerns, and most important, they should know that the world will not end if they don't get all As. You will love them unconditionally. I sure hope so. Repeat after me: "I will love them unconditionally."

Being a kid today is vastly different from my childhood. Kids grow up very fast, seeing and experiencing too much, trying to act older than they really are and rushing out of childhood as if they are escaping a bad movie. They want instant gratification for the pictures they post and the comments they make; their entire psyche is impacted by a simple click, share, and post. What a sad way to live.

If your kid suffers from anxiety and depression, you are not alone. The most important thing you can do is pay attention to any verbal and nonverbal signs that something is not right. If kids are not communicating, see if they will speak with someone else and open up; they can put up a huge barrier to keep anyone from getting in, but eventually you need to break though for their sake and yours. There are so many reasons why kids will shut you out. Some reasons are hormonal, and others are social and societal pressures. Growing up is very hard. All you can do is create a safe space and a constantly open door of communication. When you see your kid suffering, figure out what the two of you can do to move through this rocky period. Anxiety, depression, and trauma take time and patience to work through. You can't just throw a quick solution at your kid's problems. Be present and listen. Work together to help your child through a rough patch.

Parenting is a tough job. Some days you wish your kid came with directions. We make mistakes, and there are no perfect parents. One day your kid seems fine and thriving and another day is crumbling, and you are blindsided. You can do all the right things and your kid can still have emotional and social problems. If you have conflicts with your kids, tune in to how you communicate and how you treat them. Be vigilant about not repeating the bad behaviors you experienced in your childhood. The time is now to correct the wrong that you experienced as a kid—and if possible, share some of your backstory. Of course, you will feel like your advice is old and stale, and your kid will think you are from the Dark Ages. Your youth feels like it was eons ago and you feel 112 years old. Welcome to the club.

CHAPTER 10

Midlife Is Not So Bad...Said No One. Ever. Until Now

"You're never too old to play. You're only too old for low-rise jeans."
—*Ellen DeGeneres,* Seriously...I'm Kidding

You've heard it all before. Some guy you know has a midlife crisis and ditches his wife for a Harley. An unhappily married woman runs off to live her unfulfilled dreams traveling the world, freely and boldly. Others abandon their nine-to-five job for a lifelong-dream career. They take a drastic pay cut from their attorney salary to run a small East Village bakery. The one thing all these people have in common is: they are willing to face midlife boldly and brazenly and jump into a second chapter that might be scary at first but might end up being the best thing they ever did.

People make bold decisions along the way that impact their personal and professional lives, because they reach a certain point in their lives and they ask themselves, "Is this it? Is this all there is for me and my life?" And the answers are often incredibly life changing. Risks are almost always scary, but doing nothing is worse. Staying in a dark, unhappy place or choosing to jump through your stormy mess of a life to get through to the other side is brave and full of soul searching. Midlife is not for the faint of heart, but we don't have any other choice but to learn how to navigate these uncertain and oftentimes-exciting new adventures.

This chapter will feature insights from the award-winning writer Kerry Hannon, who writes for the *New York Times*, *AARP The Magazine*, *and Forbes*. Kerry shares her research and insights on how people create healthy second acts in their lives out of personal and professional necessity.

Meet Kerry Hannon

Kerry Hannon is a nationally recognized expert and strategist on career transitions, personal finance, and retirement. She is a frequent TV and radio commentator, and is a sought-after keynote speaker at conferences across the country. Kerry focuses on empowering yourself to do more with your career and personal finances—now and for the future. She is the author of a dozen books. Currently, Kerry is writing her thirteenth book, which will be published in spring 2019 and is called *Never Too Old to Get Rich: The Entrepreneur's Guide to Starting a Business Midlife*.

Kerry Hannon is also a columnist and regular contributor to the *New York Times*, AARP's work and jobs expert and "Great Jobs" columnist, contributing editor and "Second Verse" columnist at *Forbes*, and an expert and a columnist on personal finance, wealth management, and careers for female baby boomers at the PBS-produced website Next Avenue.

When I spoke with Kerry, she smartly turned the tables on the notion of a midlife crisis. She clearly sees midlife differently than most. "Is it really a midlife crisis or midlife bliss?" she asked.

"Why make it a crisis when you can be happy about it? At midlife we hit a wall, and suddenly you lose friends to cancer or you have a health crisis of your own or you lose a job. Of course, these things rattle us." Kerry meets people who have an epiphany that things are happening in their lives and they need to take charge of their life. She pointed out that we need to find things in life that bring us happiness and give us the opportunity to give back to the world. People realize they can make a difference and now is the time to do it.

Kerry shares my own point of view. "We need to listen to our inner monologue and be physically fit and spiritually fit," she said. "It's important to be nimble at this midlife stage and get centered, get quiet, and find what it is that is going to give you the core strength to move forward for this new chapter in your life." She explained that some of us have skills that we are not even aware of, and it takes friends and family to help us see what we are good at. In the updated version of her book *What's Next?* Kerry looks at how people have changed careers in midlife to do something they were passionate about, something they really wanted to do. She spoke with someone who was a lobbyist in Washington, but he had always wanted to have a stand-up act. He became a satirist in Washington, but he realized he wasn't going to make the money he needed to make following his passion, so he did some lawyering work on the side. Kerry explains in the book that it's important to make your passions work for you. She has met people who have built successful businesses and then sold them and moved on to their third act. One woman went from managing a Bloomingdale's store to opening a pet store. She uses all her skills in retail there and now has a fantastic pet store; this is a win-win, because she has a career that fosters her love of animals while using her experiences and skill set.

Kerry's books give people inspiration while instilling a can-do attitude and helping people find happiness in midlife. She believes, as I do, that it is never too old to try something else, because nothing is forever. You might do something for a short time and then switch gears. You can also weave together a couple of different things you like to do, so you have other avenues to explore. Kerry pointed out in our conversation it's like having a "cool quilt." Having a lot of interests makes life interesting.

In her book *Love Your Job* (I love that she calls it "the Suck It Up book"!), Kerry says she wants everyone over fifty to quit their whining and complaining. Sometimes we act like little children, don't we? Of course, you have the fear of needing money and wanting to be in the job market, but she helps people learn how to fall in love with their current job *again*. Instead of, "Take this job and shove it!" try, "Take this job and love it!" Kerry says you can find the joy in your job, and she helps you determine what changes you can make internally and externally to find the passion in your work again. You end up finding joy in your job and stop complaining and griping, because come on—that's not going to get you anywhere, is it?

Kerry's message is an important one. "Take your job and love it, and be grateful," she says. Make it work for you! Kerry agrees that rejection in the workplace is harsh and hurts, but you need to learn from rejection and be open. Usually, you end up being propelled in a new direction you never expected. Hopefully, you have some skills such as meditation or some ritual in your life that centers you, so you can critique yourself and ask, "What did I learn from this experience?" Sometimes you just have to tough it out, because rejection teaches us resilience, which is invaluable throughout life.

As mentioned, Kerry is a contributing editor at *Forbes* magazine and the "Second Verse" columnist at Forbes.com. She started at *Forbes* magazine in her twenties and worked in New York City and Washington. As she continued in her career with Forbes and her *What's Next?* book came out, Forbes reached out to her and asked her to write about the growing population of baby boomers and second acts. She's had a great time writing about people who have made incredible transitions in life. She also writes about what to do when you start a work-from-home business, what it's like to work for yourself, and the nuts and bolts of retirement plans. She has met some very interesting people who have made some great career changes, and gives practical advice to others who are interested in following a similar path.

In midlife, some people switch from working in a lofty corporate job to doing something meaningful for a nonprofit. Kerry pointed out in our conversation that it's not about needing the work but about wanting to work on something that is part of change and making a difference, staying mentally and socially engaged. Next Avenue is Kerry's website geared toward women. She has written several books for women, including *Money Confidence: Really Smart Financial Moves for Newly Single Women*. She gives baby boomers advice for personal finance and careers, including practical tips to help women become more confident and empowered when it comes to investing and managing their own careers.

As a writer, Kerry never takes a day off from writing. Her routine starts at five thirty in the morning every day. Because she is a morning person, her routine keeps the creative juices flowing and works extremely effectively for her. The more she writes, the better she gets, and she loves the challenge of writing different things. Her advice to writers: "You need to set deadlines and goals and be accountable to yourself. We live longer, healthier lives and we have bonus years to keep going as fast as we can go."

When I asked what self-care advice she would give, Kerry explained that having soul fitness, or spiritual fitness, and physical fitness is so important to well-being. Her soul fitness includes taking long walks with her dog and riding horses. She believes that when you take care of yourself, you exude energy and a feeling of possibility that makes people see you are someone with a positive vibe, and they will want to work with you; she says, "It's better than Botox!"

When I asked Kerry what advice she would give to someone in a career funk, she shared some insightful ideas. "If you are in a career funk, you need to realize it's all about you, your attitude, how you view something, and your internal game." She suggested that you really take a good look at yourself and write in a journal; this will help you pinpoint the triggers that upset you. Find moments of gratitude before you leave your job. What three things were bright for you? It is possible to find happiness in your job, but you need to do work on the inside. Her advice if you need to make a career change: "Go for it! But take baby steps and be rational. Know who you are and set appropriate goals. Take baby steps to get there."

And now the big question, "What about a financial funk?" Kerry said that money is the biggest stumbling block when people want to make changes in their work life. Whether you want to start your own business or switch careers, you might start with a lower salary or might not be able to pay yourself. You must gain control of your finances big-time. "A lot of people don't want to think about finances. The people who have been most successful at making career changes have been nimble; they are debt free, which gives them choices to do different things in their life," she said. Kerry said you should create a budget and take a close look at where you are spending money and where you can trim back your expenses. Then once you have a budget, you can determine what you can cut out and make your financial situation better. Maybe you can downsize your home. Most important, pay off those credit cards and tackle your debt.

If you are suddenly single, you can feel like you are floundering, because you and your partner were interdependent. Go slow and never make a rash move, such as a huge financial decision. Go through what you have and make a plan with a financial advisor. No big changes. Assess what you have and what changes you need to make. Take control of your life and make wise, well-thought-out decisions.

Kerry believes we need to have confidence in ourselves and our abilities. "Believe in yourself," she said. "You are your best advocate!"

Follow Kerry on Twitter *@KerryHannon*, visit her website at *KerryHannon.com*, and check out her LinkedIn profile at *www.linkedin.com/in/kerryhannon*.

Meet Brie Darling

Brie Darling is a singer, a drummer, an actor, and a winner of *Cake Wars*. She has been a member of the bands Fanny, Fanny Walked the Earth, and Boxing Gandhis; has performed or recorded with Carole King, Robert Palmer, and Ringo Starr; and has been a songwriter for the Pointer Sisters and Michael Jackson. Brie is sixty-nine years old and is loving life and all of her creative pursuits. I wanted to find out the story of how she became a drummer and custom-cake creator. Here's our Q&A.

Janeane: Did you always want to be a musician?

Brie: It's the only thing I have ever done. I started when I was fourteen. So, this is it for me. And I am still doing it, so I guess this is it!

JB: And how does it feel to be doing all of this? I love your singing and everything.

BD: I feel like the lucky log fell on my head. At this point in my life to be able to still be doing it and to have the opportunities still coming my way, I couldn't ask for more. My life is good.

JB: Did you always want to be a drummer, or did you start out with something else?

BD: That's a funny question, because I didn't start out as a drummer. My parents, bless them, they were the best. They encouraged us, which is an awesome thing. I have two brothers, and my mom asked, "What instrument do you want to pick?" We didn't have a lot of time to think about it. I picked piano, and my younger brother picked drums, and my older brother picked guitar. Both my parents made that happen. We didn't have a lot of money, but the piano she got us was from a thrift store, and it turned out it had a broken bridge, so it wasn't usable. We couldn't afford another one, so that one just sat in our house and we tinkered on it for a while. But a band came to audition my brother on drums, and I was sitting on the drum set when the manager and guitar player showed up, and they hired me on the spot.

JB: What?!

BD: And I didn't really know how to play, but there I was banging away on the drums. My brother gladly gave me his drum set to go play with this band, and that moment in time—I was fourteen years old—changed my life forever.

JB: Amazing.

BD: I am forever grateful. There was never, ever envy or jealousy. I took his job. I took his drums and he said, "You go, girl!" To this day, he follows what I am doing on Facebook and he shows me all the support and encouragement.

JB: Love it!

BD: That's how I became a drummer. I am an accidental drummer. I was kind of good at it and I love doing it; it just became my life. I was a drummer first, and then I found out I could sing.

JB: I love your voice. You never took singing lessons, did you?

BD: In the first band when I was fourteen, I was the drummer and I sang background. Then when I joined June and Jean Millington in the Svelts when I was sixteen, I sang my first lead vocal and that was a song by the Four Tops, "Reach Out I'll Be There." I realized I could sing. [I thought], "This is cool; this is fun!" I think with everything I do in life, I think, "This is cool," and I do it not realizing maybe I am good at it, maybe I am not, but if it is fun.... I am fortunate enough that sometimes it turns out to be good enough that it takes me to the next level. That is how I discovered I could sing, and I just love singing and playing. I am like Mister Magoo. I stumble into things and it works out.

(*laughter*)

JB: It's good because I don't hear, "Well, I didn't have the confidence." You seem like you were comfortable in your own skin, giving it a try and seeing how things went.

BD: It's funny, because in a way, you are exactly right. It's more fun than I am afraid. The thrill is bigger than the fear. I do have fears, but the thrill of it is much bigger than my fears, and that takes me out there doing it anyway in spite of those fears that I have; that is something that I like to put out there, because I think people think that the brave ones out there doing it have no fears. I am here to tell you I might look completely confident, but I wake up every day with those little nagging fears; it is something that I want to write a song about.

JB: You should.

BD: Because I think it is an important thing, and if you just do it anyway, then you beat that giant down one more day, and it's not to say that it won't come back, but at least you beat it down one more day. Hey, and some people don't have them! Bless them and that is awesome, but I do!

JB: I do, too! I heard this great line in a song, "Don't let fear take the wheel." Because it is very easy to let fear take over.

BD: Absolutely! That is so great that you say that, because people think someone like you who can talk in front of millions of people and sound confident, they think that you have no fears.

JB: Oh, so many!

BD: So, we're here to say, "We do!"

JB: Yes! Definitely.

BD: And that helps other people to know that, "Okay I have these fears [but] I can do it anyway!"

JB: I think it is really important to confront your fears. A lot of people say, "Do what scares you," but it is true because the more you do something, the more you are going to forget to be fearful. You are just going to naturally start doing that thing.

BD: Right. Or if you can beat it down one more time, then the next time you are confronted you might go, "Okay, at least I can face this one. I might not win, and you might lose, but that is okay." The more wins you have under your belt, the more you have in the bank to face another battle.

JB: Yes.

BD: The older I get, the more I realize how important it is to be a real human being instead of being a pretend one who's got it all together.

JB: Right, because who really has it all together? Come on! (*laughter*)

BD: I used to think that I was the only one who didn't and everybody else did. Everybody else had a perfect relationship—

JB: Oh, please.

BD: The perfect confidence. The best education. The smallest waist. (*laughter*) All that stuff! And now I am realizing we are all in the same boat, man.

JB: We are. It's all smoke and mirrors. That is what I call social media. "I am doing this, and I am doing that!" People have their own fears and insecurities. I think that is why there are so many selfies.

BD: Yes.

JB: You have an interesting backstory, because you didn't just do one thing. The name of my show is *Get the Funk Out!*. Do you find that having these different adventures into acting, TV, and theater helped you sort through your life and helped you stay out of a funk?

BD: I would like to say that I stayed out of the funk, but I waded in the funk a bit! (*laughter*) I am really fortunate. Things came my way and I was in places in my life where I was able to embrace a lot of the opportunities. I also lost a lot of opportunities, and I let a lot of them go, but I have to say that led me to where I am today. I am feeling pretty fortunate at this point in my life, at this age, to still have opportunities and to be where I am at. I am grateful for that.

I am not encouraging that people let things happen to them. I think it is great to go after things. I am just learning more about myself. I just found out in the last few months that I have ADHD. Who the heck knew?

JB: Really?!

BD: Yeah, I look back and think I knew that I was smart in school. I knew that I wasn't stupid, but stuff wouldn't glue to my head. I was wondering, "Why is this person next to me answering these test questions so easily after having read a chapter and the information wouldn't glue to my brain?" If I was interested in something, nobody knew it better than me, but if I didn't have a particular interest, I couldn't get it to stick.

JB: Right.

BD: If I am interested in something, you can't tear me away from it, but if I can't understand it and it doesn't make it past the barrier, it just flies away.

JB: What made you decide to go get tested for ADHD?

BD: I was having anxiety. I needed to deal with it, because it was starting to be really difficult for me just to function. I have friends and relatives who have that condition, and it never even occurred to me. Oh my God! Why didn't I know this before? And I think to myself, "I didn't." And there are certain things that come along with having ADHD that are pluses. You can be very creative. You can really focus on the things you love, which is what I recognize I have done. In a way it is a blessing, and either way I am stuck with it. It is what it is.

JB: Exactly.

BD: I just take it for what it is. I got the opportunity to do a lot of things, and I lost a lot of opportunities as well. I really wanted to get into acting. A friend of mine turned me on to acting classes, and the reason she did was because she felt it would help me being onstage for music—being able to have a better stage performance. And I took these acting classes and I really wanted to get into it, but at the time I did it there were not a lot of opportunities for minorities. There were no opportunities in television or commercials. There were none, but in spite of that a couple of opportunities did come up. I did get to do a lot of things. Most of them were artistic endeavors.

JB: I think it's great.

BD: I have a lot of creative outlets. I am grateful for them. I got to make these cakes—

JB: I want to talk about that.

BD: I worked on these houses, too, and I am grateful.

JB: The *CakeWars*. You won in 2016. How did that come about?

BD: I was watching when cake shows became popular. Duff Goldman had that show [*Ace of Cakes*, based on his shop] Charm City Cakes. I saw it and looked at it and said, "Man, I could do that!" Of course, I had never done it before, but I decided I could do it. (*laughter*)

A friend of mine has a wife who was having a baby, and I decided I was going to make them this kind of funny cake. I decided I could cover it with fondant and make it the way I envisioned it in my head.

JB: Okay....

BD: I made it and it was, uh...terrible.

(*laughter*)

BD: But it was because I didn't know how to use the materials. I knew in my head that I could do it. But here's what happened! I have to tell you this, because it is really funny.

JB: Yes, please!

BD: I made this baby head, and it was an oval-shaped baby head, and I put a big screaming, crying mouth with tears coming out of its head and funny little hair poking out of its head. Mostly, it was a big mouth screaming. I made it out of red velvet cake, because I thought that would be really cool, and I covered it with buttercream icing, and then I might have put fondant on it. Little did I know that the red in the red velvet cake would seep up through the white buttercream icing. By the time it was done, the red seeped up through the icing and it looked like the baby had a rash all over its face.

JB: Oh *no!* Eczema!

BD: Yeah! (*laughter*) I decided this is not a good thing to give to my friend. I tossed that cake and I gave him a cake for his baby's christening, and it was beautiful. So, that kind of got me into it and it was sort of accidental. I was making these cakes for my friends, and then people started telling people and then I was getting orders. The show *Cupcake Wars* was already on and I was wondering if they would ever have a *Cake Wars*. The minute I saw it was on there, I looked it up online and asked to submit. I sent in a couple of photos of my cakes and they said, "Come on," and we won.

JB: Amazing.

BD: Yes. Amazing! I think that's that weird kind of boldness where you just kind of go, "I can do that!" whether you can or cannot. Someone will call me and say, "Can you make a cake that is like—"

JB: Leopard print.

BD: Yeah. "Can you do this?" And they will come up with some weird.... This woman says, "My husband is a race car driver. Can you make a car on two wheels, on its side going around a corner?" and I say, "Sure!" I hang up the phone and go, "What did I just do?!" And then you do it. It took me a year to do the leopard-print cake, because it was a year of experimenting. It took me a year to perfect it.

JB: You mentioned you are building a house, another skill you have.

BD: I've remodeled a couple of houses, and I actually do the physical work myself, like the drywall and—

JB: Whoa! Really!

BD: Yeah! Hammering studs. And the house I live in now, I did all the tilework myself. I am not willing to carry eighty-pound buckets of cement anymore. I split one of my properties into two and I am building a smaller house, and it's so cute; it is small and it's a little house. I found an amazing contractor and I designed it, and I am over there every day. We are plotting and planning it together. I am in love with building this house, because it is just turning out so good.

JB: Exciting!

BD: It's another artistic endeavor.

JB: It's another side of your creativity.

BD: Yes, things are good in my world, but music is my main focus right now. While I am working on my music, I am working on my memoir.

JB: Oh, you are?

BD: Yes, why not? While I can still remember things. (*laughter*) This is a very special time. I am creatively and physically able to still play and still sing, and that is precious, you know?

JB: Yes.

BD: When we last spoke, I was sitting in my car in the parking lot of a rehab facility and Jean Millington, a member of *Fanny Walked the Earth*, had had a stroke; it had just happened. My point is, I know this is precious, the ability to still play drums and still sing. I am not taking this for granted. I am still doing this until I am not able to do this anymore; this is something I have done since I was fourteen years old. I just played at the St. Jude Children's Hospital benefit last night.

JB: Nice!

BD: Yes, I played drums and sang with Cherie Currie from the Runaways; it was so fun! I got to play and sing, which is awesome. I want to do this as long as I can.

JB: You should.

BD: I have a couple of other projects in the works. I am going to rock it out as long as I can.

JB: You should!

BD: My husband, Dave Darling, produced the Fanny Walked the Earth record. We also had a band in the mid-'90s called Boxing Gandhis. We put the band back together to make a new record; it's still art but it's activism. We decided to make a record to raise money for the Border Defense Legal Fund and the ACLU. One hundred percent of any money we make will go to these causes. Dave started writing songs immediately after seeing pictures of the kids in cages at the border. The record is done and mixed! We are currently talking to record companies about partnering with us to put the record out.

JB: I love it!

BD: Yeah, it's about beautiful songs. Back in the mid-'90s, Boxing Gandhis had a triple-A hit called "If You Loved Me, Why Am I Dying?" We did big, fun dance songs, but they always had lyrics that were social commentary. We called ourselves "the thinking man's party band." (*laughter*)

We called ourselves a lot of things. Porch Funk—it was a big funk band but with important messages. This record is about immigration, racial tension, the distribution of wealth, and taking personal responsibility for what is going on around you, just trying to make the world a better place. That is a record that I love with people that I love. I am just happy to be this active. I am more active now than I have been in a long time.

JB: Isn't that funny?

BD: It's crazy!

JB: That is so funny the way life works. The older you get, the busier you are and the more you are doing all these fulfilling things. I think it is great!

BD: Like I said, man, I feel like the lucky log fell on my head.

Find Brie Darling on Facebook and at *www.briedarling.com*.

Meet June Millington

June Millington is the cofounder and lead guitarist of the all-female rock band Fanny, the cofounder and artistic director of the Institute for the Musical Arts (IMA), and a singer, songwriter, producer, and writer.

She was born April 14, 1948, in Manila, the Philippines. Around the age of nine or ten, June and her sister Jean started playing ukuleles. At the end of seventh grade, while attending Assumption Convent (now Assumption College) in Manila, June heard a girl playing guitar and was immediately mesmerized. For her thirteenth birthday, June's mother gave her the perfect present—her first guitar.

In 1961, the Millington family moved to Sacramento, California. In high school, June and Jean created an all-girl band called the Svelts—which morphed into Wild Honey—that played funk, pop rock, and Motown covers. Within five years after moving to California, they met Brie Berry. Brie initially played in the Svelts from the summer of '66 to the summer of '67 and went on to join their band Fanny as their drummer after June left in the fall of '73. June and Jean, along with Alice de Buhr and Nickey Barclay, became the original members of the all-female band Fanny. Fanny was very active in the early 1970s. They were one of the first female rock bands, the third to sign with a major label (after Goldie & the Gingerbreads and the Pleasure Seekers), and the first to release an album on a major label (in 1970). They produced two top-forty singles on the Billboard Hot 100 and released five albums.

June called in to my radio show from Goshen, Massachusetts, where she is the artistic director of IMA, which she also cofounded. IMA hosts five rock-and-roll camps for girls each summer, including a recording camp, and is where her band's latest album, *Fanny Walked the Earth*, was recorded. When we spoke, she shared details about her book, *Land of a Thousand Bridges*, her backstory of how she got into music, and how she continues to maintain her passion and dedication to music and has immense gratitude to be able to do all the things she loves to do.

At an early age, June felt music was her calling.

June: I think it was a destiny that we were called to. We started playing with acoustic guitars at hootenannies, and we met a couple of girls and started to sing with them, playing Motown on acoustic, which was actually pretty hot!

Janeane: That's cool!

JM: And then a girl from our rival high school heard about us and called and asked if we wanted to start a band. Jean's boyfriend was in a surf band, and we had been singing between their sets at bowling alleys and stuff like that, so we said, "Sure!" We jumped on their equipment between sets and that was great, and then we started our band, the Svelts, and about a year later we lost our drummer and somehow Brie found out about us and joined us at a gig we were doing the summer of '66 in Sparks, just outside of Reno. We were playing about five sets a night until four in the morning.

JB: Whoa!

JM: She was underage, so she used to have to stand in the kitchen and watch through the porthole to see us play, which she did, and at some point we just said, "Hey! Just come on out!" It was about four in the morning. She just walked through that door from the kitchen to the stage and just started playing with us, and it was a perfect fit. It was like, she didn't even have to audition; it was just happening.

JB: How old was she?

JM: Maybe sixteen about to turn seventeen.

JB: Amazing.

JM: Something like that.

JB: And then at some point Brie dropped out, right?

JM: That was the summer of '67. She was only in the band about a year. After that she played with us on and off. She got married, pregnant, and ended up in LA at Fanny Hill. There were a lot of adventures that ensued. She wasn't in Fanny when we started recording in Hollywood but was at Fanny Hill doing her own thing, sometimes jamming with us, and raising her daughter. Occasionally we'd do gigs together to pay the rent, but that was under the industry radar. We were getting ready to do big gigs and tour as the record company was releasing our first album in 1970.

When I left the band in '73 and when Fanny turned into what I call Fanny point one, that was with Brie and Patty Quatro. That was the band that had the hit with "Butter Boy." Just think of it like girlfriends playing musical chairs. Except it was rock and roll and we had a PA.

JB: Amazing.

JM: It is amazing and it's worth reading my book, by the way, *Land of a Thousand Bridges*. It's iconic because there is nobody else who has had the experiences I have had and we have had. There have been other all-girl bands, but unfortunately, we knew only one and that was Birtha, also in LA, who were fantastic! We saw them play and they were girlfriends of ours also before we all started recording. We heard of the Ace of Cups who recently released an album, but we didn't see them play; they were like a myth to us and the Svelts in Northern California.

JB: So you were pretty much the only all-female band that was playing out.

JM: That is all we knew. We were the only ones certainly in the Sacramento area who were doing gigs steadily. Sometimes we did two or three gigs a night. We would do a couple of gigs, bop to an after-hours joint, and play a little more; it gave us gas money or enough money to buy toilet paper and maybe a guitar or something.

(*laughter*)

JB: Wow!

JM: That was something we had to do; it is hard to explain. I guess I could use the word "addicting," because there is something about doing music and pleasing people. Also, we knew we were challenging the status quo, and we wanted to prove that we could do it.

JB: And you loved doing it.

JM: Oh, absolutely! It was our heart and soul.

JB: You know, the name of my show is *Get the Funk Out!* and I am always so fascinated with how people stay so positive in an industry that is so challenging.

JM: When you have to do it, that is what you do. I have never had a child, but I remember asking Jean, "How do you deal with that pain?" And she says, "Oh, you just forget about it after a while. You are just so in love with your baby, and all those endorphins kick in." And I guess it is kind of the same. You play, and you get kind of high from it; it's so great, and every gig that we did was another chance to feel that incredible love and sense of community with everyone who was dancing. By the way, I thought about this a lot—in all the years of playing with the Svelts and Fanny, I never once felt racism. Sexism—yes, a lot! Misogyny—oh, yeah!

JB: Oh, yeah!

JM: But racism, no, because everyone was just loving the music and loving the dancing and it was a revolution! Everyone was united by the songs. We were creating. We were making it up. By the time we got to LA, we started to meet a lot of people who already had hits, and we played with a couple of them up north, like the Youngbloods. We started to make friends with those people who were creating that sound that is now called classic rock! They were creating it, and it is difficult for people to even imagine—there you are, and it's glorious! It's really fun despite all challenges.

JB: Right.

JM: We were up for it!

JM: You just kept going from different bands and different adventures; it's something you are just passionate about.

JM: Absolutely; it was our lives. You don't not do your life, right?

JB: You're right! (*laughter*) You just keep going.

JM: Yes.

JB: What advice would you give to musicians today, especially female musicians?

JM: My first piece would be, don't stop. Every day is different. Every gig is different. In Fanny, when we had a road crew, we had people helping us with sound; we had technicians that traveled with us, and roadies. No matter how well we prepared, the same show could fall flat for us one night—and the audience liked it, but it fell flat for us—and the next night would be incredible. That is the thing about music. You are really calling on the muses, and you never know when it is actually going to connect even with you and with the audience. Keep going, because you can't control that. All you can do is stay steady with what you know is real and true. Number two: Take care of yourself. It seems kind of pithy to say that, but for me especially, getting enough sleep has always been important.

JB: Yes.

JM: Brush your teeth. Eat well. Try to have good thoughts. Stay positive.

JB: Right. I think that is so key. If you don't love yourself, take care of yourself, it shows.

JM: Oh, I didn't even say love yourself, but that's good. I am just talking about as a task. You asked, "What advice would you give?" Certainly, love yourself, but I wouldn't have said that first because you know (*laughs*) it takes an awful long time to realize you've got to do that, too!

JM: I know! Doesn't it?

(*laughter*)

JB: But it's a domino effect, because if you are not good to yourself, and you are crabby and don't feel good about yourself, you are not going to be good to other people.

JM: Well, that is true. Absolutely. A domino effect. I like that. Another thing I would give advice about is to be grateful for everything. It was so devastating for all of us when [my sister and bandmate] Jean had her stroke; she couldn't move her right side at all. She couldn't talk. Now, she can talk. She has had speech therapy. She is such a dedicated worker. Now, she can walk a little bit. She can get out of the car by herself. I am happy she is willing to join us at a party in Davis, where she lives, and maybe sing a little bit and enjoy. Gratitude for everything for every moment means so much; it really counts for a lot.

JB: Yes. I feel like all of you are all such great role models for [us] as we age…

JM: Yes.

JB: To be grateful, to do the things you love to do.

JM: One of the things that upset me the most about Jean having a stroke, although of course that is devastating, but when we decided to do the album [*Fanny Walked the Earth*] and we were talking about why we were doing it, one of our goals was to show up in front of people and show them that you can still slam at sixty-eight, sixty-nine years old—I just turned seventy—and be proud of it! We can play like no one else can, because we started back when that music was being invented, and it was incredible.

JB: Right!

JM: We caught the fire, you know? As Bob Marley said, "Catch a fire." We really did.

JB: You did, and you paved the way for other people.

JM: Yeah, I think I have to accept that. Sometimes that is hard for me. I'm like, "Really?" We kind of knew we were doing that, but we were doing it for ourselves. However, now that that moniker is kind of put on us, I've got to say we did. I also want to acknowledge all of the other women who just never got the record deal or didn't get noticed beyond their high school days or whatever. I guess I would say we all did it together; there was an energy.

JB: Yes, absolutely. Where can people find out more about you?

JM: They can go to IMA, where I am talking to you from right now, because that is basically my life's work. We started a nonprofit for women in music—the Institute for the Musical Arts. If you go to ima.org, you can see what is going on, you can get in touch with me, and I have a pretty good Facebook presence. I guess I am kind of an oldie, because I haven't switched over to Instagram and Snapchat and all that kind of stuff. I just turned seventy, like I said, and it's kind of fun. While I'm doing the audiobook to *Land of a Thousand Bridges*, my partner Ann keeps telling me she thinks this is going to be my most important legacy, because it really puts you right in our shoes; it really puts you right in the times. Book one (*LOATB*) stops in 1975, and I am working on book two now - from the Philippines through rock and roll and picking up where it all intersected with women's music and feminism, a seriously impactful time for me. It takes you straight through to 1975, but since I left Fanny in 1973 there's a little bit leading up to the overlap, for example my magical time in Woodstock. A lot happened then for me spiritually. I really did kind of drop off the face of the earth, because I just needed to find out: Who the heck is this June Millington who everybody says is blah blah blah?

JB: Yes.

JM: The fame did not turn out to be what I thought it was; it was making me into a one-dimensional figure, which I *hated!* I needed to step out of that flat picture that was being presented in the press, because that was the only way that the press or society could see me. You couldn't actually be a real, creative woman.

JB: Awful.

JM: Yes, so I had to figure out: How do I step into that paradigm? I actually needed a way for the paradigm shift, because by 1975, I got invited to play on this album called *Changer and the Changed*, which Cris Williamson was doing, and that was my entrée into the women's music and feminism, and that was super blast off; that was 1975 and that is also when Jean asked me to go on the last Fanny tour, because they had a surprise hit with "Butter Boy." It was me, Jean, and Brie, and Wendy Haas-Mull and another woman I brought from New York, Padi Moscheta, who was in another band that I had started called Smiles, and that was 1975. So, you blast off with what I call Fanny point two. We went on the road and I played on *Changer and the Changed*, and I went on the road on Cris' first national tour in 1976. Let me tell you, that was incredible rock and roll! Feminism and rock, and that is where my book starts.

JB: So cool!

JM: I already have six chapters written, and the reason why I stopped there is because Jean, Brie, and I, and Wendy, we barely can remember what actually happened then!

(*laughter*) We were a bunch of young women just kind of snowballing into our lives! I have a tape of us playing in Memphis, and I would tape everything on a cassette, and I asked the soundman to press record, and it sounds really good! We were really good!

(*laughter*)

So when I think about all the things I have done, and I moved on to women's music and IMA and the girls' rock camp, and the music that they are creating, it's really important. I am valuing my life more now than I ever have, which is very interesting.

JB: And you are able to do what you still love, which is a gift.

Find June Millington at *www.ima.org*, and on Facebook at *www.facebook.com/june.millington.1* or at *www.facebook.com/FannyWalkedTheEarth*. You can also find her on Instagram *@fannywalkedtheearth* or support her at *www.gofundme.com/jean-millington-go*

Meet Cindy Joseph

Cindy Joseph is a wife, mother, model, makeup artist, and pioneer in pro-age thinking. I first heard about Cindy on the Second Act Yahoo! Video series. Her view on life and as a second-act game changer intrigued me. I knew she would be a perfect guest for my show. Plus, she rocked her gray locks and gorgeous, natural looks like no one I had ever seen. Here's our Q&A from the show.

Janeane: How did Yahoo! hear about you?

Cindy: I was so honored to be in that group. It was really fun. They really got it. They really understood what my whole philosophy is all about. I have been in the fashion and beauty industry for a very long time—about twenty-seven years as a makeup artist and over twelve years now as a model. I just knew it was time. It was time to stand up and say, "*Enough!* Enough is enough!"

JB: Yes. (*CJ laughs*) And elaborate on that. Tell me about that.

CJ: Well, everything is anti-age. Anti-wrinkle. Anti-every woman pushing forty. We are continually bombarded by this message that we have to look like we are in our in childbearing years. That's the only way to be interesting, valuable, attractive, fashionable, and on and on, and it's—

JB: Horrible.

CJ: Completely make-believe. I call it the last piece that we need to shed from many years ago. We got the vote a hundred years ago. We were liberated forty years ago. We have run for president. Why on earth are we holding on to this concept that we are only valuable during our childbearing years, or at least if we look like it?

JB: I agree. Some people say it's Botox or bangs. They are so afraid to age and look natural and show wrinkles.

CJ: Yes, and completely understandable. I have absolute and total compassion for every woman and myself in that area, because we were born into a society that judges us heavily in the area of looks, and then they say our looks start to fade, disappear, and go away after we turn twenty-nine!

JB: How sad.

CJ: So, we are led to believe like, "Oh, man, I am not going to get the flirtation, the fun, the attention, unless I look young." You can make a ninety-five-year-old woman blush. We love the attention. We love being valued, and we want to be valued for who we are until the day we die. And we don't want to have to do it with Botox and hair dye.

JB: Yes. Well, you are stunning. I posted your picture on Facebook and my show blog, and you should have seen the reaction!

CJ: Oh! I am so excited. And thank you for that wonderful article! I just read it before I came on the show, and I was so touched by it. You captured—you got the essence of what I am trying to say. (*giggles*) And it is so gratifying!

JB: Well, it's so important because we put so much stress on ourselves and we think that if we go out and we get the plastic surgery and lose the pounds, dye our hair a certain color, that we are going to gain the attention of our loved ones or we are going to feel better about ourselves, but that feeling better starts from within.

CJ: That is absolutely right, and I want to go back to the idea that if you do dye your hair and you get a shot of Botox and you do any of these things, I am not saying that this is dirty, bad, and wrong. I say if it makes you feel good and you are honoring yourself as a woman, and you are going for it out of enthusiasm, pleasure, and desire, then I am all for it one hundred percent. The bottom line is, if you feel good, you're going to look good. We are so judgmental of ourselves, and we are so lenient with our girlfriends.

(laughter)

I have so many girlfriends who are like, "Oh, look at this cellulite. Look at this wrinkle!" I am like, "Honey, do you have any idea how gorgeous you are? And how wonderful you are, and the more I get to know you, the more beautiful you become?" Do I say that to myself?

JB: No.

CJ: That's a whole other thing. We look in the mirror and we're like, "Oy! Look at this and look at this! *(laughter)* I've got to fix this and I have to fix that!" It's time to take off those critical filters when we look in the mirror and start looking at our own faces and our own bodies with that kind of love and support and compassion that we do with the other women in our lives.

JB: Right. I agree. Now, tell me about your backstory. You have been in the fashion industry; share a little bit about your bio.

CJ: I started out as a makeup artist in the late '70s in the San Francisco Bay area. My training came from being addicted to makeup in high school and thinking that I looked terrible without it. I wouldn't walk out without the full-on artillery pulled out. I wore base, concealer, eyeliner, eyebrow pencil, not one but two pair of fake eyelashes. It was the Twiggy days and all that. I would pore through the fashion magazines and try and try and copy this one and copy that one. And then of course, my girlfriends were like, "Do me! Do me!" I had a blast. A big part of it was just pure entertainment. But a big part of my motivation was fear, and later, when the late '60s came around, I was being affected by all the new opinions that were happening.

JB: Cindy, why fear?

CJ: Fear of not being noticed. Not being liked. Not being pretty enough. Not being in the in crowd. Not getting the boyfriend. Whatever it was that I and my friends were afraid of that was motivating our desire to wear the makeup and have the hairstyles and wear the latest fashions. If you think back to when we were little girls and we were just playing dress-up, we are not thinking about that. We're just having fun with the stuff! Just being playful and living out a fantasy: "I'm a fairy! I'm a ballerina!" or whatever. "I'm a truck driver" or whatever it may be. Our motivation has to change as we get older because of all these messages that we receive, almost subliminally from society. And then we start doing the dressing up and the makeup and the jewelry. We are motivated not by fun and pleasure but by fear. That is the key to me for each woman to really take a look at what is really motivating her.

JB: That is so important. Tell me about your parents. Were they influential with you at all?

CJ: I would say that my parents really influenced me in that they really enjoyed life. My mom was kind of no-nonsense—her mother was frilly and wanted to dress her up in pink and frills and all that, and she didn't want anything to do with it. She wanted to take drafting. She wanted to climb trees. She wanted to do all the things that boys in society back then could do. She wasn't allowed to, so she got a little rebellious. When she was out on her own and married, she decided to live her life the way she wanted to and not the way she was dictated. So, she became a self-taught architect, and she wore practical clothes and she wore a little bit of lipstick once in a while, but she really wasn't into all of that. Typically, the daughter went totally the other way.

(*laughter*)

Once the late '60s came around, I started taking a closer look and I thought, "How am I ever going to get married? If someone meets me with this mask on my face, and then it's time to wake up next to him in bed, what am I going to do? Get up before and go make my face up?"

JB: That's right!

CJ: I just started thinking, "This is crazy!"

JB: Yes.

CJ: I had an interesting experience with a girlfriend in a gas station bathroom, where we started laughing our heads off in front of the mirror and the eyelashes came off from the tears of laughter. Pretty soon we washed all the makeup off and looked in the mirror and said, "Okay, this is it. This is the real us." We left that gas station bathroom, with the least flattering light imaginable....

JB: Of course.

CJ: And said, "This is really who we are."

JB: How old were you?

CJ: I think I was sixteen years old.

JB: Good for you.

CJ: Yeah. That was a huge change. And another extremely significant time in my life was in my early forties, and I started taking courses that were really describing the nature of men and women, and who we are. Our nature. I kept hearing that women are pleasure oriented and men are goal oriented. Women are random and men are linear. I continued taking these courses, and close to forty-nine I decided to start living my life according to what pleasured me, and becoming pleasure oriented instead of goal and success oriented. That shifted everything. I also stopped dying the silver hair that started coming in around the sides of my face. I had a little bit on top since I was thirty-two, and I kind of kept that because it was a trademark, but it started coming in on the sides. I was getting pretty freaked out. Every time I looked in the mirror, I was like, "Whoa!"

JB: Yeah.

CJ: I was looking more and more like my mother. More and more like my grandmother. I went through that moment of fear, and I colored it for about six years, and then one day I am talking about age and I am talking about what a bad rap it gets. And it wasn't happening to me. I was getting happier! I was getting healthier! I was becoming more self-confident. I was becoming wiser. Life was getting better and better and better. And I thought, "Oh, my gosh! And I am covering my age. That's a little hypocritical." So, I threw the bottle in the garbage, and I gritted my teeth and said, "C'mon babe. You can do this." And my hair completely grew out. And the day I cut off the last bit of color, I was approached on the street and asked to model.

JB: Oh, come on!

CJ: Yes!

JB: Come on! Go on. Continue.

CJ: Well, I couldn't believe it myself. I looked around and looked at this girl who walked up to me, a casting agent, and said it was "a joke, right? Who sent you?" It ended up being the real deal, and sixth months later, I was signed with Ford Modeling Agency, representing all the women of my generation, and I was selling hair products and makeup and clothing and all the fun stuff. It wasn't geriatric medicine and good for your back problems. This was about health and beauty and fun. I realized I am in a generation of women who have redefined every decade of their lives. We have never accepted the status quo. We didn't in our twenties, thirties, forties, and now we are in our fifties and sixties. We are still rockin' and rollin'. We are doing things that no generation before us has ever done.

JB: It's amazing.

CJ: It is truly unprecedented. We are going back and getting doctorates and master's degrees in our seventies. We are starting new businesses, as I just did a year and a half ago. We are becoming yoga teachers. We are running marathons. Whoa! Who was doing that in their fifties in the early 1900s?

JB: No one.

CJ: It is truly remarkable, and it's not just our generation; it's the progress of science. It is learning what health really is. It's emotional. It's mental. It's physical. It's staying awake and aware and active. Paying attention. It's so exciting. The part that thrills me is that we now have an opportunity to shift the entire attitude of our society, because now the younger generation can look up and see silver hair and wrinkles as happy and enthusiastic. Full of vitality. Doing interesting and amazing things, instead of looking at misery and closed-mindedness and ill health.

JB: Exactly.

CJ: So, now the crow's feet and the silver hair can represent something positive, instead of something negative.

JB: Now, how old were you when you were approached by this casting agent?

CJ: I was forty-nine years old.

JB: Unbelievable.

CJ: I pinched myself every day for a few years. (*laughter*) I have been in the industry a long time, and this is something really new. But then I looked around and I saw all the other models in my division at the agency, and it's like, "Yeah, baby! We're doing it!!" Very exciting.

JB: You have such a youthful look to you. Is there some kind of routine you do? You must exercise, eat well. Is there something you do that you would like to share?

CJ: Well, first I am going to tell you the truth. The truth is, when I am photographed and no one is seeing me in real life, they are seeing me in images. I tell them, "Please don't retouch them. Leave that age spot. Leave that wrinkle." Women want to see real.

JB: Yes. They want to relate. They want to see someone that looks similar to them.

CJ: Yes and even in my videos that I have—I have these little demo videos on my website to show people how to use [my makeup products] the Boomstick and the Boomsilk, and they are very useful and very helpful. But I have to use a light to actually show the product going on my face. It ends up that that type of lighting is known in the industry as "beauty lighting." It's huge and it comes from the front and it makes everything disappear because you don't have any shadows. The other day I videotaped myself showing my skin, my face, and everything in different light. I've got the crepey skin hanging on my neck, I've got the little jowls going on, I've got the puffs around the corners of my mouth, I have lots of wrinkles under my eyes and the corner of my eyes, and everybody—they don't get to see it. It's either retouched or lit a certain way; it's the nature of the business and it's changing, or I would not be modeling—or women of my age would not be modeling—but we still have a long way to go.

* * * * *

Cindy Joseph passed away from cancer on July 12, 2018. According to her obituary written by Daniel E. Slotnik for *The New York Times* online, "Her career flourished as companies began to seek more mature models to appeal to aging baby boomers, and she appeared on the covers of magazines and on billboards, including one for Target in Times Square. She also encouraged models, and women in general, to embrace their age instead of trying to conceal it. And she exemplified a wave of models who have succeeded in recent years by doing just that."

A message from Julia Joseph, Cindy's daughter:

I thank everyone who has inspired and been inspired by my mom. She lived life with so much enthusiasm and we miss her dearly. Thankfully her message lives on, and I know that our joy, and your joy, is her joy.

If people want to learn more about Mom, I will be adding stories about her to my site and blog, so they can visit juliajosephbeauty.com.

CHAPTER 11

Seniors Put Us to Shame

"For what it's worth...it's never too late, or in my case too early, to be whoever you want to be. There's no time limit. Start whenever you want. You can change or stay the same. There are no rules to this thing. We can make the best or the worst of it."—F. Scott Fitzgerald

Let's face it: Growing old is not for sissies! We no longer fit into our clothes. We see gray hairs sprouting up everywhere, like the weeds in our yards (except we don't mind those as much). There's also that losing fight against baldness, and that awful muffin top. And those annoying, quirky habits we once mocked in our parents are now (oh, horror!) some of the same things we do now. We were adamant we would never become our parents, but in some strange way, here we are. We fight aging with all kinds of lotions and potions, injections and diets, but the truth is, we should be embracing whatever age we are. There are numerous people living their most fulfilled lives in their eighties, nineties, and beyond.

And those fears and phobias? Those sometimes become worse as we age. We lose our mojo somewhere along the way. Perhaps we don't even remember having a mojo or recall the person we used to be. Sometimes we can't even remember if we took those darn vitamins that are sitting right in front of us, because we are too sleep deprived and experiencing endless nights of insomnia. We are tired, cranky, and achy from past injuries, or maybe we just feel like we are falling apart and could use a body transplant. To top it off, we fail to see we are ridiculously set in our ways and think that all those things we once wanted to do are no longer possible; they seem unrealistic. We make excuses or let life take over. We foolishly believe "that ship has sailed."

But the truth is, almost anything is possible if you really want something bad enough and if you are willing to work your butt off trying. However, you must first get fed up with the person steering that ship. That would be *you!* You have to be fed up with all of your excuses and negativity. Yes, fed up with the mindset that you just can't live those dreams, play in that band, and check off those things on your bucket list. Something must change in your mindset, and it's time to kick your excuses to the curb and do whatever it is you want—*now!* Because you know what? There are people a lot older than you, or even not as healthy as you, who are not complaining about what they wish they could do or how they wish things were different. They are living in the moment with every ounce of drive they have and moving forward attacking their dreams and aspirations. Yes, they are getting it done. They are not wishing they would do things; they are actually *doing* them and coming up with more things they will achieve all the time.

People switch career paths or try new skills in their sixties, seventies, eighties, and nineties. Think you're too old to run marathons and compete in triathlons? Not a chance. Eighty-year-old men and women are out there kicking butt. Some are weight lifters, triathletes, yoga experts, skydivers, and more. There are authors, artists, filmmakers, and so many other talented people who find that their funks happened for the best reasons. We get better with age and grow more confident during life's crazy ride. You will, too.

Remember Jackie Krisher from the chapter entitled, "It's Never Too Late to Try Something New"? She's back! I wanted to hear more about her journey as a CrossFit enthusiast and triathlete. She shared more about her journey and goal of hiking Mount Kilimanjaro by the time she is eighty-seven.

Janeane: Now, Jackie, you don't have any aches and pains some days, where you say, "I just can't do this"?

Jackie: Yes, I do. I have all kinds of problems. Believe me, you name it and I have it. I have a back problem from top to bottom. I am a survivor of an airplane crash. And I have high cholesterol, I have cardiovascular problems, and I have a chronic kidney disease (CKD). And I said, "You know what? I am not going to let all of that bother me."

JB: That is great!

JK: I am going to keep doing what I am doing. And CrossFit— I got into CrossFit when I was seventy-nine years old, and today I am still doing CrossFit.

JB: And what does that entail?

JK: Google it. It's very hard. I lift weights. I do lunges. Everything is with weights. A week before my birthday, I decided to practice my deadlift. I am good at it and I love it. I put on eighty-six pounds. I thought: I was going to be eighty-six, so I did eighty-six pounds on my deadlift. Ten repetitions. Then I [would] rest and walk around and come back and do another one. I did ten rounds. So, you multiply eighty-six times ten and again ten times in an hour.

JB: Oh, my gosh, Jackie!

JK: That was a week before my eighty-sixth birthday.

JB: Unbelievable!

JK: Yeah.

JB: I know people in their eighties, and they are not nearly as active and doing what you are doing, but it sounds like this is what keeps you happy and content getting up in the morning.

JK: You know what? Ever since I was a young kid, I was always sick and I always had a problem. My back and so forth. I had a pain here and there. I used to complain and take medication. No more. I don't take any medication. I take Advil and I use ice packs, lots of vitamins, and massage. I go to a next-level chiropractor, which is a sports medicine doctor.

JB: That is great.

JK: Because when I was in the plane crash, I had two vertebrae broken, C2 and C3. They are right there in your neck.

JB: Yes!

JK: All your nerves, muscles, and ligaments come from there. So, sometimes I have a hard time; this morning I had a hard time. In my CrossFit training, I walk on my feet and hands backwards and forwards and for about forty feet; it's not easy, but it is a good exercise. I had never done that exercise before. Since I have been doing CrossFit and going to that next-level sports medicine doctor—I go when I need it, and you know what? For thirty-five years, every morning I was getting up and my neck was feeling so bad. Every day.

JB: Uh!

JK: A hot shower would do me some good. Then I started to do CrossFit, and when you start you have pain all over. They kept telling me to see Doctor George. Ever since, with him and my doctor, for the last three years, I get up in the morning and I don't have to jump in the shower. My neck doesn't hurt anymore.

JB: Incredible!

JK: Yes. Thirty-five years.

JB: I feel that you are very inspiring and I am learning a lot, because as we age, we have aches and pains and some people reach for pills and things.

JK: Yes.

JB: Between all the things you do, you figured out what works, and you sound like you are on a really wonderful chapter in your life, where you are probably the happiest you have been, maybe.

JK: You got it.

JB: Where can people find out more about you, Jackie? I googled you and up came your film, *Jackie Krisher: No Limits*, but anywhere else?

JK: I am on Facebook all the time under Jacqueline Andrea Krisher. Sometimes I go on Facebook and say, "You've got to love CrossFit!" I say what I did and people say, "This girl is an animal!"

(*laughter*)

JB: You are! You are unbelievable. Do you have a favorite thing that you love doing?

JK: My favorite thing would be the bicycle, but I fell a few times on the bicycle. I like the walking and running, and never fell, but I did fall during the biking. I got hurt pretty badly.

JB: Any advice for people that are feeling in a funk and they haven't really exercised in a while? They want to do something but maybe they won't do as much as you do. What advice would you give them?

JK: My suggestion would be to put some walking shoes on and start to walk as far as you can. Don't go one way and come back, because it is too easy to come back sooner. If you take a walk, and over a trail, then you go for forty minutes, but you finish doing an hour, because you start at point A and come back to point A. You did not go from A to B and B to A again.

JB: I see.

JK: You make a circle around whatever it is, and this is what worked the most for me.

JB: That is great.

JK: Once you are off something, it is so easy to not go again. My life is full. I think about my kids and my grandkids, but I also have to think about myself, too. I don't go anywhere if it is cold. I don't put myself in a situation where I will get sick.

When you get older, you have less of an entourage. When you work, you have so many people that you know, so many contacts, like your coworkers. But when you don't work anymore, your circle is very small.

JB: That's right.

JK: And I am proud to say that my circle-of-people range includes all ages—from newborns to ninety-year-olds. One day, I was at CrossFit and guess what? There were two guys in the class—sixteen and eighteen—and myself. They all love me. They don't want me to go.

JB: Of course not; you are very inspiring.

JK: Yes. Yes, and that makes me very happy.

JB: It should. You probably look back on your life when you weren't doing anything and think, "Wow! Look at me now!"

JK: Exactly. Just wait. I want to do the Mount Kilimanjaro. I am going to start to train for that. I want to make it. Oh, yeah.

JB: Is there a mantra or quote you live by?

JK: Stay positive at all times. Don't give up. Make new plans. Always think ahead.

JB: What advice do you have for others?

JK: Never ever give up, don't quit, work at it, and think positive.

I have no doubt Jackie will make it to Mount Kilimanjaro. She has motivated me in so many ways and changed my perceptions of aging and our self-inflicted limitations. I know I will never be as fearless as Jackie, but she certainly is inspiring. One day, I hope to be thriving in my eighties and walking with my close group of hiking friends, too; it is important to stay active mentally and physically at any age. If we don't, we get rusty and it's harder to get moving and motivated again.

After spending time with Jackie, I decided to explore the lives of other seniors who are living physically and mentally fulfilling lives. People are living longer, and some are in no rush to retire or give up a hobby that old stereotypes would deem too challenging. The older workforce is enjoying social connections and benefiting from financial and emotional incentives. Seniors know that staying active physically and mentally is essential for longevity.

Nationally and internationally, senior citizens are working and enjoying life beyond expectations and stereotypes. The National Senior Games Association started in 1985, held its first competition in 1987, and just celebrated its thirtieth anniversary in 2017; this nonprofit organization was established with the mission of "promoting adults to lead a healthy lifestyle through sport." The NSGA website (nsga.com) describes the National Senior Games as "a 20-sport, biennial competition for men and women 50 and over, and is the largest multi-sport event in the world for seniors." The NSGA has created a competition that brings participants from all over to compete in archery, badminton, basketball, bowling, cycling, golf, horseshoes, pickleball, power walking, race walking, racquetball, road racing, shuffleboard, softball, swimming, table tennis, tennis, track and field, volleyball, and other sports.

If you do a Google search for "senior athletes," you will see generations of remarkable achievements, and some of these athletes are landing in *Guinness World Records*. For those of you who think that at a certain age "the ship has sailed," *ha!* There are so many stories of people who started doing a sport or creative adventure in their fifties, sixties, seventies, or eighties and have no sign of slowing down. Oftentimes these new chapters begin because someone faces the loss of a loved one, a divorce, or a professional or personal funk. Here's a look at a few fearless, driven, and vibrant seniors who are doing things most of us would never imagine.

Ernestine Shepherd—Oldest Performing Female Bodybuilder
Age: 82

Ernestine "Ernie" Shepherd is a personal trainer, professional model, and competitive bodybuilder. According to her website, in "March of 2010, on stage in Rome, Italy she was formally given the title of World's Oldest Performing Female BodyBuilder (by Guinness World Records)." You would never know her road to fitness did not begin until age fifty-six. Faced with the loss of her sister after they had agreed to train to become the world's oldest bodybuilders, Ernestine was derailed by grief, anxiety, and depression. However, according to Lisa Capretto at HuffPost, her sister came to her in a dream and told her to follow through with their goal. From there on out, Ernestine was driven to become the world's oldest female bodybuilder, and over time, there was no need for any medications for her acid reflux, depression, and anxiety; it all disappeared.

Ida Keeling—Centenarian Track and Field Athlete
Age: 103

Ida holds masters athletics records in the sixty-meter and one-hundred-meter distances for women in the ninety-five-to-ninety-nine and one-hundred-plus age groups, and believes exercise should be done daily. In 1972, her doctor's prescription of a daily dose of Hennessy cognac helped her circulation, so she has been taking it ever since. Her advice? "Eat for nutrition, not for taste." Her diet includes cod liver oil, orange juice, and lots of fruits and vegetables. According to *Essence* online, Ida began running at age sixty-seven.

Book: *Can't Nothing Bring Me Down: Chasing Myself in the Race Against Time*

Bryson William Verdun Hayes—Oldest Skydiver
Age: 102

In 2017, the London Associated Press reported that "a 101-year-old D-Day veteran has become the oldest person in the world to skydive. Bryson William Verdun Hayes completed a tandem skydive with members of his extended family on Sunday at an airfield in Honiton, southwest England. Hayes' son, grandson, great-grandson and great-granddaughter joined him. At the age of 101 years, 38 days, Hayes broke the Guinness World Record held by Canada's Armand Gendreau, who jumped in 2013 at 101 years, three days."

Hayes said he had wanted to try skydiving when he was 90 but was talked out it at the time by his late wife. He jumped for the first time at age 100.

Hidekichi Miyazaki—Oldest Sprinter
Age: 108*

*passed away January 2019

According to HuffPost writer Yagana Shah, 108-year-old Japanese sprinter Hidekichi Miyazaki broke the world record for the oldest sprinter in 2015; he completed the one-hundred-meter sprint in about forty-two seconds!

Dilys Price—Oldest Female Skydiver
Age: 86

Dilys holds the Guinness World Record as the Oldest Female Skydiver. Known as "Daredevil Dilys," she has completed more than 1,100 jumps for disabled children's charities. According to an article by BBC news writer Gemma Ryall, at "age 54, divorced, bringing up her son and going through what she describes as a midlife crisis, Dilys decided to do a skydive for charity. She had been scared of heights but as she floated through the air, she said a fire inside her was sparked—and she was hooked."

Ryall shared that Dilys encourages older people to have a passion until the day they die. And what is Dilys' latest adventure? In 2018, at age eighty-six, she became a model for the brand Helmut Lang and was featured in its "Women of Wales" fall collection.

Jim Arrington—World's Oldest Competing
Professional Bodybuilder
Age: 86

According to writer Laura Johnson at *Bodybuilding.com*, "Jim Arrington was named the 2018 World's Oldest Male Bodybuilder by the Guinness Book of World Records, and is a 16-time body-building champion, participating in over five dozen competitions throughout his 70-year athletic career."

Tao Porchon-Lynch—World's Oldest Yoga Instructor Age: 100

In 2012, Tao Porchon-Lynch was named the world's oldest yoga instructor by *Guinness World Records* at age ninety-three. She is an American yogi of French and Indian descent. She discovered yoga in 1926 at age eight while living in India, and has been teaching yoga for over seventy years. Her résumé includes: World War II French Resistance fighter, model, actress, film producer, wine connoisseur, competitive ballroom dancer, and yoga master.

Books: *Dancing Light: The Spiritual Side of Being Through the Eyes of a Modern Yoga Master*; and *Shining Bright: Quotes and Images to Inspire Optimism, Gratitude & Belief In Your Limitless Potential*

Obviously, not all seniors aspire to become world record holders. Some prefer hobbies and individual or group activities that are less rigorous but equally enjoyable. Seniors who live alone or who have diminished physical activity due to illness or injury are more likely to experience depression and feelings of boredom and loneliness. There are numerous activities that can help decrease these feelings, reduce anxiety and stress, expand social circles, and improve overall health and mood. Here is a general list of activities:

- Painting (oil or watercolors)
- Sculpting
- Sketching

- Photography
- Woodworking
- Card games, board games, mah-jongg, and the like
- Cooking
- Yoga (such as laughter yoga)
- Exercise classes
- Stretching
- Pilates
- Learning and playing musical instruments
- Singing
- Tai chi
- Outdoor activities such as walking, hiking, biking, fishing, swimming, tennis, painting or coloring, gardening, and golf
- Crafting
- Acting
- Stand-up comedy
- Dancing
- Volunteering
- Automobile repair and restoration
- Furniture restoration
- Home repair
- Meditation
- Traveling

If you know any seniors who live alone, reach out to them. Offer to take them for a meal or invite them over. Ask them if they need anything from the store or something done around the house, or if they would like to join you on your errands. Encourage them to take up a hobby or social activity that you are part of; this will introduce them to new people and possibly improve their mood. Staying active boosts everyone's physical, mental, and emotional well-being. A small act of kindness can make a big difference in someone's life, especially someone who has no daily interactions and activities. The holidays are especially hard for people, because they tend to become depressed and miss their loved ones; this is another important time to be compassionate and reach out to people in need. Just a simple phone call can brighten someone's day. You never know the impact you can make. Invite someone along on a walk or to a social event. Befriending a stranger can open your world up for greater joy in their life and yours.

CHAPTER 12

Don't Fear Those Funks!
Enjoy the Ride

"You have brains in your head. You have feet in your shoes. You can steer yourself any direction you choose. You're on your own. And you know what you know. And YOU are the one who'll decide where to go."
—Dr. Seuss, Oh, the Places You'll Go!

No one can give you a time frame for healing or moving forward. Take small steps out of the cavernous funk you find yourself in. Small steps are better than none at all. Pick yourself up and dust yourself off. Look at your situation as life's inevitable wounds that make you stronger. Sometimes a tough period in your life gives you a new perspective, and you become a braver, smarter, new you with a suit of armor that helps you deal with the next funk thrown your way. Those twists and turns can be scary and awful, but they shape who we are and whom we can become. Try not to fear those funks, because they just might be the best thing that ever happened in the long run.

Through pain, struggle, and strife we learn how to survive and how to carry on. The battle scars of life are learning moments that teach us about ourselves and build resilience and grit. We face continual challenges and uphill battles, but we learn how to come out stronger and feel less beaten down emotionally and physically. We can teach our life lessons to our children or peers, because life is filled with constant learning moments. The only way through tough times is with determination and recognition of what you are feeling and experiencing. Whatever it is you are facing, you need a healthy mindset, a strong support network, and a survivor attitude. And once you've reached the exit door leading out of your funk, you are now a different person, probably a little beaten up and ready for a retreat somewhere. Hopefully, the painful situation you made it through left you stronger, wiser, and ready to take on anything that comes your way. Time will be healing and lead you to new paths you never expected. Be open to the changes that come your way.

Your struggle can turn out to be a blessing in disguise or just an opportunity for you to grow and expand your horizons. Of course, I am not implying that losing the love of your life to cancer or another horrible illness will turn out to be a positive experience. However, you can learn a lot about yourself in your time of grief and build new relationships while healing and moving away from your pain and sadness; this is the time to explore new interests, meet new people, and see life with a different set of lenses. Grief is tough to repair, but taking the very best care of yourself makes all the difference. You will find a meaningful takeaway from whatever it is you are going through, and discover you are no longer the same person. Change rocks us off our axis and shifts the ground beneath us; this is life's way of telling us to pay attention.

We have all had our share of funks. Funks are just part of the package in this crazy roller coaster ride called life. No one is immune to funks, unless you are made of steel and know some magic secret that you aren't sharing. Most of us know that being in a funk is unavoidable. But if you develop coping mechanisms, these tools can carry you through life. Of course, we will all have good and bad days, and days that are absolute nightmares. And if you're a woman, you might have moods that can be as unsettling as riding the Tower of Terror, especially to those around you.

We all hit roadblocks at some point or another. We experience loss emotionally or professionally. We get hurt, we feel lost and alone, but then, miraculously, something begins to unfold for some of us. We somehow figure things out, listen to others and to our own voice of reason, or even pray a little harder or perhaps for the first time in a long time. Whatever choices we make, we somehow turn a corner and begin to carry on (that is, emerge from that dark cave we retreated to). However, some people are not as fortunate; they are not able to figure out how to pick up the pieces. They turn to substance abuse, make detrimental decisions, and choose the wrong path. If you find yourself in a deep, dark place and feel hopeless, seek professional help. No one should suffer in silence or become self-destructive. There is a world of resources and people waiting to help. All you have to do is ask.

Fortunately, many people slowly and steadily pull themselves out of the vortex that had sucked them into that funky place. Your journey begins one step at a time; that is all it takes. No matter how small the step is, you begin to fight your way out of whatever you are going through. Just put one foot in front of another and begin again, because that is what we need to do, and as we make our way out of that awful storm, a little bit of light shines through and something better comes along. You just need to turn towards that light, that glimmer of hope, and trust that after the darkness, life will get better. You'll see.

Another positive outcome of overcoming a funk is, we find a dimension of ourselves we never knew existed and meaningful moments arise unexpectedly. We might meet a stranger who offers the perfect advice at the most opportune time. A new career path or opportunity arises. Being in a funk can be an enlightening and redefining experience; it enables us to dial in to what we need and find direction, and yes, it can also be frightening and fill us with apprehension. Still, change can be the best healer and inspiring at the same time.

For those of you who have ever had your heart broken (maybe even ripped to shreds and stomped to pieces), perhaps later you realized that the person you agonized over was, in fact, *completely wrong for you in the first place*! Yes, I am shouting this from the roof-tops, because a lot of you get what I am saying. You cannot realize how wrong someone is for you unless you have some distance from the situation and some time to process your relationship (that is, you finally wake up and realize you deserve *a lot* better).

A few days after ending a stale relationship in my twenties, I found a new beginning and it wasn't with someone else. I found myself returning to my passion for music, but in a very unex-pected way. I kept having a recurring dream night after night. I was seeing myself playing guitar again. For years, I had been telling myself, "One day I will take lessons again and play really well." Unfortunately, that day hadn't come. I still had the electric guitar my dad had bought me at fourteen, having kept my promise not to sell it. The problem was that I wasn't playing my guitar and it was collecting dust and getting piled on with unfolded laundry.

The persistent dream began after my breakup and continued for several nights. I saw myself playing the electric guitar in ways I never knew I could; these dreams were vivid and motivating. When you are going through an emotional time, you never know where you will find new directions and a strong motivating message. For me, I was nagged by the dreams to stop procrastinating and start playing again. Just find something that you used to love to do, because once you get going again, the feeling is invigorating and healing, and it is hard to stop your momentum.

On the third day of rocking out in my dreams (to an audience of just my pillow and two cats), I jumped out of bed and knew enough was enough. I enrolled in guitar lessons with an amazing teacher. The lessons lasted over nine years, up until I was married and nine months pregnant, waddling down the street with my Fender Strat strapped to my back, past the Berklee College of Music in Boston. I was exhilarated to finally do something about my aspirations, and not let them go to waste because of procrastination and a gazillion lame excuses.

The funny thing is, sometimes we don't even know what we want and what we need. Then life throws us a left hook and we're blindsided. Through it all, we find our way. Being lost and crumbling are part of getting back up. We choose to go down a different path, gain inner strength, or even kick toxic people to the curb because they block us from being our true selves and living our happiest, most fulfilling lives. Best of all, funks inspire and motivate us to carry on, keep going, and grow up.

Here is a summary of the steps you can take when you find yourself in a personal or professional crisis. Having a plan and thinking methodically, instead of impulsively, is a good way to start.

The Road out of Funktown!

- ⟲ Write down what happened and how you are feeling. Do a mind dump and write down every little detail. Vent and pour your heart out. Don't edit anything you write. Be your most honest self.

- ⟲ Express yourself through any creative outlet you enjoy.

- ⟲ Make sure you get the right amount of sleep. The benefits of good sleep will impact your immune system, mood, personal relationships, and metabolism.

- ⟲ See your friends and family. Spend time with people who support you and nurture your confidence and self-esteem.

- ⟲ Speak to a therapist if you feel off-kilter and helpless. Seeking help is an important part of getting back on track. Don't hesitate to get whatever help you need as soon as possible.

- ⟲ Create a plan to switch paths in your life. Make an "I always wanted to…" list—a bucket list or whatever you want to call your list. Once you have some clear ideas, share that plan with your most trusted friends and confidants. Be open to their thoughts and opinions.

- ⟲ Write down a list of things you are grateful for and focus on the positive notes in your life.

- ⟲ Take the best care of your mental, physical, and emotional health. Exercise, meditate, build new relationships, and pursue creative outlets. Long term, these will be your keys to resilience and well-being.

- ⟲ Love who you are completely and fully. Accept every ounce of your true self and make a pact to always love who you are. Be kind to yourself and others; show your-self compassion and understanding. Life can be hard, and we are stronger than we realize.

Tend to Your Garden

This is not going to be a "how to grow tomatoes" section. When I said, "Tend to your garden," I had two thoughts. You might have a real garden that is dried up and neglected, so you know what to do there; it's screaming for attention. But our gardens can also mean our family and friends who nurture us and help us grow. Take care of them, too. Make time for meaningful relationships and endeavors; they will all pay off in the end.

My garden reflects what is going in my personal life. If my garden is overgrown and a sea of weeds, this screams neglect, and chances are my life is in disarray. When my dad was sick, all I grew was weeds. Big, crazy, wild weeds took over everything. They were so ugly, we got a letter from the community association saying something like, "Fix up that ugly yard or be fined." Right before Dad passed, I picked out some drought-tolerant plants (that I wouldn't kill from neglect) and had someone help me fix up the dismal yard. I felt a little better looking at beautiful plants instead of weeds and dirt. Then I flew to Florida for Dad's funeral. I felt like I had left my family with something cheerful to look at while I was gone.

Slowly, I started spending more time outside, planting and watering again. My yard and garden reflected the healing period in my life. Flowers started blooming, and the reemergence of life made me smile a bit more. My stepmother has always been an incredible gardener, so I tried to plant some new fruits and vege-tables in our garden. For a long time, I didn't even go outside and pay attention to the dreary wilting grass and trees. I didn't care. Again, this was a reflection of my inner world, which was a wreck.

My stepmother taught me that organic fertilizer helps plants and edibles grow more. It took me a while to think about putting something with feces in my garden, but when I finally added the fertilizer and more water (duh—water is key, people) to my garden, *boom*! Mangos, zucchini, and potatoes! If you look at sh*t as something good, you can apply that analogy to your life. Think of life's sh*tty moments as fertilizer to grow something better and find a more meaningful life. Years ago, I thought gardening was *so* boring, but now I love the idea of playing in the dirt again and throwing vegetable scraps in the ground and seeing what surprises grow. When you think about it, we use feces to grow beautiful fruits and vegetables, so it can't be that bad. Now, if we can just look at our sh*tty moments as "not so bad" and figure out a way to use them to grow into something better or happier, that is the gem here. Once you feel sh*tty, it's hard not to feel sh*ttier, but eventually you will bloom again. You just have to want to thrive and rise up from the sh*tstorm. Pay attention to how you feel during this time and you might find that you wanted a change all along. In order to make that change, you go through an upheaval. Be patient, because better moments are in store for you when you least expect them to happen. In fact, some of the best moments in my life have happened when I least expected them; that's the beauty of life.

Finding Myself Through Grief

I hate public speaking. I might as well be naked in front of a large, unruly crowd and asked to sing. It's torture. When I knew

I had to speak at my dad's funeral, I had to be prepared. Preparation is everything no matter what you do. I would somehow put my discomfort aside and push aside my fear of bursting into tears, trembling uncomfortably, and looking like a mess. I thought if I were to lose my sh*t in front of all those people, no one would understand a word of my slobbering self. I kept telling my sleep-deprived emotional wreck of a self that I had better sound intelligible and keep it together. But then something surprising happened. I might have given one of the best speeches I had ever attempted; it was as if my dad were sitting in the front row and smiling ear to ear, absorbing every word. I imagined telling him how thankful I was and seeing tears in his eyes.

I took the podium and looked out at everyone before saying a word. I made eye contact with a few people, but I was overwhelmed by their feelings of grief. I stayed strong and didn't want to go there. Instead, I felt a sense of relief that Dad was no longer in pain; this was my time to breathe and share what life had been like after I moved in with him at age sixteen. By keeping my composure, I felt everything he had instilled in me, and a more confident person took that podium.

For the time I knew him, I was thankful and appreciative of everything he had ever done for me. He was the one who saw things in me I never knew I had. He saw endless possibility and determination. He saw heaps of creative endeavors and accolades. He was forgiving when I screwed up and never came down on me in a harsh, criticizing way. Writing his eulogy brought me back to self-love and finding myself in my sorrow. After the funeral, I flew back home to California, and that night I typed up the eulogy I had scribbled down in a notebook; then I did something bold. I submitted my piece to *The New York Times* for the section "The

Lives They Loved." If you look it up, you will see our silly picture and my tribute to Dad.

So, why is it I cried weeks later after reading the eulogy online? I guess I know how to put on my game face, and then I fall apart. Thanks to Dad, I began writing again. I wrote while he was sick, and I wrote while he was near death. But most important, I wrote constantly and with passion after he passed. Writing has been my healer. I just never expected to face more funks during the process of writing a book about funks, but these experiences were necessary and part of my journey. On days when writing was tough, I would tell myself to keep going. There are worse things to face.

Having gratitude is an essential part of being human; it allows you to dial in to what you should be thankful for and tune out all the noise that clouds our thinking and judgment. During a recent yoga class, I had this overwhelming moment of gratitude. I thought about how blessed I was to have such a loving and supportive husband, family and extended family, two beautiful daughters, a puppy that shifted my priorities and beliefs, a roof over my head, a safe and beautiful area to live in, and on and on and on. I was flooded with so much gratitude, I felt that I needed to consider my list of things to be thankful for more often. All the minuscule things I had been worked up about washed away; they just seemed irrelevant and unimportant. I stopped focusing my energy on the insignificance of them all.

We Are a Work in Progress

We all have personal baggage, and some of us have extensive sets of baggage we carry from youth through adulthood. At any age, you can work on yourself, work through the issues that hold you back, learn how to face life's funks, and muddle through the messy moments into bigger and better experiences. The only way through our challenging times is directly through the crazy mess, because through the upheaval and wreckage we become more resilient, a little more fearless and self-aware and, if we're doing this all right, happier.

We all go through personal and professional upheavals, but how we deal with sudden changes, challenging endings, and new beginnings makes us smarter and more insightful. When we feel broken and there seems to be no solution in sight, there really is. We just need to be open to the answers all around us and listen to our gut; that's usually the best gauge for life's direction.

There is a simple roadmap for navigating life's rocky road. Just ask yourself these questions:

Where am I in
my life, personally and professionally?

Am I in a personal or professional funk, and if so, what happened and why?

Should I seek professional help, or can I figure this mess out on my own?

What do I want to do differently in my life?

What fulfills me mentally, physically, and emotionally?

What is holding me back from moving in a positive direction?

How will I get to where I want to be?

What resources do I have?

How will I take the best care of myself so I can thrive?

Stop wasting time and wishing and hoping for things to happen in your life. Take action *right now!* Start doing and stop saying, "One day, I would like to..." Today is the day. Now is your time to get yourself out of whatever it is you are going through and get moving. Unpack your baggage and deal with whatever is weighing you down. Clean house, make changes, and create a life you want and deserve. What are you waiting for? You don't need anyone's permission to be happy and fulfilled in this lifetime.

Takeaways

⟳ Accept failure and find your lessons learned. Failure and disappointment make us stronger, and sometimes we rebound into something better. I have been known to thank my rejections and failures, because they did me a favor.

⟳ Ask for help, especially when you repeatedly try and fail at something. Something just isn't working, and you can't go it alone. Help can illuminate what's not so obvious and give you a greater sense of confidence once you do finally get something you struggled with.

⟳ Don't do something because you want to please others. Follow your own path and live your own life.

⟳ Find your passions and focus your distracted mind in the traffic jam of life.

⟳ Develop a solid group of friends and mentors.

⟳ Have downtime and never be too busy to nurture yourself and your relationships. Know when to take a time-out and practice self-care.

⟳ Create healthy routines that will keep you mentally and physically fit.

⟳ Don't fear change. Change can be the best thing for you and what you needed all along.

⟳ Try all kinds of things that interest, you especially if people try to convince you not to.

⟳ When in doubt, don't. Trust your intuition if something feels wrong.

- Push yourself out of your comfort zone and try something scary and new.

- Take care of your mind, body, and spirit.

- Don't think that having a relationship will fix you and make you feel complete—only you can do that.

- Don't put limits on your achievements.

- Find contentment in stillness.

- Have compassion and understanding for yourself and others.

- Put yourself in someone else's shoes.

- Know what to do when things fall apart and life throws you curveballs.

- Have the nerve to speak your truth respectfully and compassionately.

- Help others as if they were your own friends and family.

- Have realistic goals but don't beat yourself up if you do not achieve them. Make small, attainable goals and create a time frame. Achievements do wonders for self-esteem.

- Be you. Don't pretend to be someone else.

- Never stop learning, growing, and living your best life.

CONCLUSION

"Eat a live frog first thing in the morning and nothing worse will happen to you the rest of the day."—Mark Twain

This book was never meant to be your shield against the inevitable struggles you will face—that would be impossible and unrealistic. Throughout your lifetime you will lose people who are incredibly precious and influential in your life; the gravity of their departure will rock your world, and you could feel as if you are functioning on autopilot; this is when you need to take *really* good of yourself. You will face a slew of other losses and disappointments throughout your lifetime, but thrown into the mix will be tremendous joy, beautiful miracles, pure bliss, and heaps of gratitude.

Our ability to work our way out of life's pitfalls comes down to one very basic principle—how much do you love yourself? The way out of what you are going through is determined by your ability to love and nurture yourself in a time of crisis and upheaval. When you take care of yourself, you love and accept who you are, you realize that life will be happy again and that you are deserving of happiness; it might take time to recover, so be kind to yourself and compassionate on whatever rocky road you are facing. Don't let fear take the wheel in your journey. Cherish you and others who love you. Life can be tough, but you will find the beauty and joy in the simplest moments. See them and embrace them, because they are there for the taking.

You should finish this book knowing that you are not alone. No matter how perfect someone's life might seem, it is not. We are complex, and our scars are deep and not always visible. I like to believe that it is better to share my wounds with others, because we have all experienced life's skinned knees and emotional upheavals, and in the end, they remind us of how far we have come and how resilient we are.

My father always used to end our phone calls by saying, "Just keep going." This is what we must do. Just keep going. Be your own cheerleader in life, your own director and narrator. Take your pain, your downfalls, your hard life lessons and create something meaningful that serves a purpose. Create art if that is what speaks to you. Your pain and loss can be a lesson for someone else going through the same thing. By putting your emotions and life lessons into something for others to experience, you have created a selfless piece of art (such as a poem, a story, or a film), which becomes a vehicle that helps people feel less alone and more alive.

We are a work in progress. And if you are fortunate enough, you will have many interesting career paths and pursuits that make you fulfilled and happy throughout your lifetime. A stagnant mind and body lead to an unhappy soul. Soak in everything you can and grow. Have a variety of interests, but don't be so hard on yourself. The bumpy roads of life are followed by new joys and pathways. Explore them. Embrace them.

Instill creativity in your life, even if you don't think you have the time or the aptitude. We are all capable of having a creative, imaginative mind, but it's what we do with our abilities that matters.

I have been humbled over the past eight years by the stories and insights my show guests have shared. With the negativity, conflict, and strife in this world, there are still beautiful stories to tell and share. Those are the stories that need to be told, because they serve a purpose and provide solace. Be open to the positive notes around you. Be open to joy and the routines of life that make you smile. Seek out new people and opportunities, and never let anyone or anything bring you down and convince you that you can't get back up. Find the light in the darkest moments. Believe in yourself and see the possibilities for goodness and a life you deserve. Creativity is the elixir of youth. Mindfulness is the internal compass. Self-love is everything. Without love and compassion for yourself, you have less to give to the people in your life. Trust your gut and keep going. You've got this (even though some days you might not think so). Keep going, my friend. Just keep going.

> *"Practicing an art, no matter how well or badly, is a way to make your soul grow, for heaven's sake. Sing in the shower. Dance to the radio. Tell stories. Write a poem to a friend, even a lousy poem. Do it as well as you possibly can. You will get an enormous reward. You will have created something."*—*Kurt Vonnegut*, A Man Without a Country

BIOS

Melanie Brooks—accomplished writer and teacher

Cindy Charlton—triple amputee, inspiring speaker, and accomplished author

Scott Crabtree—founder and chief happiness officer at Happy Brain Science

Brie Darling—singer, drummer, actor, and winner of *Cake Wars*

Dr. Orin Davis—principal investigator at the Quality of Life Laboratory and head of behavioral science at Vervoe

Christine Dimmick—wellness expert, founder and CEO of The Good Home Co., and cancer survivor

Sue Enquist—former softball coach at UCLA, eleven-time national champion, six-time Hall of Famer, and founder of ONE Softball

Robin Farmanfarmaian—professional speaker, entrepreneur, author, and angel investor

Jake Ferree—yoga master and personal transformation expert

Adrien Finkel—author, photographer, comedic television producer, and founder of her My Naked Truth project

Kerry Hannon—nationally recognized expert and strategist on career transitions, personal finance, and retirement; author of over a dozen books; and writer for *The New York Times*, *Forbes*, *Money*, *U.S. News & World Report*, and *USA Today*

Cindy Joseph—Cindy passed away in July 2018 from cancer. She was on my show a while ago, and her daughter Julia and family gave me permission to include her in the book. She was a wife, mother, model, makeup artist, and pioneer in pro-age thinking.

Kalifornia Karl—professional musician and founder of Joyful Noise Music

Jackie Krisher—eighty-five-year-old triathlete and CrossFit participant

Lauren Lipton—award-winning journalist and author of *Yoga Bodies: Real People, Real Stories and the Power of Transformation*

June Millington—cofounder and lead guitarist for the all-female rock band Fanny, cofounder and artistic director of the Institute for the Musical Arts (IMA), singer, songwriter, producer, and writer

Gary Pihl—Gary Pihl, former guitarist for Sammy Hagar and current member of the band Boston

Jill Santopolo—*New York Times* bestselling author

Adam Shell—award-winning documentary film director and the creator of *Pursuing Happiness*

Jay Silverman—director, producer, and filmmaker

Elena Stowell—author, science teacher, and Brazilian jiu-jitsu practitioner

Jenna Torres—musician, singer, and songwriter

Charlie Visnic—editor and creative tinkerer

Peter Zheutlin—freelance journalist and author

SUGGESTED READING

No Mistakes: A Perfect Workbook for Imperfect Artists
Keiko Agena
TarcherPerigee, 2018

Happy Accidents: The Transformative Power of "Yes, And" at Work and in Life
David Ahearn, Frank Ford, David Wilk
Wiley, 2017

The Triumph of Rosemary: A Memoir
Judge Marylin E. Atkins
Two Sisters Writing and Publishing, 2017

50 Ways to Get a Job: An Unconventional Guide to Finding Work on Your Terms
Dev Aujla
TarcherPerigee, 2018

Ivy and the Butterfly: A Magical Tale to Color
Johanna Basford
Penguin Books, 2017

Unfu*k Yourself: Get Out of Your Head and into Your Life
Gary John Bishop
Harper One—Harper Collins, 2017

How to Be Perfect Like Me
Dana Bowman
Central Recovery Press, 2018

An Excellent Choice: Panic and Joy on My Solo Path to Motherhood
Emma Brockes
Faber and Faber, 2018

Writing Hard Stories: Celebrated Memoirists Who Shaped Art from Trauma
Melanie Brooks
Beacon Press, 2017

I Dare Me: How I Rebooted and Recharged My Life by Doing Something New Every Day
Lu Ann Cahn
TarcherPerigee, 2013

Quiet Power: The Secret Strengths of Introverts
Susan Cain, Gregory Mone, Erica Moroz
Dial Books, 2016

Quiet: The Power of Introverts in a World That Can't Stop Talking
Susan Cain
Crown Publishers, 2012

Life Lessons: 125 Prayers and Meditations
Julia Cameron
TarcherPerigee, 2017

When Things Fall Apart: Heart Advice for Difficult Times
Pema Chödrön
Shambhala, 2000

Chasing Hope: A Patient's Deep Dive into Stem Cells, Faith and the Future
Richard M. Cohen
Blue Rider Press, 2018

The Kindness Cure: How the Science of Compassion Can Heal Your Heart and Your World
Tara Cousineau
New Harbinger Publications, Inc., 2018

GET THE FUNK OUT!

The Pursuit of Endurance: Harnessing the Record-Breaking Power of Strength and Resilience
Jennifer Pharr Davis
Viking, 2018

How to Be a Happier Parent: Raising a Family, Having a Life, and Loving (Almost) Every Minute
KJ Dell'Antonia
Avery, 2018

The Rough Patch: Marriage and the Art of Living Together
Daphne de Marneffe, PhD
Scribner, 2018

Detox Your Home: A Guide to Removing Toxins from Your Life and Bringing Health into Your Home
Christine Dimmick
Rowman & Littlefield, 2018

Changing Behavior: Immediately Transform Your Relationships with Easy-to-Learn, Proven Communication Skills
Dr. Georgianna Donadio
SoulWork Press, 2011

There are No Grown-Ups: A Midlife Coming-of-Age Story
Pamela Druckerman
Penguin Press, 2018

The Patient as CEO: How Technology Empowers the Healthcare Consumer
Robin Farmanfarmaian
Lioncrest Publishing, 2015

My Naked Truth Project
Adrien Finkel
Kensington Publishing Corp., 2018

The Creative Curve: How to Develop the Right Idea, at the Right Time
Allen Gannett
Currency Books, 2018

Big Magic: Creative Living Beyond Fear
Elizabeth Gilbert
Riverhead Books, 2015

The Anti-Inflammation Cookbook: The Delicious Way to Reduce Inflammation and Stay Healthy
Amanda Haas
Chronicle Books, 2015

Money Confidence: Really Smart Financial Moves for Newly Single Women
Kerry Hannon
Post Hill Press, 2017

What's Next? Finding Your Passion and Your Dream Job in Your Forties, Fifties and Beyond
Kerry Hannon
The Berkley Publishing Group, 2014

10% Happier: How I Tamed the Voice in My Head, Reduced Stress Without Losing My Edge, and Found Self-Help That Actually Works—A True Story
Dan Harris
It Books, 2014

Social Media Wellness: Helping Tweens and Teens Thrive in an Unbalanced Digital World
Ana Homayoun
Corwin, 2018

Wherever You Go, There You Are: Mindfulness Meditation in Everyday Life
Jon Kabat-Zinn
Hyperion Books, 1994

Thriving Through Uncertainty: Moving Beyond Fear of the Unknown and Making Change Work for You
Tama Kieves
TarcherPerigee, 2018

The Good Mood Kitchen: Simple Recipes and Nutrition Tips for Emotional Balance
Dr. Leslie Korn
W. W. Norton & Company, 2017

Your Inner Critic Is a Big Jerk: And Other Truths About Being Creative
Danielle Krysa
Chronicle Books, 2016

Almost Everything: Notes on Hope
Anne Lamott
Riverhead Books, 2018

Heavy: An American Memoir
Kiese Laymon
Scribner, 2018

Vodka Is Vegan: A Vegan Bros Manifesto for Better Living and Not Being an A**hole
Matt Letten and Phil Letten
TarcherPerigee, 2018

Yoga Bodies: Real People, Real Stories, & the Power of Transformation
Lauren Lipton
Chronicle Books, 2017

The Warner Loughlin Technique: An Acting Revolution
Warner Loughlin
Howland Tilley Press, 2018

Psyched Up: How the Science of Mental Preparation Can Help You Succeed
Daniel McGinn
Portfolio Penguin, 2017

The Book of Awakening: Having the Life You Want by Being Present to the Life You Have
Mark Nepo
Conari Press, 1999

Just When You're Comfortable in Your Own Skin, It Starts to Sag: Rewriting the Rules to Midlife
Amy Nobile and Trisha Ashworth
Chronicle Books, 2018

Mindshift: Breaking Through Obstacles to Learning and Discover Your Hidden Potential
Barbara Oakley, PhD
TarcherPerigee, 2017

The World is Just a Book Away
James J. Owens
USC Libraries Press, 2017

Art of Gathering: How We Meet and Why It Matters
Priya Parker
Riverhead Books, 2018

Brain Maker: The Power of Gut Microbes to Heal and Protect Your Brain for Life
David Perlmutter, MD, Kristin Loberg
Little, Brown and Company, 2015

What's Making Our Children Sick? How Industrial Food Is Causing an Epidemic of Chronic Illness, and What Parents (and Doctors) Can Do About It
Michelle Perro, MD and Vincanne Adams, PhD
Chelsea Green Publishing, 2017

How to Break Up with Your Phone: The 30-Day Plan to Take Back Your Life
Catherine Price
Ten Speed Press, 2018

The Eat-Clean Diet for Family and Kids: Simple Strategies for Lasting Health and Fitness
Tosca Reno
Robert Kennedy Publishing, 2008

The Eat-Clean Diet Recharged! Lasting Fat Loss That's Better than Ever
Tosca Reno
Robert Kennedy Publishing, 2010

Daily Writing Resilience: 365 Meditations & Inspirations for Writers
Bryan E. Robinson, PhD
Llewellyn Publications, 2018

Mastering Stand-Up: The Complete Guide to Becoming a Successful Comedian
Stephen Rosenfield
Chicago Review Press, 2017

Saying Goodbye to Daniel: When Death is the Best Choice
Juliet Cassuto Rothman
The Continuum Publishing Company, 1995

Letters from Max: A Book of Friendship
Sarah Ruhl and Max Ritvo
Milkweed Editions, 2018

The Light We Lost
Jill Santopolo
G.P. Putnam's Sons, 2017

Back to Human: How Great Leaders Create Connection in the Age of Isolation
Dan Schawbel
Lifelong Books, 2018

Aware: The Science and Practice of Presence—The Groundbreaking Meditation Practice
Daniel J. Siegel, MD
TarcherPerigee, 2018

Flowing with the Go: A Jiu-Jitsu Journey of the Soul
Elena Stowell
Boutique of Quality Books, 2012

Frango & Chicken
Elena Stowell
Thewordverve Inc., 2018

Zen Guitar
Philip Toshio Sudo
Simon & Schuster, 1997

Ordinary Goodness: The Surprisingly Effortless Path to Creating a Life of Meaning and Beauty
Edward Viljoen
TarcherPerigee, 2017

The Strength Switch: How the New Science of Strength-Based Parenting Helps Your Child and Teen to Flourish
Lea Waters, PhD
Avery, 2017

Rescued: What Second Chance Dogs Teach Us About Living With Purpose, Loving With Abandon, and Finding Joy in the Little Things
Peter Zheutlin
TarcherPerigee, 2017

ACKNOWLEDGMENTS

For Shannon and to all of you who have lost loved ones, misplaced yourself in grief, and who have been sucker-punched by life's funks. May you spin your sadness and uncertainty into something meaningful and surprisingly wonderful. Just look for the light through the darkness, because beautiful moments await.

A huge shout-out to all the contributors in this book who allowed me to share their stories with the world; to my wonderful editor, Debby Englander, for her encouragement and belief that I had a passion worth sharing; and special thanks to Post Hill Press.

Thank you, Kerry Hannon, for your excitement when I first told you my vision for *Get the Funk Out!*. You have been a fabulous cheerleader all these years! To my listeners, show guests, supportive friends, and loving family who tune in to my show (even in your Uber and MRI scan), your support means the world to me.

If my dad could read this, here's what I would say: "You saved me in so many ways, and I thank you for loving me, believing in me, teaching me the power of hard work, and being contagiously funny." To my stepparents, Marge and Bob, who have shown me endless love and kindness since I was little. On this crazy ride, we have laughed, cried, and stumbled through too many funks together, and I adore you.

To my loves—Robert, Tovia, and Eliana. Thank you for inspiring me, cheering me on, and showing me love I never imagined. I love you.

ABOUT THE AUTHOR

Janeane Bernstein is a writer, an on-air radio personality, a voice actress, and a researcher. She earned a doctorate in Educational Media and Technology from Boston University's Curriculum and Teaching department and studied education and communications at Syracuse University. Since 2007, she has been an on-air radio personality and producer at KUCI 88.9 FM, on the campus of the University of California, Irvine. Janeane's show, *Get the Funk Out!* airs weekly and streams at *www.kuci.org*.

The show *Get the Funk Out!* features a diverse national and international guest list, including health and wellness professionals, *New York Times* bestselling authors, award-winning filmmakers and actors, talented musicians, hilarious comedians, models, producers, mindfulness experts, researchers, and so many others who have been through a rough patch. *Get the Funk Out!* is tremendously fulfilling and inspiring on many levels. Most of the conversations are organic and unstructured, creating a show that is truly unique and inspiring.

http://getthefunkoutshow.kuci.org